THE **RESILIENT** UNIVERSITY

THE
RESILIENT
UNIVERSITY

HOW PURPOSE AND INCLUSION
DRIVE STUDENT SUCCESS

FREEMAN A. HRABOWSKI III

WITH **PETER H. HENDERSON, LYNNE C. SCHAEFER,** AND

PHILIP J. ROUS

Johns Hopkins University Press | Baltimore

© 2024 Johns Hopkins University Press
All rights reserved. Published 2024
Printed in the United States of America on acid-free paper
9 8 7 6 5 4 3 2 1

Johns Hopkins University Press
2715 North Charles Street
Baltimore, Maryland 21218
www.press.jhu.edu

Cataloging-in-Publication Data is available from the Library of Congress.
A catalog record for this book is available from the British Library.

ISBN: 978-1-4214-4844-2 (hardcover)
ISBN: 978-1-4214-4845-9 (ebook)

Special discounts are available for bulk purchases of this book. For more information, please contact Special Sales at specialsales@jh.edu.

To our UMBC colleagues and students

and

To all higher education institutions that give their all
to supporting students, especially in times of crisis

Contents

Preface

The near simultaneous arrival in 2020 of a viral pandemic and racial unrest across the nation shook us. As leaders in higher education, we moved in the face of this adversity through stages of disbelief, uncertainty, and discomfort, then resilience and eventually aspiration. Sometimes we lived with all of these at once—but through it all we kept hope.

The palpable uncertainty unnerved us. One college president said that managing under these circumstances was like "driving through a thick fog." Another said, "My crystal ball is no better than yours."[1] Our colleagues described their experiences by using aeronautical metaphors that expressed both uncertainty and its attendant anxiety: "It was like flying blind," "We were building a plane while flying it," "I felt like I was jumping out of a plane and hoping that the parachute would open."

We contended with uncertainty throughout the pandemic experience. Most of us in higher education "followed the science" in determining COVID-19 protocols because science provided the best guide to creating a safe, healthy environment on our campuses. Yet the science was often playing catch-up with the virus as we pursued a better understanding of its variants, viral transmissibility, vaccine efficacy, and effective treatments. This could leave us in the disquieting position of making decisions with partial or changing information.

Meanwhile, we felt the discomfort of reckoning with racial injustice. We heeded our hearts, our friends, and our critics as we sought to discuss, understand, address, and perhaps begin to dismantle structural racism in higher education. As I wrote in *The Atlantic* with colleagues in the fall of 2020:

The knee on the neck of George Floyd aggravated an American psyche already frayed by the pandemic and stay-at-home orders. Protesters from diverse backgrounds marched in the streets across the nation demanding change. Channeling the growing public and private support for meaningful change into action requires Americans, in every sector, to engage in difficult conversations, and to be honest about our problems and deliberate in developing solutions. We in higher education are no exception. We . . . have an obligation to engage in this work, because we have become more central than ever to our students' American dreams. We hold out to our students the promises of an enriched life and social mobility, and yet we often fall short in providing these to all who arrive on our campuses.[2]

In the face of uncertainty and discomfort, leaders at all levels of an organization shape our response and determine what we can accomplish. Some people are able to tolerate ambiguity and the unknown, but most of us find it unsettling. When a situation is difficult, the longer we take to address problems, the more serious they can become. That is when we witness lack of coordination, uninformed missteps, duplicate efforts, important balls dropped, and deserved, if unwanted, criticism. When leaders work to keep people calm, hopeful, and intentional, though, we can be resilient and focus on advancing our mission. This is when we successfully navigate challenges and turn our attention back to fulfilling our purpose and advancing inclusion, the twin drivers of student success.

At the University of Maryland, Baltimore County (UMBC), as on other campuses, what made us strong and resilient through several tough years was a community that knew its values and purpose. We protected our academic program, supported student success, and promoted equity and inclusion. We drew on the strong sense of community that we had built over many years. This empowered community, its collective values, and its shared leadership formed the foundation for pulling together and doing the work during this season of uncertainty and discomfort to tackle our challenges and embrace our opportunities.

In spring 2020 colleges, universities, and higher education organizations cancelled events and meetings. Normal travel, speeches, and external meetings came to a halt for all of us. Then, that summer, as we became more comfortable with Zoom, WebEx, Teams, and other platforms for conducting virtual meetings, colleagues in institutions and organizations across the country realized that events and meetings could resume using this technology. Indeed, many realized there could be even more such meetings than ever because travel was not required.

In summer and fall 2020 a number of colleges and universities—community colleges, liberal arts colleges, comprehensives, research universities, and university systems—invited me to speak to their boards or leadership teams about my earlier work, *The Empowered University*. They read the book in advance of my talk and came ready to ask tough questions. We had robust and honest discussions.

Eventually, someone—a faculty member, the president, or board chair—would ask, "Have you at UMBC stayed true to your values, culture, and shared leadership approach as you have navigated a pandemic and a racial reckoning?" "Yes!" My answer regarding the way we handled these unexpected events at UMBC was always unequivocal. They would then discuss how they had also stayed true to their values. From there, we would explore the notion of an empowering leadership style, ways to cultivate resilience, and the challenges of addressing and advancing diversity, equity, and inclusion. These conversations inspired new thoughts about empowerment, resilience, purpose, and inclusion and *The Resilient University*, this sequel to *The Empowered University*.

This book is the story of how higher education—in particular one empowered university—fared during the crises of 2020 and the years that followed as we moved from reacting to crisis to intentional work supporting student success. It is the work of four coauthors: the work was a collective effort that pulled together academic affairs, administration and finance, and policy advocacy. Peter Henderson was my senior advisor at UMBC and my coauthor on articles in *Issues in Science and Technology, Proceedings of the National Academy of Sciences,* and *The Atlantic.* He brought a national policy perspective and significant writing experience to this project. Philip Rous, provost at UMBC, and Lynne Schaefer, vice president for finance and administration at UMBC, brought their experiences during the pandemic to the work of writing this book. I already had a strong interactive working relationship with and deep trust for these experienced administrators before the pandemic. Our collaborative approach to leading the university served us well as the crisis unfolded. While I consulted with them on high-level decisions, I made a deliberate decision to empower them, and through them to empower the campus, to make decisions and do the work. I wanted all staff members on our campus to know that they had my full confidence. They did not let me down.

We base our views in this book on extensive conversations with our UMBC colleagues—faculty, staff, and students—and colleagues from other institutions in the University System of Maryland (USM), associations such as the Association of Public and Land-grant Universities (APLU) and the National Association of College and University Business Officers (NACUBO), and elsewhere around the country. These conversations have allowed us to gather information about the experiences of our community and other campuses during the pandemic, recession, and social unrest.

As we did for *The Empowered University,* we began our research for this book by holding discussions with our UMBC colleagues. We would like to thank our USM colleagues Chancellor Jay Perman and Vice Chancellors Jo Boughman and Ellen Herbst for sharing their perspectives on how the USM and its member institutions navigated the COVID-19 pandemic in 2020 and 2021. We would also like to thank the following UMBC colleagues who discussed their roles and actions during this period as we deliberated and managed three unexpected crises and the acceleration of our work in so many areas: Lisa Akchin, Arianna Arnold, Valerie Sheares Ashby, Brian Barrio, Keith Bowman, Dana Bradley, Brittni Brown, Robert Carpenter, Katharine Cole, Helena Dahlen, Anjali DasSarma, Mehrshad

Devin, Paul Dillon, Candace Dodson-Reed, Damian Doyle, Saman-tha Fries, John Fritz, Linda Hodges, Bill LaCourse, Marie Lilly, Robert Lubaszewski, Susan McDonough, Kimberly Moffitt, Tony Moreira, Yvette Mozie-Ross, Cael Mulcahy, Janet Rutledge, Sarah Shin, Greg Simmons, Orianne Smith, Chris Steele, Karl Steiner, Jack Suess, Valerie Thomas, Elle Trusz, Shelly Wiechelt, Melody Wright, Jessica Wyatt, Nancy Young, and Lucy Wilson.

Several UMBC colleagues shared with us pieces they wrote about their experiences during the pandemic. These include Lisa Akchin, chief marketing officer, who wrote about sustaining a university brand during the pandemic emergency, and Linda Hodges and her colleagues in the UMBC Faculty Development Center, who wrote about the way they marketed their pedagogical assistance to faculty who were also working to learn instructional technology to teach online. Jack Suess, chief information officer, was very helpful to us in understanding the role of technology during the pandemic and the technology issues in higher education that leaders face in the years ahead.

Last, we would like to thank Jackie Hrabowski, Sabrina Fu, and Laura Henderson for their ongoing support of our work, and our children, Eric Hrabowski, Clarissa and Ashley Rous, Samantha and Matthew Landen, and Christopher, Geoffrey, and Julia Henderson for their inspiration.

Freeman A. Hrabowski III

Note: Each of the coauthors is also an individual actor in the narrative of the book. In those instances in which we appear as actors, we refer to our-selves in the third person.

THE **RESILIENT** UNIVERSITY

PROLOGUE

Empowerment

FREEMAN A. HRABOWSKI III

"It's not about me. It's about us."

Colleges and universities, whatever their size, are complex organizations. Every campus needs the work of many—senior leaders, board members, donors, students, alumni, faculty, and staff. A community of colleagues works together for a college or university to thrive.

Yet campus leaders bring varying styles, and campuses have diverse cultures. Because of timing and circumstances, leadership teams sometimes make decisions quickly; other times they engage in more deliberative and shared decision-making. Campus leaders differ in terms of the balance they strike between these approaches, varying in the extent to which they engage and empower others to lead, make decisions, and innovate.

The Empowered University described how our university, the University of Maryland, Baltimore County (UMBC), supported student inclusion and success through an empowering culture and shared leadership. We had deep, sometimes difficult, conversations about challenges and opportunities. We encouraged buy-in, cultivated allies and champions, and empowered change agents. Through *purpose* and *inclusion* in our leadership style, we achieved the *purpose* and *inclusion* at the center of our academic program that drove student success.

Leaders may find empowerment tricky. Sometimes to empower others we must let go; at others we must become even more involved.

I had a eureka moment at one point in my presidency. We were deeply engaged in a difficult enterprise software transition. At the end of one meeting with my new vice president for finance and administration, I said, "Okay, as a next step I will convene a meeting of the team leaders." However, she said, "No, I've got this. I will convene the meeting and take care of next steps." I was taken aback but then relented. She convened the meeting, team leaders took action, and the work on the software transition went well. I did not need to control the work. Paradoxically, the more I let go to trusted colleagues, the better I could perform as a leader, freeing my time for the work I had to do and letting others lead change in the way only they could do.

While there are times to let go, there are also times to engage. Two decades ago, when we applied to the National Science Foundation (NSF) for an ADVANCE grant to support the recruitment, success, and leadership of women in our science and engineering faculty, people asked why I—as a man—would want to be the principal investigator (PI). I said, "Men should be as concerned about the advancement of women as women are." I signaled to our campus that this work was important and a priority. I was PI, yet I also had seven other co-PIs. We were a team.

Most important, I demonstrated that I was both curious and vulnerable. I made it clear that I was learning and that others should as well. I could admit when I did not know something—in this case, how women experienced the faculty career ladder in science at UMBC and other research universities. I could ask others for help in understanding the problem, seeking solutions, leading the effort, and doing the work. In doing this, I was not just learning myself but also modeling that behavior.

It is ironic that we lead academic institutions—places of learning—yet as leaders, we sometimes act as if we already know everything. We do not, however, and we should not pretend to. Here are questions I often contemplate as a leader: Am I curious? Am I secure enough to be vulnerable? Can I admit it when I do not know something and need to learn or when I am wrong and have made a mistake? Can I empower others to help or, more important, lead the work? When do I let go and when do I engage?

We exercise leadership in a cultural context. Eric Weiner writes, "Culture is the sea we swim in—so pervasive, so all-consuming, that we fail to notice its existence until we step out of it. It matters more than we think."[1] Indeed, the culture on each of our campuses matters because it limits or enables what is possible in the daily work we do and for any long-term change we seek.

We should assess the elements of our campus cultures because they may have implications for what we can accomplish. We see our campus culture in our vision and mission statements, as well as the goals we establish in our strategic plans. We also see it in the values we hold, the norms we adhere to, the attitudes we express, the behaviors we exhibit, and the actions we take. We live our culture in the questions we ask, the initiatives we support, the effort we put into our work, and the achievements we measure and applaud.

If we find that our culture, values, norms, and behavior do not align with and support our goals, then we have work to do in changing that culture, as difficult as that may be. I have said in public— at a White House Summit—that "culture change is hard as hell." But this is not an excuse to ignore it. Because higher education matters, it is our responsibility as campus leaders to embrace the work of culture change when it is a prerequisite for the work we want to see.

How do we change culture? A playbook for change might involve several strategies. First, we acknowledge that an organization as complex as a college or university does not have one homogenous culture, as much as we talk about our campuses as if they do. We find that people hold different values and norms across divisions, colleges, and departments. Still, leaders can stimulate the identification of key values, norms, and behaviors that form a core culture, such as student success, inclusive excellence, shared leadership, community, and putting people first.

Second, we can stimulate discussions that lead to a new understanding of problems and solutions. We have conversations that sometimes are difficult, especially as they touch on sensitive issues. We consider the quantitative and qualitative information available. We create a shared understanding of problems, opportunities, solutions, and risks. The goal is, ultimately, to agree on actions and work together. In performing these tasks, we create a shared narrative of where we have been, where we are, and where we are going.

Third, we can identify those with power—from prestige, position, or the ability to persuade—who can be important to shaping our core culture and values. We can work with these individuals in several ways. We can also identify those with initiative who may serve as change agents and leaders of innovative work.

Fourth, sometimes action speaks louder than words. Discussion gets us only so far. Then action can demonstrate what is possible and change minds. In the late 1980s I encountered opposition when I sought to create a new program for high-achieving Black undergraduates in science and engineering at UMBC. Some objected to a program focused on one race. However, the biggest problem was that faculty—most of whom were well intentioned—had not seen Blacks succeed in the natural sciences and engineering on our campus, so they could not imagine what that might look like. I suggested that we start the program and consider it an experiment, with evaluation embedded from the start, and see whether concerted actions could make a difference. Soon, faculty who were used to Blacks who did not perform well in their classes changed their attitudes when the students we brought in began to not just succeed but also earn top marks. This experiential learning changed what we thought was possible. It changed our culture.

Last, to change the culture we sometimes need to change the people. This can happen naturally with turnover. When I was president, demonstrated commitment to diversity and underrepresented minority student success was one of the characteristics we looked for in applicants for key campus positions.

Culture change takes dedication and commitment over a long period. It happens incrementally, with conversations, faculty and staff buy-in, people willing to step up as change agents, and new investments to support the work of those agents and the success of those investments. Then one day we notice that the culture has noticeably shifted. Moreover, that changed culture then enables further innovations, initiatives, programs, and actions.

In an empowering culture, we cultivate a "habit of mind" that is intensely reflective. We look hard in the mirror—noting strengths and weaknesses, assessing our opportunities and challenges, asking what we are doing and why. We encourage ourselves to think about how we can do our work differently and better.

To create this culture, we empower administrators, staff, faculty, and students so that anyone can be a leader in identifying and implementing the work we need to do. We begin to create it by embracing shared governance. When we work with faculty and staff senates and student government organizations, we are more transparent, we gather information, we learn, we create opportunities for community members to participate in and support both decision-making and action. Shared leadership is more than shared governance. It also engages and supports those who raise issues and are willing to work with campus leadership to solve problems, start initiatives, and do the work.

My experience has been that we have better ideas to consider, more effective action, and less resistance when many people pull together. Senior leaders develop a vision, using an inclusive process. They then encourage deep engagement with those who will be responsible for whether we realize that vision—namely, our colleagues. We work collaboratively to develop goals and work plans. We agree on our expectations, assign responsibility, and set deadlines. Leaders remain part of the work, providing support, feedback, and resources.

At UMBC we leaned into shared leadership. While I was president, the provost, the vice president for finance and administration, other leaders, and I participated in faculty senate meetings. The president of the faculty senate and the chair of its academic budget and planning committee were members of my President's Council, which met biweekly. My leadership team and I embraced long-term consistent interaction and conversations among campus leadership, faculty, staff, and students. We held campus retreats, our strategic planning process was inclusive, and we held periodic focus groups with campus groups. We increased communication with campus to provide both care and transparency. We established incentive grant programs for faculty to encourage work in such areas as course redesign and entrepreneurship.

An empowered university, a collective culture, and shared leadership enable change, yet individuals still must choose to act. There are many reasons they might not do so. People may be comfortable with the status quo. They may not believe in the work or understand how change benefits them, the university, or society. They may experience uncertainty and fear in the face of change. They may perceive the risk of loss or failure and may not have the courage to act. They may not believe a goal is achievable if the outcome is yet unseen. They may perceive that sustainable change requires long, organized, and sometimes expensive commitments of time, energy, and resources that can feel overwhelming.

They may understand that change also requires grit and improvisation. Sometimes the chosen path turns out not to be the best because of unanticipated obstacles or challenges. At these junctures, successful change agents find ways to change course or obtain new information or resources so that they can get on a new, more effective path to success.

For those who feel that the status quo is preferable to or more comfortable than change, what is the incentive to do the work? What nudges people who say, "If only I had the time and resources, then I would do it"? What is in it for them to engage in the work, especially if the work of change arrives on top of their regular work?

For some, the work is its own reward, and we may have little work to do in motivating them. They have a passion for excellence or a particular purpose. The work has meaning for them, and they derive pleasure from either success itself or what it achieves. Change often happens when these people perform tasks beyond their regular duties. They take on the extra work because that is where they make the difference.

For others, we must engage and persuade. Engagement demonstrates respect for community members with whom we work who feel empowered by being part of the process of change, whether it is general culture change or the work of a specific initiative. Engagement provides opportunities for explanation, information sharing, and discussion. It provides opportunities for persuasion. Persuasion is the work we do to convince others to join and contribute to the work. At the end of his tenure as president, Harry Truman is said to have remarked, "He'll sit right there and say do this, do that! Poor Ike. It won't be at all like the Army." Presidential power stems not from command but from persuasion. Successful leaders and change agents work to persuade others about the nature of a problem, the benefits of a solution, and being a part of the solution. In an empowered community, persuasion is a two-way street. Conversation sits at the center of community, empowerment, engagement, and persuasion.

We remind ourselves that "success is never final." It is never final because once we achieve success, the work continues. We must sustain it. We have to combat backsliding among our staff and train new people joining the team to do things the new way. We also have to protect the innovation from those who wish to contest, undermine, or repeal it. Success is also never final, because the world is constantly evolving. We can always be better. There is always more to do.

In 2018 UMBC experienced two unexpected events: an upset victory by our men's basketball team over the University of Virginia in the NCAA tournament, and a student protest on our campus about sexual assault. The first experience was exciting and joyful, as we became "America's team" for a weekend and basked in the media glow; the second was serious and painful as the protestors challenged us to have the courage to do better with regard to sexual assault and

Title IX. We responded the same way each time: we focused on our values, we asked hard questions, we listened carefully, and we took actions that emerged from broad discussion and analysis.

UMBC emerged a better place each time, but success is never final. In 2020 we encountered two more unexpected events that shook us. In March we confronted the COVID-19 pandemic. The WHO declared COVID a pandemic, and Maryland governor Larry Hogan issued an executive order closing state agencies and imposing other public health restrictions to contain the spread of COVID-19. Soon, we had closed our physical campus and moved instruction online for at least the rest of that spring semester. Then, just as we were getting our bearings with regard to that crisis, we reeled in May from the tragic murder of George Floyd and the subsequent nationwide outpouring of grief and anger about the lingering challenges of structural racism. We began deep conversations about race and institutional change.

Even if a small group is involved at the outset, real change happens when we pull people together from across the campus community to do the work over time, as seen in each of these four examples:

- The basketball team won the NCAA tournament game, but the community worked together to reap the rewards and advance UMBC as an institution.
- Several student groups led the sexual assault protest, but the community worked together over two years to build a new approach to and organization for Title IX and diversity, equity, and inclusion at UMBC.
- Our crisis management teams led the initial campus response to COVID-19, but as the pandemic became a long-term circumstance, teams from across the campus did the work that kept us safe, deployed new policies and technological tools, and sustained our mission.
- A small number of people confronted leadership with their concerns about race, but we soon expanded these conversa-

tions to bring in the entire community through forums and the establishment of an Inclusion Council.

This resilience was possible because we had created a campus culture that allowed us, in unexpected situations, to focus on our values, ask hard questions, listen carefully, and take action.

Our colleges and universities have important work to do. Higher education matters. The success of our nation depends on how we manage our higher education institutions in a twenty-first century that demands informed, educated, and thoughtful citizens, as well as a skilled and knowledgeable workforce that can drive our economy. We need educated people who understand our problems and opportunities, and who create novel solutions. Student success matters. The importance of higher education to students and their families for economic success and social mobility has never been higher and will only increase in the future. Entrance to the middle class—once attainable with a high school diploma and a manufacturing job—can today be secured primarily though postsecondary education. College is also an opportunity for personal growth, attaining life skills, and better understanding the human condition and the world around us.

Yet the story of higher education in the United States since World War II is an unfinished success story. In 1965, 10 percent of Americans age 25 and over had earned a bachelor's degree. By 2021 this had climbed to 38 percent. However, we see significant disparity in attainment by race. Bachelor's degree attainment for Asians is now 61 percent, for whites 42 percent, for Blacks 28 percent, and for Hispanics 20 percent.

Meanwhile, only 60 percent of full-time students who begin at a four-year institution complete a bachelor's degree from that institution in six years, a percentage that David Kirp recently called "a scandal." If that is a scandal, what do we call it when the six-year completion rate for Blacks or Hispanics is just 40 percent?[2]

Serious, sustained change is hard work. When the change we want to see involves race, diversity, differences, and inclusion, it can be even more challenging, as these are topics most Americans are not comfortable discussing. When change is the right thing for us to attempt, we must nevertheless engage and persist.

My colleagues and I are, at this writing, seeing two contradictory trends with regard to diversity and inclusion in higher education. The first trend is encouraging: many higher education institutions and companies want to do more to recruit and support underrepresented racial and ethnic minorities, women, people who are LGBTQ, and people with disabilities. Many universities and corporations are creating DEI (diversity, equity, and inclusion) positions than ever. The new president of UMBC is hiring a vice president for institutional equity and chief diversity officer (CDO).

Establishing a chief diversity officer position is just the first step. For a CDO and their staff to be successful, leaders must be clear about expectations, provide resources, and vocally support the CDO. Expectations are critical. What does our diversity work mean for culture? For representation and inclusion? For outcomes? One of the challenges we are seeing is that some of those recently hired into diversity positions at colleges and universities become discouraged and leave when their expectations and those of leaders, or the goals of their work and the culture of the institution, do not align. When this happens, the cause of diversity and inclusion is undermined or, even worse, seen as just a cynical exercise of "checking the box" rather than work that supports substantive change.

The second trend we are seeing, as colleges and universities commit to DEI, is its politicization. In Florida, Texas, South Carolina, Virginia, and other states, governors and legislators are now contesting DEI. They are asking public colleges and universities to detail their DEI activities and the resources they have committed to them. In some states, legislators have introduced bills limiting DEI efforts, instruction about certain topics related to race, and more. At public and private institutions, some trustees are asking— and not in a good way—"How woke is the campus"?

In our work supporting DEI, we must be strategic in the language we use. The goal is not to win an argument. That is a short-term victory. What matters in the long game is engaging one another, seeking common understanding, and finding solutions that work for all. I have often found it helpful, in this work, to speak of "being fair" and helping students "of all backgrounds." Like Rev. Dr. Martin Luther King, Jr., I quote the nation's founders, who spoke of freedom and equality for all.

The long game is important. To enact change we must set long-term goals, always keep in mind what works to accomplish them, and do the work. When we created the Meyerhoff Scholars Program in 1988, for example, we did not expect immediate results. In fact, we knew that our students had to complete four or more years as undergraduates and then about six or so years as doctoral students before we saw the outcome we wanted—a PhD in a tenure-track faculty position. That is at least a decade of studies!

After the tragic death of George Floyd, students, alumni, and faculty raised concerns with me and other leaders about experiences they had faced. We did not expect to make all things right immediately, knowing how hard it is to change human culture and behavior. We created an Inclusion Council to provide advice to our new Office of Equity and Inclusion and charged it with, among other things, providing recommendations for long-term actions that would improve campus climate and promote equity and inclusion. Some might see creating a committee as kicking the can down the road. Sometimes that is the intent. For us, though, the intent was to create, through community input, a shared understanding of problems and solutions. After receiving the report of the Inclusion Council, we then established an Implementation Team that we charged with assessing and prioritizing recommendations and developing an implementation plan and schedule.

Some presidents I have worked with have expressed the concern that they cannot say some of the things I can say because I am Black. If they say them, pushing back in any way in conversations about race, others may label them as tone deaf, uncaring, or even racist. Yet it does not have to be this way. A leader who is self-assured and willing to be vulnerable can set up conversations so that, if uncomfortable, they can be civil and productive, resulting in shared understandings and collective action.

Leaders should begin with the notion that any issue is everyone's issue if we cherish justice and equity. As I noted with regard to our ADVANCE grant, men should be as interested in gender and the advancement of women as women are. Similarly, whites should be as interested in race and the advancement of underrepresented minorities as Blacks, Latinx peoples, and Native Americans. Straight community members can be LGBTQ allies. They may already be relatives.

Having set that context, leaders must attend to their mindset. Begin with empathy. Can we imagine ourselves in someone else's shoes? Bring humility. Are we willing to place ourselves in vulnerable or uncomfortable settings? Be willing to engage in conversations. Do we ask questions, listen, and learn?

What are the outcomes we seek when it comes to diversity, equity, and inclusion? The answer may begin with numbers and representation. A critical question is whether we are seeing numbers and representation increase, not just in the aggregate but in all areas and disciplines. Still, numbers are only the beginning.

We have many questions to ask. Are people staying in their studies and supported? Are students doing well academically? How do they feel? Are they learning how to work with people different from themselves? Are faculty faring well on the road to tenure? Are we doing what we can to ensure that those underrepresented minority faculty who come up for tenure do so with a solid CV and portfolio that will lead to a successful tenure bid? Have we advised/mentored them? Have we made sure they have the time and space to do their research? Can we make sure we do not overwhelm them with service demands? We should ask staff how they are doing in their careers. How do they feel about their work environment? Do they have opportunities for professional development and career advancement?

Words are powerful. They translate our thoughts into actions. We in higher education have used many words to describe the difficult, conflicted journey we have lived since early 2020: fear, anxiety, apprehension; coping, flexibility, exhaustion; excitement, innovation, growth. They capture how challenging the work has been as well as the moments of opportunity. We have selected six words— vision, openness, resilience, courage, passion, and hope—to offer a realistic and constructive approach to leading campuses, empowering colleagues, and creating resilient institutions that foster student success through purpose and inclusion. Each of the chapters in this book focuses on one of these:

- Vision: Vision articulates our purpose. Here we discuss the role of a diverse higher education community in meeting society's challenges and opportunities, and the responsibility of each college or university to achieve academic goals in light of these.
- Openness: Openness is our approach to realizing our vision through shared leadership and an empowered community. Here we discuss how asking probing questions, engaging in productive conversations, and keeping an open-mind, especially under conditions of uncertainty, help us work toward solutions and capitalize on opportunities.
- Resilience: Resilience is about focusing on purpose, persisting in the face of challenges, and getting back up when knocked down. It is about grit. We create resilience in our campus operations by drawing on existing institutional resources, planning for contingencies, and generating an urgency about the work. Here we discuss how supporting the people who make up our campus community and providing the resources they need leads to that resilience.
- Courage: Courage is needed to make challenging decisions, on the one hand, and to be true to our values, on the other, so we can achieve inclusion and equity. Here we discuss how summoning the will to create a safe, equitable, inclusive, multicultural community supports the academic program and the people who make up our community.

- Passion: Passion lies at the center of our work in supporting student success. Here we discuss how staying deeply focused, despite disruption, on our mission—supporting and improving student success, research and creative achievement, and community engagement—has allowed us to achieve long-term goals and sustainability.
- Hope: Hope allows us to cultivate an optimistic outlook, by understanding that we have been through tough times before and that we will get through this. It allows us to persevere, overcome, and build anew.

1

Vision

What Is Our Vision?

To be intentional in the face of daily demands and frequent crises, leaders must hold fast to an institutional vision that serves as a moral compass, an organizational inspiration and aspiration, and a constant, long-term focus for decision-making as we carry out our mission. This vision is what we are collectively striving for, even if it is unclear how to achieve it. It provides the opportunity to be proactive rather than reactive, and there have been so many opportunities to be reactive in recent years.

Developing an institutional vision serves many purposes. By using a broad, inclusive process for creating a vision, we develop communal goals for the institution and achieve the deeper buy-in from colleagues necessary for making the vision a sustained reality. By remaining true to this institutional vision, we keep our eyes on long-term aspirations, even when short-term crises disrupt our work. By clarifying and communicating our institutional vision, we can answer critics who question the value of higher education. Cheryl Norton, former president of Slippery Rock University, writes: "Remember, you are building for the future. Consequently, any vision should support the development of the institution's identity and long-term brand. Initiatives that constantly change or are not consistent with the institution's purpose can confuse constituents."[1]

Long-term organizational growth and prosperity require a vision.[2] The process for developing such a vision should begin with campus conversations in which we—administrators, staff, faculty, students, and alumni—ask good questions, share and analyze data, challenge our assumptions, have difficult discussions, and focus on the work that will support and advance our mission. The work we identify for achieving our goals should be realistic and measurable, and yet it can be aspirational as well. "Ask why not," says Cheryl Norton.[3] By doing so, an institution can grow in new ways. An inspiring vision with broad buy-in can also bring a sense of urgency to the work that is sometimes missing in big organizations, public or private, for-profit or nonprofit. Urgency brings energy; a lack of urgency can leave an organization moribund.

Most colleges and universities have a vision or mission statement. These statements generally focus on teaching, research, and service. Regarding teaching, they focus on the liberal arts, the kinds of students they serve (undergraduate, graduate, professional, distance learners), and the values they apply (academic rigor, intellectual curiosity, student support). Liberal arts colleges often note the centrality of the residential experience. Community colleges focus on affordability and transfer and career success. Regarding research and creative achievement, they discuss how the institution supports discovery, advances knowledge and art, and drives innovation. Regarding service, they note the importance of the land-grant mission and extension, patient care, community engagement, economic development, and career opportunity. Vision statements may include diversity and inclusion as core values and the responsibility of developing leaders and citizens. Institutions often note how they serve their state, nation, and world, and often strive for global impact. Many research universities set "world class" and "preeminence" as aspirations.

At UMBC, our vision statement is this: "Our UMBC community redefines excellence in higher education through an inclusive culture that connects innovative teaching and learning, research across disciplines, and civic engagement. We will advance knowledge, economic prosperity, and social justice by welcoming and inspiring inquisitive minds from all backgrounds."[4] This vision focuses on the importance of student success, research, and creative achievement. It centers inclusion and the success of students of all backgrounds. It emphasizes the need to have real-world impact through our students, our alumni, and our faculty, and through community, regional, and national partnerships. It says we can always be better and asks us to be innovative in a way that makes us a model for other institutions.

This was a vision we held onto and returned to in the midst of disrupting crises. We used an inclusive process in which the UMBC community crafted the vision statement. This process included a campus survey and discussions at an annual university retreat that involved nearly two hundred faculty, staff, and students.

For some campuses, "excellence" is a code word for exclusion. For these campuses, rigor means "it's hard to get in and it's hard to succeed." At our annual fall convocation, former president Hrabowski used to tell students that at some institutions they say, "Look to your left, look to your right. Only one of you will make it," while at UMBC, we say, "Look to your left, look to your right. If you put in the work, all of you will make it or we have not done our job." We speak of "inclusive excellence," which is based on high standards and high support. If we admit you, we must help you graduate. It is our moral responsibility.

Student success has several dimensions. Students succeed when they persist in college and complete their degrees in a timely manner and in their intended majors. They succeed when they learn to ask good questions, listen respectfully to others, think critically, understand the importance of evidence, and construct, present, and defend evidence-based positions. They succeed when they gain knowledge and skills that serve them after graduation and have experiences in college that change their perspectives on themselves and society. They succeed when they have postgraduation plans for further study or jobs.

Like more and more institutions, we at UMBC, a university with fourteen thousand students and four thousand employees, put considerable resources into student support. We seek first to use data analytics to understand student strengths, weaknesses, and skill gaps. The tools we use to provide support include introductory course redesign, faculty pedagogical development, community building, living-learning residence halls, bridge programs, first-year seminars, tutoring, research experiences and internships, and interventions by academic advocates for at-risk students. We take this very seriously.

We seek to provide students with an education that allows them to have fulfilling personal lives, successful careers, and positive civic engagement. In the process, we hope to educate students who will solve society's problems. Indeed, it is ironic that people are questioning the value of higher education at a time when the people who are solving our nation's problems are highly educated. A recent Pew Research Center survey showed that getting the COVID-19 vaccine was correlated with level of education: 89 percent of those with an advanced degree and 81 percent of those with a college degree had received at least one dose of the vaccine; meanwhile just 69 percent of those with some college, and 61 percent of those with a high school diploma or less formal education had been vaccinated.[5] If we had done better at educating more Americans both in general and about viruses and misinformation in particular, perhaps our experiences since the beginning of 2020 would have been different.

There may be no better example of the way higher education can prepare our students to solve society's problems than that of Kizzmekia Corbett.

Higher Education Matters

The Coronavirus Vaccine Team at the National Institutes of Health (NIH) downloaded the SARS-CoV-2 genetic sequence on January 10, 2020, the day the Chinese government posted it online. The team, housed in the National Institute of Allergy and Infectious

Disease (NIAID), got right to work developing an RNA vaccine using the spike protein of the virus as the immunogen. They were prepared. Dr. Barney Graham, deputy director of the NIH Vaccine Research Center, Dr. Kizzmekia Corbett, scientific lead for the vaccine team, and their colleagues had been working on vaccines for the Middle East respiratory syndrome (MERS) and severe acute respiratory syndrome (SARS) and conducting research on coronaviruses for years. They had a vaccine partnership already in place with Moderna, a pharmaceutical and biotechnology company, that would allow the team to deliver a COVID-19 vaccine using Moderna's mRNA platform. Just 66 days later, Moderna took the vaccine into its phase-one clinical trial, an astounding speed for vaccine development, which typically takes years.[6]

In this story, we can see the power of education to transform lives. Kizzmekia Corbett grew up in rural North Carolina. A teacher recognized her abilities and guided her toward activities that would nurture her talent. During a summer in high school, she participated in Project SEED, a program of the American Chemical Society, which allowed her to work in a research lab at the University of North Carolina. At age 17, she matriculated at UMBC, where she participated in the Meyerhoff Scholars program, which focuses on inclusive excellence in science and engineering. Corbett earned her PhD in immunology at the University of North Carolina and took a postdoctoral fellowship at NIAID under Dr. Barney Graham, who later became her boss in the NIAID Vaccine Research Center. Recently, she became assistant professor of immunology and infectious diseases at the Harvard T. H. Chan School of Public Health.

We can also see the power of education to change or help society. Dr. Anthony Fauci, NIAID director, said of Corbett, "Her work will have a substantial impact on ending the worst respiratory disease pandemic in more than 100 years."[7] The Partnership for Public Service recognized Corbett and Graham as the Federal Civil Servants of the Year for 2021.[8] In December 2021 *TIME Magazine*, as part of its "Person of the Year" edition, recognized Corbett and Graham as the "heroes of the year," an honor they shared with Katalin

Kariko and Drew Weissman, who had pioneered mRNA technology at the University of Pennsylvania.[9] In addition, Corbett, who double-majored in biological sciences and sociology at UMBC, has worked on the effort to urge the vaccine resistant, especially in the African American community, to be vaccinated.

This is the essence of higher education: to provide a quality education that enriches a student's life and also allows her, working in a team with other educated people, to impact our society—a cultural, social, political, economic, or, in this case, public health impact. Our vision must include understanding our society, the role of a diverse higher education community in addressing society's problems and needs, and the responsibility of each college or university to achieve academic goals and support students in light of these.

We should also appreciate the long-term federal investments that made this outcome possible. From 1999 to 2003 Congress appropriated funds to double the budget of the NIH. During this period, NIAID built the Vaccine Research Center, where the SARS-CoV-2 vaccine was developed under Graham and Corbett. It was also during this period when Kariko and Weissman received their first NIH grants that supported their work on mRNA. Where would we be today if we, as a society, had not made these investments that laid the foundation for the later work of the coronavirus vaccine development team?[10]

Every institution points to alumni like Dr. Corbett who have received honors or publicity for their work and influence during the pandemic. We have applauded other high-profile alumni who have made a difference. Dr. Jerome Adams, a 1996 graduate, was the US Surgeon General, and Dr. Letitia Dzirasa, a 2003 graduate, is the Baltimore City Health Commissioner. They both served the public during the pandemic. Just as important, we have highlighted those who typically labor without fanfare but also make a difference. Maggie Kemper, a 2014 graduate, is a COVID unit nurse at Johns Hopkins Hospital, and Trent Gabriel, a 2014 graduate, a dental resident at St. Barnabas Hospital in the Bronx who filled in when needed to test doctors, take vitals for patients, and fill pharmacy prescriptions.

Many alumni pitched in to make masks, face shields, and biomedical products. Potomac Photonics, owned by Mike Adelstein, a 1996 graduate, produced several thousand face shields early in the pandemic, sending them to hospitals in Maryland, New York, and Florida. They also produced microfluidic chips for companies to use in the development of COVID-19 vaccines and medications.[11]

Across the country, colleges and universities have highlighted the many thousands of our alumni who have been serving on the front lines of health care. Many fall 2020 alumni magazines showcased their stories. The University of Maryland School of Nursing—like other such schools—has even graduated several classes early as area hospitals find existing staff are depleted, overwhelmed, or exhausted. Whatever institution they graduated from, these graduates bring purpose, knowledge, skills, clarity of vision, and drive to realize their potential and make a difference in the world around them.

Our alumni make a difference in many fields, and we see the power of education in their stories. Adrienne Jones, also a UMBC alumna, is addressing some of our most difficult public policy challenges. Jones serves as Speaker of the Maryland House of Delegates, the first woman and African American to hold that position. During the unprecedented 2021 General Assembly session, held virtually because of COVID-19, Jones laid out an ambitious racial and economic justice agenda to address disparities in health care, homeownership, banking, and business. Other major legislation introduced during the session also addressed inequities, including the Blueprint for Maryland's Future, an education reform measure, and one-time funding for historically Black colleges and universities. Rounding out the session, the Assembly also passed major legislation on criminal justice and police reform.[12]

Dr. Kafui Dzirasa, who attended UMBC and participated in the Meyerhoff Scholars program before earning the MD-PhD at Duke University, is confronting challenges in mental health. Today, he is the K. Ranga Rama Krishnan Associate Professor of Psychiatry and behavioral sciences at Duke University Medical School. The pioneering work of Dzirasa and his team at Duke focuses on the ways that genes interact with the environment when a person is under stress, thus modifying normal neural circuits. Based on this research, Dzirasa envisions a day when doctors can use neuroelectrical stimulation to treat such illnesses as depression, bipolar disorder, and addiction.[13] The National Academy of Medicine recently elected Dzirasa as a member, and the Howard Hughes Medical Institute named him an HHMI Investigator.[14]

Kaitlyn Sadtler, after attending UMBC, earned her PhD in cellular and molecular medicine at the Johns Hopkins Medical School, did a postdoctoral fellowship at the Massachusetts Institute of Technology, and is now an investigator and director of the immunoengineering section at the National Institute of Biomedical Imaging and Bioengineering at NIH. There she is leading the national study estimating the number and percentage of US residents who have had COVID-19 without presenting symptoms. The results of this study will help complete our picture of the transmissibility of this coronavirus, helping other scientists understand how it spreads and what can stop it.[15]

Higher education matters. It empowers students for life, careers, civic engagement, and citizenship. When asked if college was useful, the large majority of college graduates said it was, according to a 2016 Pew survey.[16] Among respondents, 93 percent said it was somewhat or very useful in helping them grow personally and intellectually, 84 percent reported somewhat or very useful for opening doors to job possibilities, and 82 percent agreed that it was somewhat or very useful for developing skills or knowledge for the workplace.

While graduates still report positive college experiences, the US population in general is reporting declining approval for higher education. Pew reported that, in 2019, about half of the US respondents surveyed believed that higher education is having a positive impact on society, down from 63 percent in 2015. Meanwhile 38 percent responded that higher education was having a negative impact, up from 28 percent. Pew reported a partisan divide, with 67 percent of Democrats saying that higher education has a positive impact, down from 72 percent, and 59 percent of Republicans responding that the impact is negative, up from 37 percent.[17]

While the drop in approval ratings for higher education concerns us, the issues driving those trends are familiar: tuition, workforce development, free speech, and the ways we understand our society and polity. Pew investigated these to clarify partisan differences in the issues of concern.[18]

- Democrats especially, but also a majority of Republicans, are concerned about tuition levels.
- Republicans especially, but also a majority of Democrats, are concerned that students are not getting the skills they need to succeed in the workplace.
- A large majority of Republicans, but only a small minority of Democrats, believe that (1) there is too much concern about protecting students from opinions they might find offensive and (2) professors are bringing their political and social views into the classroom.

These results are not surprising. Elected officials and political candidates have made into political issues college costs (tuition-free college, student debt), the content of education (American history, critical race theory, workplace skills), and free speech on campus (controversial speakers). This is a double-edged sword. We should absolutely debate and clarify these issues, educating the electorate about how a college education is financed, how structural racism affects individuals and our society, and so forth. The vitriol of political debate in the contemporary United States, however, with partisan-aligned news and social media echo chambers, often turns up the heat without shedding light. This polarizes some Americans and turns others off.

As leaders in higher education, we must, without apology, make the argument for the value of our work. There are many resources for us to draw on to make the case. For example, the National Association of College and University Business Officers (NACUBO) has recently made available a slide deck that helps a speaker make the argument that higher education makes available more opportunities, more prosperity, and more benefits to our communities. Higher education institutions create jobs, increase tax revenues, grow the local economy, provide health care, improve food security, and engage in the research that leads to new ideas, innovation, economic growth, and national defense. Meanwhile, obtaining a college degree can boost lifetime earnings and retirement savings. College-educated citizens are more likely to vote and volunteer and are less likely to be unemployed or on public assistance. The benefits are both private and public.[19]

What we begin with, then, is that higher education matters. However, there are many unresolved issues that have been with us for some time and that we still must face. We in higher education cannot ignore these issues, as they affect both our campuses and our society. We must look in the mirror, ask how we, as institutions, have contributed to these problems, and then work intentionally to address them, keeping our long-term goals in mind even in the face of short-term disruptions.

The Times They Are A-Changing, But the Song Remains the Same

The United States is a dynamic society with deep, difficult challenges. Since the founding of our country, we as Americans have fought over—sometimes literally—race relations, immigration, gender roles, electoral participation, economic opportunity, and inequality. Today's partisan divisions, #MeToo movement, racial unrest, and policy debates are the current, urgent versions of older challenges still disputed and unresolved. The United States also continues to change as globalization, demographics, technology, and communications have shaped our population, economy, and social structure over the past 150 years. In this century, the evolution of partisan-aligned social media, the emergence of global terrorism, and the existential threat of climate change have added fuel to political, policy, and environmental fires. Then, in early 2020, as we already struggled with all of those contentious challenges, the COVID-19 pandemic upended our society, economy, schools, and campuses in ways that none of us imagined.

All of these issues find their way to our campuses. During 2020 and 2021 the myriad ways our campuses and society were interconnected were clear. All of us—on campus and in our country—struggled with political division, an economic recession, structural racism, and a public health crisis on a scale that none of us had ever experienced. The higher education community and our society are still navigating these crises and the work they have brought us to ensure the health, safety, and success of our community members.

While these crises combined to deeply and unexpectedly disrupt our campuses in 2020, none of the related issues were new to us: equity, finance, teaching and learning, business operations, and more. We already understood their importance and, in many cases, were already working on them. What was different about 2020 and 2021 was that crises accentuated these concerns, and our colleagues sometimes accelerated their work in response. And yet, in most instances, the work is still not yet complete. The issues and work that accelerated during these crises are ongoing, and we have the chance to create something new on our campuses and in our society as we continue this work.

Though we had resources and colleagues to draw from, few of us anticipated and planned for a pandemic. We navigated COVID-19 and the recession it engendered in real time, often making decisions with partial information. Our campuses followed different paths, but regardless of the decisions we made, this experience has changed us all. Most obvious, we found that we could adapt to disruption quickly when needed. We moved work and instruction online and have since moved them again into hybrid environments where we are sometimes online, sometimes in person, and in either case using new digital tools. Some faculty have found that the experience of teaching online has prompted them to rethink course design, pedagogy, and student engagement. (There is nothing like experiential learning.)

While we sought to manage during a pandemic, we also saw national unrest over structural racism and a divisive presidential election. Our experiences with these have led us to think more deeply about both inclusion and the way we educate our students. We need more understanding of and conversations about the history and current reality of structural racism and other issues. We have to think more deeply about preparing our students to be citizens. We must focus on developing media literacy in our students. How do we teach them—through every course—to be critical thinkers who can absorb, analyze, digest, and understand information? What is the role of the university and its faculty in an age of mass information, misinformation, and disinformation?

It is challenging to tackle these issues when we are exhausted from all that the pandemic has demanded of us. However, we must summon the will to carry on because even without the pandemic, we would still face critical issues in higher education. Many students have challenges accessing and affording higher education. Some wonder if the benefits will be worth the cost, a reasonable question for anyone to ask. Research shows significant returns, on average, for those who earn a bachelor's degree, but not everyone who starts at a four-year institution completes a degree within six years; 40 percent do not. The quality of the education delivered to students remains an issue, though new understanding of the ways students learn and faculty adoption of new teaching methods are making some headway. We are still in the middle of a conversation about how to make our campuses inclusive and equitable. We are challenged as well to support student well-being and mental health. Moreover, we do all of this while managing institutional financial stability and investments in facilities and technology.

Student Success

Many are now questioning the "value" of a college education. This has been driven in part by politics and "culture wars," yet there are also legitimate concerns about completion rates and mounting student debt. Those who start college, take loans, and do not complete a degree often face considerable financial hardship. It would be no wonder for someone in this situation to ask, "Is it worth it?" If immediate employment at decent wages—something increasingly available in today's temporarily constrained labor market—is a viable alternative, then a young person might select that as the better choice in the short term instead of postsecondary education.

Our response must be to redouble our efforts to increase student success—the completion of a quality postsecondary education by many more of our students—rather than concede that postsecondary education is not for everyone. We know there is value in what we offer, and we acknowledge that postsecondary education can take many forms to fit the needs of each individual. Students may work toward a certificate, an associate's degree, or a bachelor's degree to support their aspirations. Here, though, is the point: when we see a family that has sent at least one person to postsecondary education (community college or a four-year institution), we typically see a family that wants to send other family members. When our institutions shift more wholly to a student-focused mission that facilitates learning, retention, and completion, then we will succeed as institutions, students, and a nation.

Since higher education has private and public returns on investment, it is both an individual and public policy concern. At the state and national levels, we should be concerned about both educational attainment and the quality of the education attained. Attainment issues include increasing access and affordability, raising college retention and completion rates, and reducing time to degree. Quality issues include curriculum, pedagogy, course redesign, and inclusion. When we think about curricula, we should ask whether we are providing students educational opportunities that match their life goals (individual returns) and educating them to be productive workers, citizens, and leaders in the twenty-first century (public returns).

TABLE 1

Six-year graduation rates of first-time, full-time freshmen (fall 2012 entering cohort) at four-year institutions, by selectivity of institution and race/ethnicity, 2018

	Total	White	Black	Hispanic	Asian	Pacific Islander	American Indian/ Alaska Native	Two or more races	Non-Resident alien	Distribution of institution
All four-year institutions	62.4	65.9	42.4	56.7	75.5	49.1	40.6	57.7	71.5	100.0
Open admissions	33.6	40	20.2	29.1	40.8	17	15.5	27.2	46.1	27.2
90% or more accepted	45.1	49.8	25.5	37.8	51.8	33.7	29	38	54.6	8.9
75.0% to 89.9% accepted	58.3	62	38.4	50.5	63.4	43.6	41.8	51.4	62.8	18.0
50.0% to 74.9% accepted	63.4	67.3	45.7	56.6	72.1	53.2	43.6	58.5	70.3	31.6
25.0% to 49.9% accepted	71.8	76.5	48.2	67.3	81.5	67.1	54.9	70.8	77.4	11.2
Less than 25.0% accepted	90.1	92.1	71.6	87.5	94.5	72.8	81.2	90.7	91.2	3.1

Source: US Department of Education, National Center for Education Statistics, Digest of Education Statistics.
https://nces.ed.gov/programs/digest/d17/tables/dt17_305.40.asp
https://nces.ed.gov/programs/digest/d19/tables/dt19_326.10.asp

The completion agenda has been a national priority for much of the past two decades, yet we still have much left to do. Nationally, just 60 percent of undergraduates who start at a four-year institution will graduate in six years. David Kirp has called this "the college dropout scandal."[20] The scandal is worse than that figure alone reveals, as graduation rates vary significantly by institutional admissions selectivity and by race/ethnicity.[21]

We see these institutional differences in completion rates (table 1):

- For institutions that admit fewer than 25 percent of applicants, just 3 percent of institutions, the six-year completion rate is 90 percent.
- For those that admit 25 to 49.9 percent, about 11 percent of higher education institutions (HEIs), the rate is 72 percent.
- With those that admit 50 to 74.9 percent, about one-third of HEIs, the rate declines to 63 percent.
- Those admitting 75 to 89.9 percent, 18 percent of institutions, have a rate of 58 percent.
- Institutions that admit 90 or more percent of applicants, 9 percent of HEIs, have six-year graduation rates of 45 percent.
- If an institution has open admissions, as is the case for one-quarter of four-year institutions, the six-year graduation rate is 34 percent.

- For-profit institutions, regardless of selectivity, have an average six-year completion rate of 25 percent.

Meanwhile, just one-third of community college students—who make up more than one-third of postsecondary students—complete a credential or an associate's degree within three years.[22]

For academic year 2019–2020, 12.7 million undergraduates and 3.4 million graduate students attended public or nonprofit four-year institutions; about 1.3 million undergraduate and graduate students attended for-profits; and another 7.7 million attended community colleges.[23] Millions of undergraduate students begin at these institutions and never complete a degree.

If our vision in higher education is to increase student achievement and degree attainment, it is clear we have much more work to do. Transformation would occur when we, as a nation, say that these rates and the disparities across institutions are not acceptable and take steps to address them.

To develop strategies, we must disaggregate the data. First, higher education institutions are diverse. They vary by selectivity, which is correlated with control (private or public) and type (community colleges, for-profit institutions, online universities, comprehensive universities, liberal arts colleges, and research universities). Second, there are distributions within each of these institutional categories by race and ethnicity that add to the "scandal." Asian and white students beat the average for each type of institution by 3 to 10 and 2 to 6 percentage points, respectively. The graduation rates for Hispanic students lag the average by 3 to 8 percentage points. The rates for Black students lag institutional averages by 13 to 23 percentage points.[24]

When we tackle access, affordability, retention, and completion, we must take into account important differences by race and ethnicity. For the 2012 entering cohort, six-year graduation rates were as follows:[25]

Asian, 76 percent
Non-US citizen, 72 percent

White, 66 percent
Two or more races, 58 percent
Hispanic, 57 percent
Pacific Islander, 49 percent
Black, 42 percent
American Indian / Alaska Native, 41 percent

We must place both institutional diversity and racial/ethnic equity at the center of our work when developing effective interventions to address student success. Then also center the diverse aspirations of students, whether they are seeking certificates, associate's degrees, or bachelor's degrees to meet their life and career goals.

We do not have to settle for mediocrity. At UMBC our admission rate has been about 60 percent. Over the past three decades, we have doubled our six-year graduation rate, which is now 70 percent with another 10 percent transferring and graduating from another institution. Our six-year completion rate for Black students is slightly ahead of the overall rate for our student population. We have accomplished this by simultaneously improving the academic program for all students while implementing strategic initiatives to support students from marginalized groups.[26]

Our holistic approach has several components. We began by ensuring that we admit students who are prepared for the work, and we implemented a first-year experience to support new students as they acclimate to college. This includes a new student book experience, first-year seminars with small class sizes, a mini-course on navigating college, and living-learning communities to facilitate belonging and academic support. We have facilitated course redesign, particularly for introductory courses, to make them more supportive and to improve learning through such practices as problem-focused and team-based learning. We have developed special disciplinary scholars programs for advanced students and evolved our academic advocacy program for those at risk of failing.[27]

Complexity

During the pandemic, we heard a great deal about transformation in higher education. What does that mean? Is it about being bold? To continue to achieve our vision, does it mean that we should consider a major shift in who we are or what we do? Are we to sustain changes made during the pandemic or undertake additional changes to shift our cultures, programs, and actions in order to meet our goals and support our students? We need to have conversations about what each college and university wants and needs to be.

There are many reasons to innovate in higher education. New initiatives can boost student access, retention, and completion. New approaches to pedagogy, course structure, or technology-enabled teaching can improve student learning. Changes in our culture and programs can increase inclusion and social justice, increase faculty diversity, support students of all backgrounds, and address mental health issues among students. New business processes can increase operational effectiveness and efficiency, improving the experiences of staff, faculty, students, and alumni, as well as potentially saving resources in the long run. New thinking about fundraising can increase institutional revenues.

We in higher education have a conflicted relationship with change. Many joke about how slowly our campuses change. There are those among leaders, administrators, staff, faculty, alumni, students, and parents who resist change because we are comfortable in our current situations or we are invested in the status quo. Institutional culture, inertia, and powerful interests constrain what is possible.

While this conservative view of institutional change has a powerful hold on our imagination, a small industry has emerged in books and articles whose principal narrative is that higher education is on the verge of transformational change. Authors of these works see a paradigm shift in which technology, new entrants in content delivery, changing student demand, and shifting financial structures collectively transform educators, educational delivery, the content of courses, and outcomes for students.[28]

These two narratives of slow progress and transformational change are at odds, and we do not agree with either. In our view, institutions change in myriad ways: we add new programs, we discontinue programs or operations that no longer add value, we change some processes incrementally, and we overhaul operations in other areas as innovations allow.

Surely, there is resistance to change, but that does not mean change does not happen. The percentage of high school graduates enrolled in postsecondary institutions has increased from about 50 percent in 1975 to nearly 70 percent in 2016.[29] College degree attainment has nearly quadrupled from under 5 percent of Americans over 25 in 1940 to 37.7 percent in 2022.[30] Undergraduate enrollment has increased from 7.4 million in 1970 to more than 17 million students today.[31] Along the way, the enrolled students have become increasingly diverse with significant change in the demographic composition of the student body. The struggles of the modern civil rights movement and continuing efforts to make our institutions more welcoming to students of many backgrounds, including gender, gender identity, sexual orientation, race, ethnicity, nationality, religion, disability, and more have made our campuses significantly more diverse. We have also witnessed breakthroughs in knowledge as well as changes in disciplines, curricula, and course offerings. We have seen significant investment in and deployment of information technology to support education, research, and business operations. Our students have laptops and smartphones, and our campuses have ubiquitous Wi-Fi.

Similarly, we do not foresee that future change will be sudden and complete. A few years ago, for example, many argued that MOOCs—massive open online courses—would soon disrupt higher education, college courses would become "unbundled," and brick-and-mortar campuses might disappear. Online education has arrived. Organizations like Coursera and online universities like University of Maryland Global Campus, Southern New Hampshire University, and Purdue Global occupy an important and growing new sector in the higher education landscape. Our sudden shift to online teaching during the pandemic suggests we will continue to evolve in the digital space as well. Yet, brick-and-mortar campuses and in-person teaching and learning persist. Change happens, yet much of the change we have seen over the past six decades has been incremental. Today, many of the issues we are struggling with have been with us for years, even decades. It is our job to continue to ensure significant progress in these issues going forward.

The type and extent of change may depend on the type of institution and the students it serves. KPMG International recently argued in a report that the deployment of digital technology and changes in consumer demand will disrupt the higher education sector.[32] However, the report argues that there will be differential changes across institutions. A small number of colleges will not be able to adapt and will close their doors or merge with others. Some will need to transform their vision, mission, goals, and operations, including more online instructional delivery. These may include comprehensive institutions and those that have high percentages of older students. Still others, research universities and selective liberal arts colleges primarily, will optimize their academic programs and operations rather than engage in large- or whole-scale transformation.

Arthur Levine and Scott Van Pelt have recently presented the argument that an already underway decades-long process of technology adoption and changes in consumer preferences will substantially change higher education.[33] They argue that students, who are digital natives with near-universal access to digital devices and the internet, have expectations as consumers that will change how higher education is delivered. Content will be increasingly unbundled and digitally available anywhere, at any time. Students will also be able to choose from a variety of providers and a range of outcomes, from a degree to a certification of knowledge or skills. The universe of higher education providers will expand to include not only traditional institutions but also a far larger number of nontraditional content producers and distributors, including nonprofits and for-profits. The pace of change has been accelerated, Levine and Van Pelt argue, by the recession of 2008 to 2009, which increased demand for job skills, and the pandemic of 2020 to 2022, which significantly increased technology adoption.

This is a formidable argument that we take seriously, though we see the consequences of these technology and consumer developments differently. Our experience has been that they are making higher education more complex rather than transforming it. They will add to what we do, or change the mix of what we do, rather than displace it. This is a critical difference. Our higher education institutions are already complex organizations, and leaders will need to adapt to manage their organizations as they become even more complex. We will still have residential campuses, we will still have in-person classes, and we will still offer undergraduate and advanced degrees. What will change is the adoption of digital content, technology, and knowledge-based credentials in addition to what we already offer. For any given college or university, an optimization strategy might involve transforming some areas, increasing effectiveness in other units, doing nothing (for now) in still others (because things are okay for now, resources are scarce, and so on), and perhaps discontinuing some practices.

These are not challenges as much as opportunities to enhance what we deliver and to provide our graduates with more personalized experiences and outcomes. In the report noted above, KPMG parsed the student experience into the learning experience, the personal experience, and the customer experience.[34] We can improve the customer experience by increasing the effectiveness and efficiency of our operations, enhancing the ability of students to conduct online and in-person business with the institution. We can improve the personal experience by enhancing student life and having the courage to make our multicultural campuses more welcoming and inclusive. We can improve the learning experience through course redesign, the adoption of digital content, and rethinking the appropriate mix of in person and online course delivery.

Taking advantage of these opportunities is not simple and automatic. It requires shared vision and leadership based on openness, resilience, courage, purpose, and optimism.

2

Openness

Success Is Never Final

With the recent popularity of the Netflix series *The Chair*, even the public is learning about the complexity of higher education. As that series has demonstrated, college and university leaders face complicated challenges, even without having to contend with a pandemic. They inherit long-standing issues that predecessors may or may not have tried to address or may have swept under the rug. New issues and crises surface that are the results of others' actions. Very often, the issues—tenure, academic freedom, curricula, academic programs, gender, social justice, technology, budgets, or business operations—are complex, with conflicting ideas and agendas that require nuanced investigation, deliberation, and decision-making. They can easily take up all of one's time, leaving little room to pursue strategic change. Institutional culture may limit one's choices.

On the flip side, it is also hard enough—and often exhausting—to manage a crisis, like a pandemic. When faced with an emergency, we focus on the urgent, immediate decisions and putting out fires. How do we navigate a disruptive event so that we not only emerge whole but enact needed change as well? How do we keep our eyes on our vision so that we continue to work toward our long-term goals despite today's troubles? Winston Churchill famously quipped,

"Never waste a good crisis." Can we see and seize opportunities in times of crisis?

At UMBC, we reminded ourselves frequently that "success is never final." We can always do more to realize our vision for our campus and our students. We can improve our current programs and operations. We can adapt our work to address the challenges and opportunities that arise from demographic, technological, economic, social, public health, and other changes in the world around us. To do so, we must remind ourselves of our vision and our long-term goals; we must align our culture and values to support that vision and those goals; we must remain open to new ideas; and we must empower the people in our community to lead and do the work.

Leadership Characteristics

When we think of leaders, several characteristics leap to mind. We expect leaders to have imagination, create an institutional vision, and lead strategic thinking and planning. We think of people who have the ability to make difficult decisions, even with incomplete information or in the face of competing interests or claims. They build trust, leading people individually or in teams. They are driven by values, have integrity, and are able to communicate effectively in small meetings and to larger audiences. They are stewards and shapers of culture and community. They maintain a strong sense of optimism, especially in the most difficult of times, balancing realism and hope. Successful leaders have grit or perseverance to get the job done.[1]

Given the need for change, a university president must become the "Chief Innovator," leading change across campus, according to Grant Thornton in a recent report on the state of higher education. In a way that echoes what we have discussed in *The Empowered University*, the report says that, as chief innovator, the president should lead the institution and shape its culture by changing norms, fostering collaboration, and enabling innovation. "Chief innovators will maximize the potential of those on their team and empower them to take on operational responsibilities that might previously have been within the purview of the president."[2]

We might argue that the president and other senior leaders should serve as the "chief" in many domains: chief strategist; chief empowerment officer; chief fundraiser; chief diversity, equity, and inclusion officer; chief innovator; and chief optimist. Still, although the successful president may be "the chief," they succeed by empowering others to work together in developing strategic plans, creating sustainable budgets and infrastructure, facilitating inclusion, and innovating in academic programs. In healthy organizational cultures, senior leaders learn about the work of their colleagues, their challenges, and opportunities. The provost, for example, should learn about budgeting and administration, other vice presidents should learn about our academic programs, and so on. This fosters a collective view of the organization.

Defining Openness

While academia is the locus of discovery that requires openness, our institutions can be rigid, bureaucratic, traditional, and siloed.

An institutional culture of openness is one that is open to new ideas, information, and perspectives and is willing to change, innovate, and take action based on new information. This culture is open

- To the notion that we can be better: success is never final
- To new ideas: leaders and change agents can advance innovative solutions
- To sharing information, evidence, and data: transparent in evaluation, deliberation, and communication
- To inclusion: staff, faculty, and students across the institution can be participants, partners, collaborators, leaders, and change agents
- To collaboration: willing to break down silos to create cross-institutional teams that undertake innovative initiatives

- In planning: inclusive in the planning process and flexible in revising plans in real time as needed
- To an interdisciplinary approach to knowledge: supporting a broad range of approaches to understanding the human condition, the natural world, and technology
- In the curriculum: open to supporting inquiry into the full breadth and depth of history and society, particularly with regard to marginalized groups
- In education: encouraging faculty to innovate in their approaches to teaching, course design, and the use of digital resources

Culture

Creating a culture of openness and empowerment is no simple task. It requires intention, communication, engagement, work, and time, but it is worth the effort. A quote generally attributed to management consultant Peter Drucker is "Culture eats strategy for breakfast." This notion reminds us of the power of institutional culture. An institution's culture or even the culture of one part of an institution can impede progress and change if it does not align with the change desired. Therefore, to move forward we must address the culture of our institutions, aligning vision, values, missions, goals, strategies, investments, and actions.

Leaders of the empowered college or university help their colleagues aspire to be open-minded, which is challenging, never-ending work. We strive to "look in the mirror," evaluating ourselves and being honest about what we see as challenges and opportunities. We collectively keep an open mind, especially under conditions of uncertainty, as we work toward solutions. We seek to be curious and ask probing questions. We share data and information, and we engage in productive, sometimes difficult, conversations. We pull people into the work, creating buy-in, empowerment, and opportunities for colleagues to become change agents. We build cross-institutional teams and collaboration. The results are worth the challenge.

At UMBC our town halls provided one vehicle of many for open communication. University-wide town halls have focused on teaching and learning, research and creative achievement, racial healing, inclusion and free speech, and internationalization and globalization. Others, organized by a division or college, have focused on issues around mental health, diversity and inclusion, and similar topics. One example is a town hall we held in 2021 to hear from Muslims in our campus community about their concerns. What was evident in the conversation was that when people get to know each other better, we have greater trust and can work together toward solutions.

We are also in the process of cultivating a culture of assessment in our community, another institutional characteristic that involves long-term change. We have included evaluation as a component of several important campus initiatives, including the Meyerhoff Scholars Program, i-Cubed (an experiment on STEM education interventions funded by the National Science Foundation [NSF]), and BUILD (an NIH-funded initiative on STEM education). We have also been building a data analytics practice over a decade or more. We started this work by creating an institution-wide data warehouse, one of the first of its kind at a university. We have since focused on evolving the analytic tools and capacity to explore and understand the student experience, especially for different groups, so that we can enhance student success. It can be challenging to find the time for intentional analytical work when you are trying to deal with current crises, but data assessment can provide insight even in the midst of a crisis.

Tensions

Even an "empowered" campus characterized by shared leadership has tensions or conflicts to work through that are complicated and require difficult choices. For example, the need for speed in decision-making and communication during a crisis often competes with both the need for more information and the importance of broad collaboration. Finding the right balance requires subjective judgment that often shifts depending on the issue and the stakeholders. Sometimes the level of communication is not sufficient or it is difficult to find internal communication channels that reach those interested. Sometimes we rush communications only to hear from groups that they would have liked to have been consulted. Sometimes it is not clear whether to make a quick decision without full information so that people know where things stand or to defer a decision until more information can be gathered, thereby leaving stakeholders with limited ability to plan. When we do not get it quite right, we regroup and try again, often rebuilding any trust lost from missteps.

Opportunities for open communication, whether in town halls or through shared governance groups, can reveal areas of tension or disagreement. It is tempting, especially when one faculty group is vocal on an issue, to assume that all faculty members think alike. Indeed, conversations in our faculty senate have demonstrated the opposite. For example, when we discussed a return to campus and in-person teaching, some faculty were in favor, others skeptical or concerned, and still others opposed to it. Those opposing a return to in-person teaching had significant, legitimate concerns about health and safety for faculty and students. We developed an approach that encouraged a return to in-person teaching but let faculty decide for themselves which modality to use. As we will show in chapter 5, there were significant differences in the mix of modalities across our three colleges (and even across different academic programs within colleges) for the fall of 2021 and 2022.

Uncertainty

What the major challenges we have been facing—the pandemic, an economic recession, calls for racial justice—have in common with higher education is uncertainty. We should never forget the sense of doubt and helplessness we all felt until a COVID-19 vaccine proved effective. The shutdown completely disrupted life as we knew it. Economic activity shrank, politics was as mean-spirited as ever, the media focused on COVID-19 deaths and racial unrest, and our campuses closed and teaching went online.

In 2021 we did not know the impact the Delta variant would have or whether we would need a booster shot. Then came the Omicron variant, a new source of uncertainty and unpredictability about how transmissible and life threatening it would be. The uncertainty around Omicron led to an immediate and dramatic drop in the stock market, numerous restrictions on international travel, and countless stories in the media even before science could give us answers. As we emerged from the Omicron wave in early 2022, we began to speak of COVID-19 moving from a pandemic to an endemic disease that we would have to live with for the long-term, creating further questions about the path forward.

To be sure, uncertainty is not new in the human experience, but these simultaneous crises have increased our awareness of uncertainty, the challenges it presents for decision-making, communications, work, and life in general, and the ongoing stress it causes for all of us in our community. Through two challenging years, we learned the importance of remaining calm in the midst of the storm, following the science, listening to people affected by the adversity, and preparing for the possibility of future financial challenges. Yet we have also learned to keep our eyes on our vision and mission and invest in critical long-term priorities, such as student success and high-priority research.

Following the science is the best path, yet this can be complicated. Science provides the best information available for decision-making. Yet, while we would like the information to be clear and complete, the science is often happening in real time during a pandemic and is playing catch-up with the virus. So, as much as we would like definitive answers, we often have to sit with the discomfort of uncertainty as we scramble for information and face decisions with incomplete information. We ask ourselves and colleagues to remain open minded as we pass through these periods of uncertainty, knowing that we may need to change our minds about decisions and change course as a situation evolves and we learn more. Science does not guarantee a good outcome every time, but it provides the information we need to make the best choices that will, on average, lead us to good outcomes.

In the early days of the pandemic, for example, we were often challenged, in "following the science," to understand what best practice was. Frequently, different sources—the White House, the Centers for Disease Control and Prevention (CDC), the state, and the various experts who appeared on news networks—provided different perspectives, information, and advice. Changes in the prevailing advice, guidelines, and restrictions over time just compounded the uncertainty and complexity. This occasionally led to significant tension, but we learned the importance of being open, flexible, and adaptable, particularly in the face of uncertainty. We also learned the importance of grace and trust, knowing that we were, as a community, putting people and their safety and health first.

Empowerment

University leaders bring a range of leadership styles to their work. Some adopt more top-down decision-making, while others consult and delegate more broadly. During the pandemic, leaders who decided to quickly reopen campuses and bring students and faculty back for in-person courses were more likely to do so in a top-down fashion. In some instances, community reactions against these decisions forced leaders to backtrack. A more collaborative approach was often slower in terms of process and outcome, but broad community consensus gave the campus more buy-in. A recent example of top-down decision-making was board approval of a proposal at one research university to require civics literacy for all undergraduates. Higher education media reported the president took the proposal for this requirement to his board without endorsement from the faculty. While there had been faculty involvement, the faculty senate had not approved a way forward. Critics from the faculty and others argued that the university's requirement would benefit from broad collaboration with and endorsement from the faculty, particularly with regard to the content of such a requirement. The board decided essentially that time had run out and would proceed without faculty support.[3]

We took a much more consultative and interactive approach to management, though this can take different forms. Early in in his tenure, former president Hrabowski was typically deeply involved in the details of academic and administrative decision-making and supervision. Over time, however, he learned that he did not need to get so far down into decision-making and supervision. He found he could rely on his talented team to carry out the work independently. At one point during the challenging implementation of PeopleSoft at UMBC, he met with the vice president for administration and finance to develop a plan for dealing with several difficult aspects of the implementation. At the end of the meeting the president said, "Okay, I will convene a meeting to move this forward." Then the vice president said, "No, I will handle this." It was a eureka moment. The president understood that he could let go, stand back, and trust his vice president's leadership. This is the essence of empowerment.

In a consultative environment, an important question for presidents and other leaders to consider is how involved they should be in managing operations or solving problems. If leaders lean in too far, they can be accused of micromanaging. If they lean out too far, they can be accused of being too distant. The answer often depends on the issues, circumstances, people, and their relationships. Hiring capable people and developing relationships of trust simplify decisions about who can and will handle certain issues.

In times of crisis, leaders can facilitate decisions and implementation with an empowered culture and shared leadership. An existing collaborative culture among the leadership team serves as a foundation. Planning, decision-making, and execution require far more coordination than usual among leaders and units during a crisis. A highly distributed organizational structure allows many hands to contribute to the work required, allowing us to rely on individuals with the appropriate expertise. Indeed, shared governance includes more than organizations such as the faculty or staff senates but also organizational units to which decisions are distributed. Coordinating individuals and groups can be a challenge, requiring frequent leadership meetings, good internal institutional communication, and both trust and faith in leadership.

Leading change requires us to engage our campuses, asking ourselves and our colleagues to ask good questions, raise issues, gather and discuss data, and have the difficult conversations that are often required to move ahead. As leaders, our job is to educate ourselves and others about the issues, then persuade colleagues, cultivate allies, and nurture change agents.

We should focus on empowering those who will lead change, often serving as guides or coaches rather than directors or supervisors. Indeed, anyone can be a leader in higher education regardless of one's formal title. Program directors, center directors, department chairs, deans, vice presidents, provosts, and presidents are positions of power and responsibility. These positions provide platforms for leadership and innovation. Yet, change agents, regardless of formal title, can lead innovation that makes a difference in teaching and learning, the student experience, research, or business operations. Change agents—whether formal or informal leaders—develop ideas, persuade colleagues to join them, gather resources, and champion change.

We must encourage this buy in for the work of change. Changing the culture can require both the values that motivate the work and the empowering settings that facilitate it. Yet motivation to do the work is complicated. Some will undertake it because they see it as a cause or a mission. Some will do it because they understand that doing the work will enhance their reputation and career. Others will need further incentives to align their motivation with institutional goals and benefits. This could take the form of explicit job goals outlined in performance reviews or the inducement of bonuses for those individuals or teams who accomplish certain goals during a particular period.

We have sustained shared leadership during the pandemic through a pandemic response organization that is highly inclusive in committees of staff, faculty, and students. The broad participation in our pandemic response planning committees not only aligned with our values but also was critical for navigating the crisis. It helped direct decisions to those best positioned to make them—at the level of the system chancellor, the president, the provost or vice president for administration and finance, deans, department chairs, or individual faculty and staff. The pandemic governance structure, moreover, facilitated information sharing and brought together people who would not normally interact in their regular jobs. This provided opportunities for new conversations, relationships, and even potential short-term or long-term innovations.

Collaboration

Closely related to empowerment is collaboration. Very often, we are siloed in our work. We have tasks before us in our organizational domains that are important and need to be done. Yet collaborative work is necessary and useful when more than one group is involved in the work, or collaboration is the key to innovation or productivity enhancement. Collaboration offers opportunities for sharing information and perspectives that lead to new ideas and innovations that can carry the institution forward.

Organizational management during the pandemic was, by its nature, collaborative. The pandemic impacts reached every corner of the university. Lynne Schaefer, vice president for administration and finance, and Philip Rous, provost and senior vice president for academic affairs, led the CPCC, composed of administrators, faculty, and staff from across our campus. The CPCC coordinated a broader set of people in five work groups focused on the academic program, research, operations, student affairs, and events. These groups brought together faculty and staff from across colleges and units to problem-solve and develop policies.

Developing reasonable and workable COVID-19 policies required input from people in different divisions and colleges. CPCC work groups sought expert advice and insights about the needs of faculty and staff in units across campus. Their frequent meetings provided conversations that allowed us to share information and concerns, learn from each other about what does and does not work, and develop policies applicable across different settings—often a challenging but achievable task.

We already had collaborative initiatives prior to the pandemic. For example, the Division of Professional Studies (DPS) and the Department of Information Technology (DoIT) had collaboratively developed over the previous decade a training program for online teaching. During the pandemic, they modified this into a program called PIVOT to train faculty who had had to move quickly to online teaching in March 2020 and would continue to teach online that fall. To support PIVOT, DPS and DoIT collaborated with faculty across departments who had previously taken online course training. These faculty members served as ambassadors between departments and DoIT and as mentors to their fellow faculty.

In addition to the pandemic, another recent example is our strategic enrollment planning and implementation process. Rous and Schaefer led this effort, bringing together leaders from the provost's office, the office of undergraduate education, enrollment management, student affairs, administration, DoIT, and finance. All of the vice presidents, deans, and vice provosts were involved, along with associate vice presidents for finance and communications. The Strategic Enrollment Plan Committee developed goals, actions, and related metrics to increase both enrollment and retention. A number of departments, including Enrollment Management, Marketing, DoIT, and the graduate school, and college representatives worked together to implement a new customer relationship management (CRM) system that would allow staff across the university to engage more effectively with prospective and current students.

In many cases, people working on COVID-19 subcommittees or other collaborative initiatives had neither met nor worked together before. Not only did their interaction lead to richer conversations and better outcomes for the initiatives but the staff found these collaborative activities to be personal growth opportunities. They learned from each other about technical details, organizational needs, innovative solutions, and ways to initiate change.

Planning

Change can happen. The experience of 2020–2021 has shown that we can enact change swiftly and completely if we want to or are forced to. In early 2020 we offered the overwhelming majority of our courses at UMBC in person on campus, and 95 percent of our students took all of their courses in person. We had invested in the technology that would allow online and hybrid instruction, and we had a program to train faculty to use it, but only a few faculty had taken steps to embrace the possibilities offered by technology-enabled education. No one would have predicted that we could convert all of our instruction to online delivery because they had not yet seen it done. And then we did it. After the World Health Organization declared COVID-19 to be a pandemic, we closed our campus and in the space of two weeks shifted our instruction online for the remainder of the spring 2020 semester. This was hardly an isolated development as higher education institutions across the country took the same course of action. But the need for a swift and complete transition, virtually overnight, took our collective breath away.

We can choose change instead of waiting for external forces to compel it. It takes imagination, planning, community action, and persistence over time. For example, in the 1990s we decided to establish a research park on our campus, as it would signal our intention to center research and economic development as features of our mission. Many were skeptical of or hostile to the idea. Faculty in the arts, humanities, and social sciences expressed concern that the endeavor would siphon resources away from their fields. Residents in the town of Arbutus, neighboring the location of the proposed park, opposed it on the grounds that biotechnology companies might accidentally release deadly pathogens or toxins into the environment. Others opposed the park because it would be located in a tract of woods that they sought to protect. Campus leadership worked hard to allay fears and negotiate with the concerned parties over a lengthy period. Eventually, we were able to acquire an existing building from Lockheed-Martin and demonstrated what was possible. Further negotiations led to a scaled-down but still sizable park, along with a conservation zone that preserved a sizable wooded area and created a buffer between the park and Arbutus. Today, the park is home to more than 140 firms, including many startups, as well as operations for two federal agencies. These entities create jobs, engage faculty in research, and offer internships and jobs to students.

In a world of greater uncertainty, planning becomes more, not less, important if we choose to be proactive. When things are certain, one can plan and stay the course until one's plans are realized. If things are uncertain, however, then planning is more important because one must think about and plan for different scenarios—and be ready to change course and plan again if and when circumstances change. Indeed, strategic planning itself has evolved—become a living thing rather than a document that is supposed to be an immutable guide for the future.

The experiences of the higher education community during the crises of 2020 to 2021 have led us to understand the importance of planning and making decisions under conditions of uncertainty. We need planning to prepare for uncertainty, planning that acknowledges the need for flexibility and the need to change course as conditions shift. While we did not fully "prepare" for a pandemic we did not anticipate, we at UMBC and other colleges and universities were prepared because we had many resources in place that we were able to draw on: a sense of community, staff who were willing to go above and beyond, technological tools, a strong financial planning process and a budget reserve fund, an approach to online learning and a program for training faculty in it, and so on. We did not need to acquire or invent these in the midst of a pandemic, whereas others did.

Still, how much constant stress can a person, a leadership team, and a campus endure? Before the pandemic, the average presidential tenure had been declining over the past two decades.[4] The received wisdom is that this has been due to either scandals or an increase in the number or intensity of stressors leaders face, such as university finances, political interventions in governance, technological and demographic change, campus unrest, alumni and donor demands, and so on. In late 2021 and 2022 many presidents announced their departures (including coauthor Freeman Hrabowski), prompting some to suggest that the wave of resignations and retirements may be stimulated by the stress of the pandemic though few retiring leaders cite that as a reason.[5]

We cannot assume that presidents are departing because of stress. Hrabowski, for example, had been talking with colleagues about the right time to retire. In fact, he put his retirement on hold twice, first as the university worked its way through a reorganization and recommitment of our work on Title IX, and, second, because of the crisis stemming from COVID-19. He and others have felt it is important to maintain existing leadership during crises. As the situation evolves from pandemic to endemic, however, they are now leaving, creating a large number of presidential openings in 2022 and 2023.

As presidents are leaving, candidates should be looking at the health and strength of a presidency at a given institution, asking a range of good questions. Is the president leaving on amicable terms? What is the outgoing president's relationship with constituencies and stakeholders? What are the strengths of the current leadership team? Are there trust and collaboration? What has the university accomplished under this president? What challenges and opportunities lay ahead?

Communications

During the Trump administration, many campus leaders felt compelled to communicate their positions on policy changes affecting higher education institutions, students, faculty, and staff. This began with the Trump administration's executive order (EO) on January 27, 2017—just a week into its term—regarding the denial of entry into the United States of citizens from seven countries (often referred to as the "Muslim ban"). While the EO was in effect, as many as 700 travelers were detained and 50,000 visas were revoked. The ban affected students, faculty, and researchers affiliated with universities across the country, including UMBC.

In our case, we communicated, through a campus email, our disapproval of the EO, our commitment to aid any faculty and students affected by it, and then following through on our commitment. And so it went, with Charlottesville, DACA, the treatment of immigrants at the border, the murder of George Floyd, and more. Then President Trump, late in his term, issued an EO withholding federal funds from any contractor or grant recipient that offered training that promoted "race or sex stereotyping or scapegoating." We worked closely with David Gleason, our general counsel, to understand what we could and could not do under the EO and what we could and could not say in a campus communication.

Then COVID-19 arrived in 2020. Campus leaders had to make what were often unprecedented and uncertain decisions. The decisions along with the subsequent policies for how campuses would operate generally required detailed explanations for who could or had to do what and when. These communications covered COVID-19 issues (testing, contact tracing, quarantine), campus access (who could come to campus, with what stipulations, and with what requirements for masking, distancing, and hygiene), teaching (which courses would be in person, hybrid, or online), events (registration for online meetings), and more.

The role of campus communications evolves as the social, political, public health, media, and technology contexts of university operations change over time. This trend began well before the COVID-19 pandemic that accelerated it. In an environment transformed by social media, for example, we now use campus communications—by email, website announcement, and Twitter—to provide information and perspectives about campus affairs, community events, national news, and even global developments. Meanwhile, over the past decade, our student body has become more diverse and more international. Because of this, students often expect the university to comment on international as well as national events.

Because of these developments, communication teams at universities across the country have increased attention to internal communications during the past four years and even more intensely during the months since the start of the pandemic. As campus leaders, we have benefited from experienced staff who help us with internal communications. They help us manage writing, relationships, tensions, and trade-offs around communications. The time and resources devoted to internal communications, however, has meant that there has been less time and fewer resources available for external communications, which are also critical. One staff member brought into our communications team in early 2020 to focus on external affairs spent all of her time over the next 18 months focused on internal work due to COVID-19. This is not unique to our campus but rather is a nationwide trend.

Working with campus leaders, our communications staff have drafted emails and created and updated websites about the COVID-19 pandemic. Five years ago, staff would assist in writing perhaps two or three leadership communications per year. During the pandemic, this increased to as much as two to three per week. Staff have crafted these frequent updates with a focus on ensuring that they are "credible, trustworthy, and compassionate." Their goal has been to provide transparency and sustain community rather than to provide "spin." As such, they have been as matter of fact as possible.

Communications staff have also assisted leadership on communications around social and policy issues as they have emerged. These communications are sensitive, focusing on critical events and developments in our society and such topics as the pandemic, immigration, race relations, global events, and the presidential election. Speaking on behalf of the institution on these topics, the president can find this work challenging. She can say what she believes, she can try to take a balanced approached, or she can use communications as opportunities to educate the campus community. These are difficult choices to make. They must be tailored to the specific issue at hand. They must be careful to allow the leader to stay true to their values yet not cut off other points of view and opportunities for dialogue.

Someone will always be unhappy, and some on our campus have criticized communications for being too measured or too slow. We have found that a helpful approach is broad consultation with campus organizations whose members are affected by an event or policy. When we have engaged in this consultation, those groups that have been involved in discussions prior to a campus communication have generally been supportive of the issued statements.

It is helpful for leaders to listen to different voices, speaking with groups, faculty, staff, students, and other stakeholders to understand an issue, perspectives, concerns, and, where appropriate, possible actions. We have often issued joint communications that have been written and signed by the university leadership along with shared governance leadership. This enriches the communication and demonstrates openness, discussion, and agreement. Yet, consultation takes time and reduces the speed with which we can issue a communication.

On the other hand, we found during the pandemic that because there was so much at stake—including life and death —many on campus wanted leaders to speak on behalf of the institution. That is, deans, department chairs, and faculty did not want to explain a situation or policy because they feared they might not get it right. People wanted to be careful, so decisions and communications became more top-down despite our efforts to be collaborative and empowering.

To be consistent in our approach to campus communications, we developed a decision-making process for issue-related university statements. This process contains a set of guidelines of questions designed to ascertain the best course of action. The rubric includes these "qualifying questions":

- Is this an issue/event that affects members of our community?
- Are we receiving direct communication from students, faculty, staff, alumni, and/or campus groups about this issue/event that asks or suggests a need for a university response?
- Does the university have something relevant to add to the public discussion?
- Can we elevate work by campus partners who are offering resources, support, and/or education related to this issue?

If the answers to some or all of these questions are "yes," then leaders may wish to issue a statement. The next steps then involve pulling together a team to coordinate the writing process, consultation with experts and stakeholders, compiling a list of the relevant work on campus related to the issue, and identifying who should convey the final message (i.e., president, provost, shared governance leaders, or other campus leaders).

During the pandemic, we embedded communications staff in our COVID-19 response operations, involving them from the outset, which has enhanced our work in this area. This strategy requires more staff time from our colleagues in communications, but it places them "in the room where it happens," thereby increasing their knowledge of developments in real time, reducing the time needed for offline discussions about communications, and providing opportunities for conversations about communications strategies as decisions are made. This is a new approach for our campus. The University System of Maryland used this approach at the system level as well. Not all campuses have used this approach. It has worked for us and we recommend it.

Events play a critical role in campus communications. Many staff members, across colleges and divisions, reported how moving an important campus event online in 2020 was a major accomplishment—technologically and logistically. Moreover, in most instances, the events were not just successful but often exceeded expectations with many more participants than we had when we held events in person. Events for students included Convocation, the New Student Book Experience, Involvement Fest (an event encouraging participation in student groups), and Undergraduate Research and Creative Achievement Day (URCAD). A "Together Beyond" post-election discussion organized by the Center for Democracy and Civic Life trained many students and others to lead group conversations after the election. Events for administrators, staff, and faculty included our Fall Opening Meeting, the University Retreat, and Staff and Faculty Service Awards. Staff in alumni and donor relations noted that online events were "game changers," because the virtual event mode allowed many more alumni to participate; increased participation led to increased alumni giving.

Other campus events included Retriever Talks and a series of Town Halls framed by "The Empowered University" as an organizing theme. The town halls had large numbers of participants, eager for information or connection with campus and colleagues. They provided a way to bring people together, tackle a range of issues important to the campus from research to race relations, and sustain a community feeling.

In addition to communications and events, our staff members have also developed other initiatives to advance our university. One of these was the Meyerhoff Impact Campaign. This initiative included advertising in the *New York Times* and a dedicated website called "The Ripple Effect." This site provides information about the Meyerhoff Scholars Program, evidence of its impact on participants and the university, reports about replication at other campuses, and opportunities to donate in support of the program.

Crisis communications, to be useful in both the short and long term, must be credible and must sustain community. They cannot be about spin. They must provide clear information as a public service. The university's reputation is on the line. They must have compassion for the reader or viewer who will be impacted by the crisis or development discussed. Our sense of community hangs in the balance. Online events such as town halls that have focused on sensitive issues and provided opportunity for participation have also given voice to many who had concerns, including those with chronic health conditions or caregiving responsibilities and those who are from disadvantaged, underrepresented, or vulnerable groups. This can strengthen a sense of community, though only if this participation and sense of empowerment is sustained.

Jack DeGioia, president of Georgetown University, took an innovative approach to campus communications during the pandemic. He initiated two video series in the fall of 2020. The first, "Georgetown This Week," is a continuing weekly message to the campus providing an update and reflections on the university's response to COVID-19. The second, "Georgetown Now," was a series of virtual "daily conversations" in fall 2020 with members of the Georgetown community. He designed these series to provide helpful information but also stimulate a sense of community, signaling, "we're all in this together."[6]

3

Resilience

Grit amid Uncertainty

Every campus has a story. The narratives we use reveal what our culture embodies and who we are. We evolve over time and so do our narratives to better capture our current thinking. We used to say at UMBC, "It is cool to be smart." We wanted our community members and our public to know that we were not just intelligent but even proud to be "nerdy." Over time, we grew concerned about the focus on "being smart" because being smart is often perceived as a fixed state: often people think either you are smart or you are not. We replaced this notion with a focus on "high expectations" and "grit."

With this subtle change, we make it clear that, with high expectations, hard work, and appropriate support, any student at UMBC can succeed. Since the 1990s, long before Angela Duckworth's book *Grit* focused our attention on passion and perseverance, we talked about the need for grit. (In fact, our original mascot at UMBC in 1987 was a Chesapeake Bay retriever called "True Grit," a statue of whom is located in front of our administration building.) With this change from "being smart" to "having grit," we were signaling that we encouraged passion and hard work and were shifting from a "fixed mindset" to what Carol Dweck and others would later call a "growth mindset."[1]

The idea of grit applies not just to our students but also to all members of our campus community. This grit is "perseverance of effort combined with the passion for a particular long-term goal."[2] This notion has been central to our success, as we have grown from a new campus in the Baltimore area in the 1960s into the research university we are today with partnerships across the Baltimore-Washington region, the nation, and the globe. The campus has accomplished this by setting high expectations for all of us, including leaders, administrators, staff, and faculty, and working intentionally over time to implement, sustain, and achieve innovations that have driven our evolution.

In an April 2020 interview with the *Chronicle of Higher Education*, Leon Botstein, president of Bard College, likened planning for fall 2020 amid the COVID-19 pandemic to "driving a car in a thick fog. You go very slowly."[3] In a December 2021 interview with *Harvard Magazine*, Lawrence Bacow, president of Harvard, said, "My crystal ball is no better than yours," and "All plans are subject to change."[4] These quotes remind us of a notion with the somewhat whimsical name of "coddiwomple," which means to travel purposefully toward a vague or an as yet unknown destination. Although hikers in England coined this slang term to describe wandering in the hills, it nonetheless conveys the sort of grit and resilience that we, and others in higher education institutions, have used to navigate the COVID-19 pandemic. We moved slowly, but deliberately and purposefully, through a dense fog toward an unknown destination, getting up again each time we were knocked down: *This is grit amid uncertainty. This is resilience.*

When we looked back at 2020 and the combination of a COVID-19 pandemic, economic recession, racial unrest, and political division, the first metaphor that came to mind was "the perfect storm." This is a much-used metaphor, to be sure, but it seemed to fit. Yet, when we took a second look at what we went through, we realized that it did not fully capture the situation. When a storm hits, even a perfect one, you hunker down and wait it out until life returns to normal.

If the power is out, you wait until the lights come back on, breathe a sigh of relief, and go back to what you were doing.

Since early 2020, however, we in US higher education have not been in one passing storm but an unending series of intense storms, and we are not going back to what we were doing before. The storms have changed us—our campuses, business operations, and work. A more apt metaphor for what we are going through might be that of "climate change" instead of "perfect storm." As with global warming, our environment has changed. We are addressing both the causes and effects of this change. We are reacting and adapting but also working to shape proactively the future we will live in, even if that world is "an as-yet-unknown destination."

We vividly recall the shock and fear that we all felt in 2020. We faced a deadly pandemic, political chaos that only increased uncertainty and undermined an effective response, and a looming financial disaster. At one point, our vice president for administration and finance described our budget situation, as we were closing dorms and facilities, reimbursing fees, and receiving word from the state that their revenues were eroding. She said we could see a budget shortfall of as much as $80 million out of an overall annual budget of about $500 million. At a nearby large research university, the president made local and national headlines by sharing a projection that the institution could face hundreds of millions of dollars in budget cuts and then announcing immediate actions including layoffs and a one-year suspension of retirement contributions. (The university later provided the retirement contributions retroactively, after it became evident that the university's revenues had not declined as significantly as projected.)

In the meantime, our serious situation required a community response. We acknowledged that we not only had to respond to the health threat posed by COVID-19 but also had a serious budget problem. We reminded ourselves that we had found our way through hard times before and that we would get through this as well. We had to keep hope alive, work on encouraging positive attitudes, and think calmly and carefully about our strategies even as we "drove through a thick fog" of uncertainty. Eventually we found our way through the budget nightmare with a combination of short-term choices, drawdowns from our reserves, and federal stimulus funding. We did not lay off any staff and sustained our academic program.

The voyage through uncertainty and crisis requires resilience, courage, purpose, and optimism. Resilience is critical and has three dimensions:

- Institutional resilience involves creating an organizational structure and the human, financial, and digital resources that sustain the institution both during normal operations and during a crisis or challenging operational environment.
- Community resilience involves cultivating other key resources—including shared values, a sense of community, mutual trust, grit, and optimism—necessary to sustain ourselves during challenging or uncertain times.
- Personal resilience is built on hope, purpose, strong relation-ships, and a sense of physical and emotional security.

All of these are much more effective if built over time, ideally when we are not in the midst of crisis so that we can be ready when we are.

Many Paths for the Journey

Leaders of US colleges and universities faced a set of complicated challenges when the World Health Organization declared COVID-19 a global pandemic in March 2020. Should we close our campuses? For how long? Should we shift teaching and learning online? Should our staff work remotely? What support should we provide to faculty, staff, and students to make these transitions? With the stress of on-line learning, should we provide our students with a pass/fail grad-ing option? Should we make admissions tests optional? Should we hold commencement in person or online? What changes should we make to the tenure and promotion process? How should we ad-dress the steep projected budget shortfalls? In what ways should we aim to change arrangements with contractors for food, janitorial, and other services? What negotiations should we pursue with vendors to change our contracts? Should we reimburse students for their fees for services they would not receive during a campus shutdown? Should we require COVID-19 testing, masks, and physical distancing for all those we allow on campus? With the availability of a vaccine, should we mandate it—and later boosters—for our campus?

As leaders, we did not respond the same way across our institutions, but we all had to decide what to do in the face of these challenges. Some decisions were easy and others more difficult. Sometimes we got things wrong. We had to decide whose expert guidance we would follow, who would participate in decision-making for the campus during the COVID-19 crisis, and when and under what circumstances we would allow community members to return to campus. These decisions varied by leadership style, institution type, public or private control of the institution, and the political or cultural context of the state where the institution is located.

Institutions found many paths for the journey through the pandemic. While most colleges and universities shut down their physical campuses in March 2020 for some or all of the rest of the spring semester, higher education institutions made a range of choices for fall 2020. *The Chronicle of Higher Education*, working with the College Crisis Initiative at Davidson College, described those choices as follows:[5]

- 10 percent fully online
- 34 percent primarily online
- 21 percent hybrid
- 23 percent primarily in person
- 4 percent fully in person

The rest were "other" or undetermined.

There were variations across institution type. The larger the institution, the more likely they would be primarily or fully online, though some large public universities, such as Purdue, the University of Illinois at Urbana-Champaign, the University of Arizona, and the University of North Carolina at Chapel Hill, and large private universities, such as Notre Dame and Liberty University, brought their students back. Smaller institutions, from 500 to 2,000 students, were much more likely to be fully or primarily in person, although some that planned for in-person instruction changed their minds. Berklee College of Music in Boston, Goucher College in Baltimore County, and Salem College in North Carolina all planned to bring students back but changed their plans to online instruction over the summer.[6] Meanwhile, public two-year institutions were the most likely to be fully or primarily online, followed by public four-year institutions. Private, nonprofit institutions were more likely to be hybrid or fully or primarily in person. Location of the institution also shaped decisions. Those in cities, suburbs, or rural areas were more likely to use the online modality, but those in towns—"college towns"—were more likely to bring students back to campus for in-person instruction.

That does not end the description of the paths institutions took. Some institutions brought all—or nearly all—of their students back to campus in the fall of 2020, but within that context some were fully in person, others were primarily in person, and some were hybrid. For example, to hedge their bets, some institutions split their semester into two "modules," during which students would take half a semester load. This provided the institution the opportunity to switch between modalities with each module should the need arise.

For some institutions, another decision-making factor was the percentage of students who live on campus, live in neighboring communities, or commute. For larger institutions with a substantial number of commuters, like UMBC, the high percentage of students living off campus in surrounding communities or at home and commuting led us to remain primarily online. It is one thing to have a relatively self-contained campus with more than 90 percent of students living in residence halls. With testing, those colleges could almost create a protective "bubble." Yet, when many students are on and off campus daily, the opportunities for COVID-19 transmission increase substantially. We did not return to primarily in-person instruction, therefore, until a vaccine was widely available.

An article in *Nature* in the late summer of 2020 described our choices for the fall of 2020 as "a vast unplanned pandemic experiment."[7] "In the absence of any national strategy for tackling the coronavirus pandemic," Emma Marsh wrote, "colleges and universities in the United States are on their own when it comes to deciding whether and how to bring students back for the autumn term . . . Many are relying on their own experts, resulting in a wide range of approaches, from telling students to attend online classes from home to bringing everyone back and testing them three times a week." She also noted that more than 1,000 US four-year institutions would bring students back that fall despite the fact that the United States had seen the largest number of COVID-19 deaths of any nation.[8]

Most institutions that had students on campus had masking and physical distancing requirements, but COVID-19 testing was variable. Some institutions tested each student two to three times per week, some used random COVID-19 surveillance, and others used pooled samples with follow-up testing of individuals when their pool tested positive. At the University of Arizona, two professors tested wastewater to detect COVID-19 in the population of specific residence halls.[9] There were other decisions to make as well. How to handle breaks? Should we hold commencement in person or online? Should we go ahead with athletics and when? Do we require athletes to wear masks, even if practicing or playing outdoors? Again, institutions made a wide range of choices.

How well did it go? Some colleges had relatively low COVID-19 transmission rates, but others faced crises, sometimes immediately. The leadership of University of North Carolina at Chapel Hill decided to bring students back to campus in fall 2020, but just a week into the semester the number and percent of students testing positive—one-third—led them to move all instruction online.[10] A similar outbreak at Notre Dame led to the same outcome.[11] *USA Today* reported on September 11, 2020, that 19 of the 25 towns with the highest COVID-19 cases per capita at the time were college towns.[12]

One of the key restrictions for a safe campus in fall 2020 and beyond was limiting social gathering. Of course, social gatherings are a mainstay of the college experience, creating an immediate battleground. Partying surely led to outbreaks at some campuses that had to shift back online. One liberal arts college in the northeast had a spike in cases after two unauthorized large student gatherings on one spring 2021 weekend. To bring the spike under control, all classes went online for two weeks. The college required students to remain in their residence hall rooms unless they were picking up meals or going for solo walks or exercise outside. The lockdown worked, bringing case levels back down to zero.

The Unexpected and the Uncertain

COVID-19 was not the first health care crisis we faced. In 2009 we were troubled by the health news out of California and Texas. We learned that health officials had identified H1N1 influenza, also known as swine flu, in those states. They warned that this flu strain was spreading and might become a pandemic. Ultimately, it did not. At UMBC, however, we responded at that time by developing a pandemic response plan, adding this new aspect to our existing campus emergency plans.

Our experiences with H1N1 remind us that we in higher education have faced emergencies before the arrival of the COVID-19 pandemic and will do so in the future. Sometimes, these emergencies affect only one institution, as in the case of the Northridge earthquake or flooding of the Iowa River that caused $750 million in damage at the University of Iowa.[13] Sometimes, they can affect multiple institutions as the H1N1 influenza threatened to in 2009 and the SARS-CoV-2 virus did in 2020.

In February 2020 Jay Perman, the new chancellor of the USM, gave his first remarks to the USM Board of Regents. He began his report with a list of the recent accomplishments of USM institutions and then turned to the issue on everyone's mind, COVID-19. He summarized a meeting about COVID-19 he had held the evening before with health experts. They had highlighted for him how uncertain the trajectory of the disease was, describing three possible scenarios. In the first, best-case scenario, the disease would produce a relatively small number of cases in the United States and disappear. In the second, the disease would produce a wave in the spring, abate during the summer, and possibly return with a wave in the fall. The third, or worst-case scenario, would be that the disease would turn into a pandemic that would significantly disrupt society, higher education, and the operations of our campuses.

It was not yet clear which scenario would play out, but Perman noted that we could learn from history about how to manage the disease. During the 1918 influenza pandemic, the leaders of St. Louis kept the city under tight public health restrictions, while those in Philadelphia lifted them just before a large holiday parade. The difference in case and mortality rates between the two cities was substantial; the citizens of St. Louis of course fared much better. The lesson was that, whatever the uncertainty, following scientific and public health expertise would lead to better outcomes.[14]

We now know which scenario played out. What was astonishing to us all about the COVID-19 pandemic was how quickly it came, how it shut down our society for months in the spring of 2020, how it exacerbated inequities in our society, and how it divided us politically. The public health lockdown to combat the spread of COVID-19 led to an economic recession that exacerbated inequities in the economy. Many lower-income workers found themselves either unemployed or in vulnerable "frontline" jobs. The disease itself affected the elderly and communities of color disproportionately, revealing significant health disparities. The response to COVID-19 split our nation politically, with conflicting ideas and information about the disease, ways to manage it, and the efficacy of masks and vaccines. These crises were compounded when the shocking death of George Floyd in May provided yet another example of racial disparities in policing and criminal justice—one that catalyzed protests across the country by US citizens of all backgrounds.

COVID-19, of course, also affected our campuses, and we scrambled to respond. At UMBC, leaders and staff in student affairs and
the campus health center began to monitor the developing public
health situation, calling the first staff meetings about COVID-19 on
campus in January 2020. About a month later, it became clear to our
leadership that a more formal response was required, and we declared an emergency in late February 2020. The president activated
our Crisis Management Executive Team (CMET), an established
group of predetermined senior leaders. The CMET then established an Incident Command Team (ICT), led by the UMBC chief of
police, to manage all operational aspects of the emergency. Over
the next week and a half, we would take a series of steps that would
lead us to a campus shutdown for an unknown period:

- March 10: We cancelled classes for March 12–13, the last two
  days before spring break, and said that classes would be
  online for at least two weeks following spring break.
- March 11: The WHO announced that COVID-19 had been
  designated a pandemic.
- March 12: Following emergency orders issued by Maryland
  Governor Lawrence Hogan to limit the spread of COVID-19,
  we announced that we would close our campus for students,
  faculty, and staff on Friday, March 13. Essential employees
  were to check with their supervisors to learn whether they
  needed to report to campus.
- March 13: We announced that the university would remain
  closed through March 18 for staff and through March 22 for
  students. The university would reopen on Thursday,
  March 19, though facilities would remain closed. Employees
  would begin working remotely on March 19. Faculty would
  prepare for teaching online beginning March 23.
- March 19: We announced that courses would be online for the
  remainder of the semester and that we would not be holding

an in-person commencement for the Class of 2020. (See box
for the email communication to campus.)

- March 21: Our campus community had its first COVID-19 case.

In March 2020 we journeyed through the "dense fog" of the early
pandemic toward an "as-yet unknown destination." Clearly, at first,
we thought our campus closure would be temporary. Yet it was not
long before the situation became clearer to us. The pandemic would
not be over soon. The CMET extended the closure of the university's physical campus through the remainder of the semester, with
only critical, approved employees allowed. Almost all staff would
work remotely. Faculty would convert their instruction online. Students would complete their spring courses virtually.

UMBC was not alone in this crisis. With some variation, this experience occurred on campuses across the country as we collectively
found our own paths through the uncertainty of this unexpected

---

Excerpt from Letter to UMBC Campus, March 19, 2020

Dear Members of the UMBC Community,

Many are calling this period a defining moment for humankind, and
history will judge us by how we respond. As the COVID-19 crisis continues to
unfold, we want you to know how proud we are of the ways that our community of inquiring minds has already been adapting. Thank you for all that you
are doing to support one another, your families, and fellow citizens during
these challenging times.

Campus leaders are meeting daily to navigate this rapidly changing
reality, and we are working closely with USM Chancellor Jay Perman, other
System campuses, and shared governance groups to plan necessary transitions in teaching, learning, research, and the daily life of our campus
community.

We have had difficult decisions to make, and we have made them with the
understanding that the health and safety of our community must be our top
priority. In partnership with the University System of Maryland, we have
determined that this means extending distance learning for the remainder of
the spring semester. During this time, UMBC will remain open for student
support services and business operations. In accordance with guidance

provided by the Governor, employees will continue to work remotely whenever possible.

To our undergraduate and graduate students: We know you have been concerned with what happens next, and we are all feeling for you and with you. There is so much you hoped to do this semester, and it is such a disappointment to have these plans interrupted. Online instruction begins on Monday, March 23, and will continue throughout the semester. Faculty have been working with the Division of Information Technology and each other to ensure the highest quality of instruction.

To the Class of 2020, in particular, please know we recognize how hard you have worked to achieve your goals. We are very sorry that we will not be holding in-person Commencement ceremonies this spring. We know how difficult this is for you, your families, and your friends. Just know this is not the end. We may not be having the in-person ceremony, but we will find ways of recognizing you and celebrating your achievements.

A special thank you to our faculty and staff who have been doing everything they can to provide emotional, academic, and other types of support to our students.

Over the coming weeks, patience and understanding will be essential as all of us adjust to these changes. We know that many students, faculty, and staff have questions, and we are committed to providing information and support. Pressing concerns we have heard include the following.

- We know that the shift to distance learning may have financial implications for students and families. We are working closely with USM to establish a system for refunds. We will announce more details in the days to come.
- Students who normally live on campus will soon receive information about the process for safely retrieving their belongings. Until this is established, students who have left campus for spring break will continue to be unable to access their residence halls. Students with an urgent need to retrieve items from their residence halls prior to this announcement may contact Residential Life.

We appreciate your patience and partnership as we move forward together in this new reality. Most important, we hope all of you and your families remain safe and healthy.

President Freeman Hrabowski and Provost Philip Rous

Full post at: https://covid19.umbc.edu/latest-campus-communications /post/91427/

crisis. To protect the health and safety of our students, faculty, and staff, most colleges and universities ended up in the same place that we did, through whatever series of steps they took, moving instruction online for the remainder of the spring 2020 semester and shifting to remote operations.

We operated under this emergency structure for about six weeks, at which time the university leadership moved to a longer-term governance structure to manage the public health emergency. We established a Fall Planning Coordinating Committee (FPCC), under the leadership of the provost and the vice president for administration and finance, which oversaw campus policies and operations going forward. Of course, the mission of the FPCC was to focus on what the campus would do in the fall 2020 semester. As the pandemic wore on, we changed its name to the COVID Planning and Coordinating Committee (CPCC) with responsibility for planning and decision-making for the duration of the pandemic.

The FPCC/CPCC established five work groups focused on key operations:

(1) *Academic Planning*, whose mission was to determine policies and processes for the spring 2021 academic program
(2) *Research and Creative Activity*, which set policies and processes for faculty and students to return to campus in phases, as safe, to resume work in laboratories, work spaces, concert halls, art studios, and other places of creative activity
(3) *Students*, which oversaw student engagement and well-being
(4) *Community Engagement and Events*, which made decisions regarding meetings, events, and event spaces, including athletics.
(5) *Operations*, which oversaw operational issues with regard to both on-campus and remote operations while campus was closed and when reopened on a very limited basis

Most campuses instituted some sort of pandemic response organization, typically consisting of committees, subcommittees, and/or work groups to identify issues, gather information, consider options, and make decisions or recommendations. Smaller institutions adopted simpler response organizations, while larger ones often adopted more complex ones to coordinate across a broader array of colleges and divisions. Some of these organizations were more top-down in their structure, while others were more inclusive and bottom up.

With this structure in place, leadership and decision-making became increasingly complex on our campus. Much of our regular work did not stop while we mobilized to develop policies, practices, and actions to address the public health and budget crises we faced. So, with the FPCC and then the CPCC, we developed a second, parallel organizational structure for crisis management that operated alongside our regular organization. This meant that many of us wore multiple hats.

To make this work, we needed broad involvement of community members, which we accomplished through the five work groups under the CPCC, which had a strong coordinating and decision-making role. We increased internal communications to educate campus community members broadly about guiding principles, priorities, and approaches, using campus-wide emails, town halls, websites, and social media. To the extent possible, we clarified roles and responsibilities and instituted accountability through frequent check-ins with group leaders, an ongoing record of meeting agendas, and requirements for reporting to the CPCC.

The CPCC soon learned that coordination across the five working groups was both challenging and critical. Decisions made in one group often depended on or affected those made by others. It took about six weeks to iron out how to handle this. The CPCC included the leaders of the work groups, but working out differences between two or more groups often required additional meetings of the CPCC co-chairs and the work group leaders. Through these meetings, the CPCC co-chairs could clarify roles and responsibilities and then negotiate differences that remained.

These were challenging times. *Harvard Magazine* recently captured the state of play at that university:

From the decision to depopulate the campus in March 2020 through the 2021–2022 regimen (social distancing, masking, testing and contact tracing, and near universal vaccination), Harvard's safety protocols effectively limited infections and staved off unsettling course corrections—like the midterm return to remote instruction [in Fall 2021] at other schools. Beyond the tangible health benefits, [Harvard president Lawrence] Bacow noted, the community's embrace of effective protective measures mattered because "Everybody's tired, we all have data on the impact this is having on student mental health"—and on faculty and staff members' well-being.[15]

At UMBC, we too put people first and, during the pandemic, this meant putting the health and safety of our community members foremost in our thoughts as we planned and managed. UMBC leadership, crisis management teams, and others took advantage of public health experts on campus to develop initial emergency procedures and then adjusted them as needed—more or less restrictive—from time to time as the situation warranted. Because of our cautious approach, the number of COVID-19 cases among our community members was relatively low compared to the surrounding community, our state, and other campuses.

Resilient Operations
Strong and Resilient

During the pandemic, we operated with parallel management structures that intersected but were responsible for different dimensions of the organization. We continued with our regular structure while we created and managed a pandemic response structure as well. For success, it is critical to pay attention to both of these structures, hard as it is with many personnel wearing multiple hats.

We all know the key operational aspects of colleges and universities. In a recent report, KPMG outlined the key strategic capabilities that colleges and universities should cultivate and draw on for short-term sustainability and long-term growth as they provide rich academic, engaging social, and satisfying customer experiences for students. Among these capabilities are the "ability to operate the business with efficiency and agility to fulfill the customer promise," "an ability to harness data, advanced analytics, and actionable insights" to assess situations and enable change, a "digitally enabled technology architecture" that supports operations, teaching, and research, "an aligned and empowered workforce that inspires people to deliver" on promises we have made, and an "integrated partner and alliance ecosystem" that works with the university and adapts as circumstances arise or needs change.[16]

Having strong resources is critical for long-term sustainability and certainly helpful in a crisis, yet leaders need to develop additional tools to build a resilient institution that is also managing a crisis. Andy Altizer and colleagues have outlined lessons learned from our recent experiences about preparing for a future pandemic. They recommend that we "ensure that executive leadership supports the need for pandemic response planning and resources," "develop crisis response teams and resources ahead of time," "leverage existing resources and establish partnerships," "plan, but . . . plans must be flexible, adaptable and expandable as circumstances change," "expect resource shortages so line up vendors in advance to get ahead of supply chain problems," and "communicate often and through multiple platforms."[17]

We see these lessons as applying to any institution and almost any crisis. At UMBC we did fairly well with regard to pandemic operations, though we found several critical areas where we initially fell short and needed to reinforce our operations. We had a pandemic response plan, developed during the H1N1 epidemic scare. It was outdated and insufficient for addressing the scope of the COVID-19 crisis, though, so we rewrote it in the midst of our early response. We had a Crisis Management Executive Team that would and did take charge during the pandemic. The CMET and its Incident Management Team worked well in providing leadership and management for the first six weeks of the crisis before a longer-term crisis response organization took the lead. Our executive team was deeply involved in the pandemic response. Our provost and vice president for administration and finance led our CPCC. We benefited from being part of the University System of Maryland, which included a medical school whose experts provided guidance to us and to others in the system and the state.

We were in a relatively good position to manage because of resources we had at our disposal, often because of deliberate actions we had taken over previous years, but we also needed to improvise. We leveraged existing resources we had built over time, including shared community values, enhanced financial reserves, strong digital and information infrastructure, and committed faculty and staff. We did not anticipate supply chain issues (i.e., personal protective equipment [PPE], cleaning supplies, construction materials), so we experienced delays and shortfalls in the early months as did most colleges and universities.

As did most institutions, we ramped up internal communications during the pandemic. We embedded our communications staff in the IMT and the CPCC from the outset so that we considered communications in our decision-making process and so that communications staff would be up to speed on what we were doing. (Nonetheless, we heard from some campus members that there still was not enough communication.)

Despite the restrictions we put in place to battle COVID-19, we were able to conduct business operations, manage academic affairs, provide a quality educational program, gradually bring faculty and students back to campus for research and creative achievement, and offer campus events online.

Challenges, Mistakes, and Burnout

Still, as Altizer and colleagues warn, mistakes and burnout are both likely. Within the context of the COVID-19 pandemic, indeed, mistakes or at least differences of opinion were very likely. We followed the science (public health guidance), and yet the expert advice kept changing as the disease changed or the experts gained new insights into how the virus operates. Therefore, what might appear to be a good decision could very easily result in a bad or unwanted outcome. On our campus, as on many others, we soon learned to offer "grace" to each other as we navigated a challenging situation.

In spring 2021, for example, we made a late decision with regard to classroom density that forced the registrar and some departments to revise their class schedules, resulting in extra work for fall 2021. We had required that students had to be spaced at least 6 feet apart in our classrooms. This reduced density meant that we could not offer many classes—especially our larger lecture courses—in person because we did not have classrooms large enough for them with students spaced out. We had anticipated that we would keep this restriction in place for fall 2021, but it became clear to us that COVID-19 vaccines would be available to students during the summer rather than the fall, making higher classroom capacity an option. We also had more information about how K-12 schools had fared, which gave us hope that higher capacity was possible without undue risk. Based on this new information, we shifted from the 6-foot distancing requirement to classroom capacity designations that would effectively allow 3-foot distancing. Suddenly, more courses could be in person. By this time, some departments had already completed their class schedules. This meant extra work for those departments and the registrar as they revised the modalities of their offerings. Despite this new opportunity to offer classes in person, some faculty wanted to come back and others did not, which led to further discussions.

We had our differences and challenges. We sensed an ongoing tension between following the science and the anxiety levels of campus members, particularly those faculty and staff who had young children or cared for older adults. Indeed, among our community members we had diverse perspectives, divergent leadership styles, and different tolerances for risk and uncertainty. We also found, moreover, that neither the faculty, the staff, nor the students had "one view," but that there was a range of views among each group.

What made the shift in our classroom capacity policy more frustrating was that we desperately needed a new scheduling process. Before the pandemic, we had been working on the development of a new process and the acquisition of digital tools that would support it. While we strongly value our adherence to shared leadership at UMBC, we soon discovered through our shared governance discussions that there was much discord on how to proceed. So, when the pandemic hit, we shelved the discussions for the time being. Yet COVID-19 and its classroom capacity issues soon shined a light on how important it is for us to address this. Revamping the process will involve centralizing it, clearly delineating new roles and responsibilities, and deploying new digital tools, as well as holding discussions about how this will benefit the university as a whole in the long run.

As for burnout, we did not anticipate how critical this issue would become. For one thing, we did not know how long the pandemic would last. As it became evident that colleagues were exhausted from the heroic work they did "above and beyond their normal duties," we had to remind them to take time off to relax and recharge. We also went out of our way to show our awareness of what our colleagues have done to support our institutions in this challenging time through our words of appreciation and celebrations of hard work. Though some people have left for a variety of reasons, for the most part (and so far), we have avoided the "great resignation" and the "great disengagement,"[18] though we are aware that other campuses have not.

Strategic Choices

Since March 2020 we in higher education have had conversations we might not otherwise have had about our academic program and administrative operations as we have scrambled to address the challenges of COVID, a recession, and racial unrest. Our work, under stressful circumstances, has challenged our values and posed hard choices. We have accelerated work in some areas, paused work in others, changed course in some of our work, and added new work to address emerging challenges and opportunities. We have had to make tough choices.

We had to make decisions about how much we could focus on the long term during the pandemic, which required much focus on the short term. The level of innovation required to manage the crisis could not be maintained without impacting the "performance engine" of the organization. As a result, we made decisions to selectively defer some ongoing initiatives, including priorities from our strategic plan, while focusing on key long-term initiatives that would create and sustain new approaches as we emerged from the crisis. Several initiatives pushed off to the future included an instructional space scheduling initiative, the implementation of a new budget model, and initiatives to enhance athletics revenue. Meanwhile, we focused our long-term resources and work on implementing the many initiatives under our strategic enrollment plan (SEP). These included staffing and policy changes made in support of student success (i.e., added academic advocates, implemented the 90-credit degree audit, limited repeats, documented incomplete grade agreements), implementing new software (customer relationship management, or CRM) to build and manage a pipeline for new students, and significant new research endeavors.

For capital projects, we made similar choices about what would best support our campus as we emerged from the pandemic. While we put several capital projects on hold, we continued work, for example, on modernizing our recreation center (the Retriever Activities Center). We also moved forward with a critically important new Center for Wellbeing, which now houses university health and counseling among other student services.

Networks and Community

We benefited from being one among twelve institutions in the USM, led by a new chancellor, Jay Perman, who was also a medical doctor and well positioned to understand and manage a public health crisis. We were able to draw on USM resources, including the University of Maryland Baltimore Center for Vaccine Development, the USM center for course redesign, and experts in online education at the University of Maryland Global Campus. We also benefited from system-level committees that deliberated issues and challenges and offered opportunities for the exchange of information on what campuses were trying. Even if we did not follow the example of other campuses, understanding their data, choices, and practices informed our decision-making in positive ways. In addition, some public health decisions, including that to impose a vaccine mandate for fall 2021, were made by the system and applied to its member institutions. This took pressure off individual campuses when potentially controversial decisions were needed.

We also benefited from the external networks of campus leaders and experts. Our president at the time, Freeman Hrabowski, had frequent interaction with higher education leaders around the country. Other leaders on our campus could also tap networks, in particular through commissions of the Association of Public and Land-grant Universities (APLU) on research, student affairs, communications, and government affairs. Our vice presidents had recently or currently served on the executive committees of several of these commissions. Our then vice president for finance and administration had recently served as chair of the National Association of College and University Business Officers (NACUBO), and our vice president for information technology was a former board chair of Educause. We also benefited from the expertise offered to us by Dr. Lucy Wilson, an infectious disease physician and professor in our department of emergency health services. Dr. Wilson is a respected expert in her field, served as an advisor to Maryland Governor Larry Hogan, and brought insights from her experience and those of her colleagues around the country.

We were also well positioned because of who we are as a campus. When the pandemic broke, our leadership set the right tone by recognizing the seriousness of the situation but also communicating a sense of hope. Our values supported our work and we stuck with

the two guiding principles we had developed earlier: we would protect our academic programs and put people first. We had previously developed resources for crisis and emergency response. In
2008 the USM Board of Regents required each system campus to
write an emergency operations plan. Then, in response to the H1N1
influenza epidemic, we also wrote a pandemic emergency plan,
which gave us something to start with in 2020, although we had to
make significant revisions to it. In January 2020, just before the
pandemic, we also funded a new position for an emergency manager. He came on board just in time.

Two powerful resources for our campus have been our empowering culture and strong sense of community. The notion of UMBC
as a community, which we cultivated prior to the pandemic crisis,
served us well during it. We cannot argue that everyone was happy
all the time; indeed we had many who dissented on a range of decisions. Yet, overall, our community members felt a sense of belonging and ownership that helped us stay strong and united in our
work. The pandemic may have closed our physical campus, disrupting our sense of place, but we sustained our culture and community
through shared leadership, collaborative work, campus communications, and online events.

In preparation for our campus retreat in January 2021, we fielded
a survey to retreat participants, asking them to name our campus
"superpower," and 225 responded. The results are in figure 1, a word
cloud that shows the frequency of terms by their size. "Community"
is the biggest word in the cloud, followed by "people" and then "students," "faculty," "diversity," "inclusive excellence," "shared governance," "ability," and "grit."

We had a culture that brought strength to our work. At the center of our culture is an authentic commitment to shared governance
and shared leadership that both included and empowered people
in the work. Our culture also encompasses a notion of "grit" in which
staff and faculty were already willing to go above and beyond in their
work: during the pandemic, they stepped up. We also had positive
relationships with partners that enabled collaborative agreements

WHAT IS UMBC'S SUPERPOWER?

FIGURE 1. Word Cloud for "What Is UMBC's Superpower?" UMBC Campus Retreat, January 2021

to share the burden of the pandemic. These included Chartwells, our food services provider, ABM, our housekeeping contactor, and the Maryland Economic Development Corporation (MEDCO), which had financed the Walker Avenue Apartments on our campus. MEDCO worked to maintain the financial solvency of the apartment complex despite revenue loss from students vacating apartments during the pandemic. These external partners worked with us to determine how to share financial losses that stemmed from the campus closure and to follow similar policies and practices to combat the spread of COVID-19.

Our recent book about leadership, culture, and innovation at UMBC, *The Empowered University: Shared Leadership, Culture Change, and Academic Success*, had, since its publication, become part of the culture of the campus that it had described. Our campus embraced the notion of an "empowered university." The book and the title were useful for framing campus conversations during the pandemic and building participation and community. A series of forums on campus were entitled "The Empowered University." The forums included a university-wide retreat and more specific events focused on teaching and learning, research, internationalization, and racial justice. This notion of an empowered campus was useful for establishing an authentic approach to shared communication, information, experiences, and decision-making.

Academic Program

During the pandemic, we made several short- and long-term decisions about our academic program, some relatively easy, others more difficult.

Our decision for admissions to be temporarily test optional was easy. At the beginning of the pandemic, the College Board and ACT suspended administration of their tests due to health concerns. Many students could not take an admissions test, and those who had taken it junior year could not retake it to improve their scores during their senior year. As officials relaxed COVID-19 restrictions in various parts of the country, students with means sometimes traveled to those locations where they could take the tests. This was not available to everyone and, therefore, created equity concerns. For these reasons, USM presidents and provosts discussed this problem at system-wide meetings, and each USM institution admitting undergraduates came to the same policy decision: make these tests optional. We had a general campus consensus in favor of this decision, and we have continued this policy for the time being. We will, however, need to make a long-term decision about whether to keep this admissions option. There are differences of opinion about what to do and why, so this will be a challenging conversation. The decision will depend, in part, on how those students admitted under the test-optional strategy fare in terms of grades, learning outcomes, and persistence relative to other students.

Our decision on whether to implement and then terminate a pass/fail grading option was more difficult. We decided to allow a pass/fail grading option for students in the spring 2020 semester but discontinued this policy for fall 2020. Some students and faculty were quite vocal about retaining this policy for that fall, because they continued to experience the stress and challenges of online teaching and learning. The Academic Planning work group, however, believed it was in the best long-term interest of undergraduate students to receive letter grades that would better communicate their actual level of achievement to graduate and professional programs to which they might apply.

Meanwhile, the decision to provide online instruction beginning March 2020 was clearly the right path forward until we had the tools to minimize the health risks for our community. Providing online instruction, however, required substantial work in a short period, and while outcomes varied, the transition was a huge accomplishment. First, the move to online teaching and learning presented a significant mental and technological shift for faculty. Orianne Smith, president of the Faculty Senate, called this shift an "existential crisis" for many faculty. After years of working in one mode, many found their jobs had changed significantly and overnight. Many took advantage of training and support for online teaching during the two-week campus shutdown in March 2020, and then the overwhelming majority (about 75 percent) of faculty took advantage of training for online teaching when it was offered more broadly in the summer of 2020.

Our Division of Professional Studies (DPS) had been providing faculty with training in online course delivery for a decade. Few had taken the training, but when the need arose, we quickly scaled up the program to meet demand with a program we called PIVOT. At the start of the pandemic, Sarah Shin, associate provost for academic affairs, convened a PIVOT working group at the suggestion of the provost. This working group was composed of representatives from DoIT, DPS, the Faculty Development Center, Student Disability Services, and the dean's offices of our three colleges. The group met regularly throughout the first year or so of the pandemic when online instruction was in full gear to develop initiatives for supporting faculty throughout the summer and into the fall of 2020.

Faculty learning communities led by 25 PIVOT faculty mentors from across our colleges were central to program success. These faculty members had previously taken the DPS training for online teaching. They supported the discipline-based learning communities, logging in every day, hosting office hours, responding to questions from their group, demonstrating course designs, and explaining how to use online tools. They were exemplary models of peer engagement during a time when many faculty needed this support from fellow faculty. The administration supported this effort, compensating mentors for their time and providing stipends to faculty who took the PIVOT training course.

The shift was also an adjustment for students who had a range of experiences as they transitioned from largely in-person learning to online instruction. The effectiveness of online teaching varied from course to course and instructor to instructor. Some students missed the in-person learning environment, though others found that the online environment had significant advantages, such as asynchronous access to recorded lectures and other resources. Sarah Shin also led the FOLIO (Fostering Online Learning Improvement and Opportunity) workgroup established to provide training and support to students encountering new modes of instruction, helping them to be successful in online instruction. This group was composed of representatives from the Academic Success Center, Student Affairs, OIA, DOIT, the Graduate School, and Student Disability Services, and included faculty and student representatives.

The FOLIO group's charge was to generate a plan to ensure that all UMBC students can operate and learn effectively online. This included establishing an all-encompassing "care package" site that is attractive and easily accessible to students with all the available services and resources in one place, which faculty can point to (e.g., Retrievers Return Roadmap Student Sections), and developing tools to help faculty promote effective student social engagement in their online classes. The FOLIO group also planned and implemented the

Academic Ambassadors program, through which graduate and undergraduate student volunteers were trained to provide support to fellow students during pandemic-induced online learning.

Student Affairs

Despite a closed physical campus, we sought to sustain the student experience in the virtual space. For example, Student Affairs staff moved online our annual fall "Involvement Fest," an event for students to connect with student organizations and groups. This was a significant, and successful, undertaking. An article in the student paper, *The Retriever,* quoted one student as saying the virtual Involvement Fest was a "game changer" for her. Despite attending UMBC in a virtual environment in fall 2020, she was able to connect with a student group that allowed her to engage with the campus while having fun or engaging in meaningful work. More than 4,000 UMBC students are engaged with student groups, so keeping this alive was important as a way of sustaining the student experience.

Student affairs also sought to sustain traditions at the center of student life. A key question staff asked themselves in the summer of 2020 was, "How do we make sure that students understand our traditions when they are new to UMBC and not on campus?" How do we communicate to them that it is cool to be inclusive or to go to a soccer game? To address this, student affairs created "Tradition in a Box." Student Affairs mailed a welcome box to new students that included a UMBC soccer scarf and a UMBC mask. As it happened, they sent them the day before a final group of new students registered through "late registration." The mother of one student wrote to say that her daughter, who registered late, was disappointed that she did not get a box when several of her friends did. The tech staffer in student affairs who had pulled the names for box distribution said he had not thought about the late-registration students. He personally drove out to Frederick, Maryland, to deliver a box to the student who was upset. The student's mother later wrote to say she had never seen her daughter so happy! This is an example of both sustaining UMBC culture and of staff going "above and beyond."

Student affairs also had infrastructure in place before the pandemic to address public health, diversity and inclusion, and civic life. The student health center quickly became the locus of UMBC's COVID-19 testing program that UMBC staff developed with input from UMBC experts. Student affairs established the I3B Center (Initiatives for Identity, Inclusion, and Belonging) during the campus effort to develop a new approach to Title IX in 2019 to 2020. This center focused on supporting students of all backgrounds. In a participatory and inclusive way, our Center for Democracy and Civic Life provided programming for campus conversations around social and policy issues as well as the 2020 presidential election.

Research and Creative Activity

Despite our worst fears with most laboratories closed for much of the year, our research and creative activity during 2020 went well under the circumstances. The Office of the Vice President for Research conducted a business continuity exercise during the first two weeks of March 2020. All staff worked from home, and the office made adjustments based on this exercise so that it was ready when we shut down the campus on March 13. With great care, a committee including faculty leaders overseeing Research and Creative Achievements gradually brought faculty and students back to campus in a phased process so that they could engage in their work in person, on campus, and in a safe manner. Because we had already created the position of Associate Dean for Research in each of the colleges, these individuals were able to provide a critical bridge between the campus-wide effort to oversee research/creative activity and the faculty in each of the colleges. Before summer 2020 the RCA committee had a process for a very limited number of faculty to apply to return to campus due to special circumstances, often having to do with specialized equipment. Then, the first phase of return to campus began in the summer of 2020. The numbers on campus gradually increased as we moved to new phases, depending on current recommendations and restrictions from public health officials.

Despite the limits on access to campus and the time conflicts that some faculty experienced with caregiving, UMBC faculty did remarkably well with research. UMBC increased research expenditures during the 2021 fiscal year, achieving its highest level over the past decade. The federal government facilitated this by granting special approval for research faculty on federal grants to work remotely as needed and possible. Meanwhile, faculty and graduate students also wrote funding proposals that led to a record number of research awards for UMBC, and spent significant time writing manuscripts for publication during remote work.

Most important, in February 2022 the Carnegie Classification of Institutions of Higher Education placed UMBC in the category of doctoral universities with very high research activity category. This put UMBC among just 146 institutions popularly known as Research 1 or R1. In 2022, 39 private and 107 public universities were in this category. "This historic moment for our campus is an outcome of long-term strategic priorities and investments in the research and creative achievement community at UMBC—people, facilities, and programs," said Karl Steiner, vice president for research. President Freeman Hrabowski added, "This milestone reflects our commitment to excellence across the disciplines, from the humanities to the sciences."[19]

R1 status is not just about research and creative activity per se but also about student success. At UMBC we have made a point of pulling undergraduates as well as graduate students into research, scholarship, and creative activity. Learning by doing reinforces what students learn in the classroom, builds their practical skills, and helps them to identify with both the work and the discipline. At UMBC, we like to say, "It takes researchers to produce researchers."

Human Resources

In addition, we benefited from particular strengths in human resources, digital infrastructure, and budgeting, which we will now discuss.

A Community of Colleagues

In *The Empowered University*, we wrote, "When outsiders comment on the successes or failures of a university, they often focus on the institution's president, who tends to get the attention, the accolades, or the blame. This view of a university is misguided, because it takes a community of colleagues working together to make a university thrive for its students and faculty."[20] Today we can add, due to our experience during the COVID-19 pandemic, "and because it also takes a community of colleagues working together to make a university resilient in a crisis."

It is, perhaps, a truism that "an organization is only as good as its people," and yet the people who work in an organization determine whether it thrives in good times and is resilient in a crisis. Financial resources, digital tools, and facilities are all critical, too, but without committed and capable people, an organization is not sustainable.

As we are writing this book, employees across the United States are turning the US labor market upside down. Many more employees than usual are leaving their jobs in what many are calling "The Great Resignation." Some are leaving because their employers have required a return to the in-person workplace and they do not want to risk getting COVID-19 or comply with a vaccine mandate. Some temporarily laid-off workers and others have asked themselves on return, "Why am I here, and is the pay worth with the work?" "Majorities of workers who quit a job in 2021 say low pay (63%), no opportunities for advancement (63%) and feeling disrespected at work (57%) were reasons why they quit," write Kim Parker and Juliana Horowitz of Pew Research.[21] Still others have found that, with significant turnover in the workforce, they are finding better opportunities, in house or elsewhere. They seek work that is more interesting, better pay and benefits, opportunities for advancement, or preferable working conditions.[22]

Korn Ferry recently reported, "Employees are now starting to ask very human questions about the work they perform. Why am I doing this? What is it for? How can we do it better? Many are choosing to leave their jobs. The competition to attract new talent is growing faster than ever."[23] An opinion piece in *The Chronicle of Higher Education* put an even finer point on this, saying, "Right now, your best midlevel manager is updating her resume. Your hardest working director is controlling his excitement after learning the salary range of a private sector opening. Your most trustworthy entry-level professional is writing a resignation letter because her new corporate position doubles her pay and doesn't require nights or weekends. Two years of pandemic life have left campus staff members beyond burned out. They are done. And they are leaving or thinking about it in droves."[24]

Information technology departments at universities have been particularly hard hit. Mark McCormack, senior director for analytics and research at Educause relates that IT staff faced unique demands during the transition to remote teaching and work that have burned out staff. *The Chronicle of Higher Education* recently reported that at one Virginia institution four members of a ten-person IT team recently left. Two did not want to comply with the university's COVID-19 vaccine requirement. Others got tired of workloads that increased during the pandemic or found that corporate positions offered higher salaries.[25]

At UMBC our Department of Information Technology (DoIT) has fared relatively well with support from our Office of Human Resources (OHR). In the past year, four out of 80 of our staff in DoIT have left for positions elsewhere in higher education or the private sector. That is high for this department, but compared to attrition nationally, 5 percent annual turnover is still relatively low. DoIT has worked with OHR over the years to provide key staff with promotions, reclassifications, or critical retention increases (in-grade salary adjustments) in order to retain them. They worked together during the pandemic, continuing this practice in order to keep DoIT strong at a time when they were in high demand.

The "Great Resignation" has not been a problem for us at UMBC except in pockets, including—rather ironically—in HR. Overall, as OHR worked with DoIT and many other departments to retain employees, our turnover was lower than normal in 2020 and was similar to what we experienced prepandemic in 2021. We know of very few staff who have left UMBC for both a higher salary and the opportunity to work remotely full time. Moreover, we have experienced these results despite a 15-month hiring freeze that often increased the workloads of staff when their colleagues departed. However, our OHR lost 12 out of its 21 staff in just 12 months, raising important questions about staff retention and career paths that are specific to that unit but of general concern as well.

In many ways, 2021 became "The Time of Great Opportunity" for staff who were looking to change jobs, but we should not just chalk up departures to this historical moment without learning lessons for the future. Most of our staff who left positions in HR either retired or moved to higher-level jobs elsewhere. Could we have retained at least some of these staff? Many sought upward career mobility that was blocked by long-term employees who liked their jobs and had no intention of leaving. Indeed, our staff continue to rate our university as a "great place to work," and our culture makes our working environment a congenial place. Still, this is not necessarily enough for those seeking opportunity. Could job reclassifications, in-grade pay increases, or creative career paths have encouraged departing staff to stay? As a midsize public university, we continue to have challenges competing with other institutions that can and do offer higher positions and salaries for staff. We also have challenges in creating career paths for staff in very small units for which there are just one or two staff positions. Staff will move up by changing jobs and units within the university or to another organization, unless we find creative ways to support them and their growth.

In-Person and Remote Work

In March 2020 the World Health Organization declared that COVID-19 had become a pandemic. We all know how our lives changed. Most colleges and universities closed their physical campuses. If we were faculty or students, we shifted from mainly in-person classes to online instruction through the 2020–2021 academic year. We shifted back to a mixture of in-person, hybrid, and online classes in fall 2021. If we were administrators or staff, we began working remotely, generally from home from mid-March 2020 until a phased return to campus in July and August 2021.

To make remote work possible, flexibility and technology were central to our success. Our OHR provided supervisors with toolkits and training that offered guidance on how to manage staff working remotely. OHR also developed a process for supervisors to request that specific staff work on campus rather than remotely. Senior leadership approved a small number of staff to work on campus. Following federal requirements, OHR also developed a process to provide paid administrative leave for staff who were unable to complete their jobs remotely but were not allowed to work on campus, as well as paid sick leave for employees who were sick with COVID-19 or caring for a family member with COVID-19.

Because of these shifts, we found ourselves in new situations that affected people in different ways. There were advantages and disadvantages to working remotely for staff and faculty:[26]

- Some missed the camaraderie of the office, including water cooler chat, impromptu meetings, and opportunities to stop in to talk with a colleague. Others were happy to be working from home. They liked the solitude.
- Some missed their commutes, which provided time to listen in the car to an audiobook or the news, or time on the train or subway to scroll through email or read a book. Others did not miss the commute at all, the early wake up and the nerve-wracking stop and go traffic on the interstate.

- Some liked the boundaries between work and home lives. For them, it was great to be in the office, focus on work for the day, and have space from the demands of family. They liked putting on their office attire and going out into the "adult world." For others, working from home meant you could sleep later, work in comfortable clothes, and juggle work and home life throughout the day. They liked the opportunity to spend more time with family and even supervise the online school day for younger children.

Many found the shift to remote work, in combination with the fears and uncertainty of COVID-19, created significant stress and increased anxiety. This was even true for some who said there were benefits to working from home. We experienced grief for the loss of "normal life" as we adjusted to changes in routines, family life, work, shopping, and more. Doing all of these from home could be very isolating, even if one did connect virtually through online classes or meetings. Or, by contrast, others now living in a house filled 24/7 with spouses, partners, children, relatives, housemates, and others found this could produce its own brand of stress or tension from being too close.

The return to work on campus was also stressful. Returning to offices "frozen in time" after more than a year had a surreal quality to it. The calendars on the wall still said "March 2020." We found handwritten meeting notes on our desks from February 2020 and other papers about work that was coming up that April and May.[27] For us, the return of staff to campus in the summer of 2021 also occurred just as the Delta variant of COVID-19 was beginning to surge. This created uncertainty about policies and practices and additional fear for some returning employees.

A big question for us, as for others in higher education, was whether to implement a vaccine mandate for students, faculty, and staff. This decision loomed over us in the summer of 2021, and we began conversations about the pros, cons, and technical details of implementing a vaccine mandate. Fortunately for us, the USM leadership decided to implement a system-wide vaccination mandate, so we did not have to directly tackle this difficult decision. Still, there were details for us to work out about verifying vaccination status, deadlines for vaccinations, and a process for waivers, exemptions and compliance.

We had an indoor mask mandate in place for employees and students returning to campus over the summer of 2021. We required them to wear a mask indoors at all times, unless working alone in an office with a closed door. We had hoped to lift that mandate as the pandemic eased further with vaccinations, but we were not able to do so in 2021 because of the increase in COVID-19 cases and growing evidence of breakthrough infections with the Delta and Omicron variants. In fact, in the late fall of 2021 we even required that people on our campus must wear KN95 or equivalent masks and were providing them free to community members.

We were aware that this indoor mask policy had its downside. When we shifted to remote work, employees were eager to return to work, because of our sense of community and the practical reality that you can get a question answered when you run into a colleague in the hallway or in the elevator. Once we were back on campus, however, the mask policy stifled these opportunities and benefits. Many staff who have offices went directly to them on arrival and closed their doors so that they could take their masks off. The amount of interaction we had hoped for on our return to campus was much lower than expected.

Our policies continued to evolve as the public health situation did, with an aim to discontinuing the mask mandate. By March 2022 the Omicron spike had come and gone with case levels per capita dropping back to where we had been in July 2021. At this point, the conversation focused over whether COVID-19 had become endemic rather than pandemic and whether, between COVID-19 cases and vaccinations, we had achieved something like "herd immunity." In this context, we revised our mask policy again. At this point, we no longer required masks except in the classroom. Staff who did not have an office were particularly happy to have this policy change, as they had been wearing masks for 8 hours a day.

The pandemic was challenging for staff and their supervisors, as we all found that working remotely was very different from working together in an office environment. With no differentiation between the office and home, some staff felt as though the workday had become almost 24/7. Many were learning new processes and had additional responsibilities related to the pandemic. Managing a remote workforce put supervisors to the test. The Professional Staff Senate, with the support of the Non-Exempt Staff Senate, brought forth a list of requests for the consideration of management, most of which had to do with respecting boundaries and providing relief for staff with caregiving responsibilities at home. We brought these requests to the Vice Presidents and Deans Council for its consideration, and those requests that were appropriate were incorporated into the Supervisors Toolkit. We also formed a broadly representative Staff Return to Work on Campus work group, with a charge of providing advice and recommendations to the administration and HR in particular, on how to support staff as they physically returned to work on campus.

The work condition that dominates conversations today is the availability of telework, which we discovered to be workable and productive for many employees when virtually everyone worked remotely in 2020 and 2021. In a recent survey, the University of Wisconsin at Milwaukee found that nearly 75 percent of their staff found working from home improved their lives. As the *Chronicle of Higher Education* commented, "They wanted a flexible schedule and work-from-home opportunities, forever."[28]

Like many colleges and universities, the pandemic experience led to discussions about telework and its benefits and costs. Prepandemic, we had a limited telework policy. Shifting to remote work changed our mindsets about what is possible and most effective from both an institutional and staff perspective. As we have returned to on-campus work, many staff who enjoyed remote work or certain aspects of it would now like to continue telework going forward on either a part-time or full-time basis. We are experimenting more broadly with telework to ascertain what is optimal for staff across varied units. We have revised our telework policy to encourage supervisors to allow their staff to continue some level of telework as appropriate. We did this on a trial basis for the fall 2021 semester and, with the arrival of the Omicron variant, we continued it into the spring 2022 semester.

We will adjust our policy in the future depending on the outcomes of this experiment. We will balance the competing demands as we do so. We want to promote staff well-being and productivity, to be sure. We also want to promote community, which we facilitate when people are together on campus. We also need staff on campus to be available when students, faculty, or others visit our offices.

Digital Infrastructure

Our resilience in the midst of a pandemic that demanded a shift to online teaching and operations depended heavily on our ability to use a strong digital infrastructure. Colleges and universities have been procuring, implementing, and using technology for decades. The shift to remote teaching and operations during the early months of the pandemic pushed our institutions to accelerate the use of technology across all our activities: teaching, research, advising, meetings, events, fundraising, alumni outreach, and business processes. The pandemic condensed the "long term"—what we thought would take a decade—into a very short period. For campuses everywhere, what was responsive in the short-term and strategic in the long run briefly became one.

UMBC was in a better position than many colleges and universities in March 2020 when it came to technology because of the tools and processes we already had in place. Other universities were buying tools, learning about them, and deploying them at the same time. By contrast, we had invested strategically over time in online and digital tools, had begun a transition to the cloud before many of our peer institutions, and had hired new staff in instructional technology. We did not have to license any new digital tools to adapt to remote teaching and work. Our staff had learned how to use and deploy the tools whose adoption we would draw on. Our work involved ramping up use of existing tools rather than starting from scratch, though the scale and pace of deployment was beyond anything we had done before.

Our DoIT played a central role in spring 2020 in the process of helping staff and faculty transition quickly to remote work and teaching. Our vice president for information technology, Jack Suess, chaired the operations group that reported to the CPCC. This position allowed him to learn needs across units in real time. He worked with his team in DoIT to figure out how they could best contribute solutions for the challenges we faced on a daily basis. By late March, they had rethought the roles and responsibilities of DoIT staff and restructured their organization to meet the university's immediate needs. Damian Doyle, deputy CIO and senior associate vice president for information technology, recalled, "A large portion of this was working with different units to help ease concerns, and facilitate training and make sure they understood we were there to help them through this transition, and to get them any tools or technologies they needed to be successful."

Many of the tools we used will be familiar to our colleagues in higher education. We had WebEx, which we used as our platform for online meetings, while other institutions were licensing that product or Zoom. We had DocuSign for digital signatures that linked to PeopleSoft and other data sources, and student employees trained to work with offices to convert signature processes from paper to digital. We had Blackboard to support our faculty in course delivery, running it in the cloud through Amazon Web Services.

Rolling out and adopting these tools required collaboration and intensive work from both DoIT and those who would own the tools and use it in their work. For example, for WebEx to work properly, staff had to get up to speed on its use, including scheduling, links, screen sharing, and recording. We also needed new norms to make it work for everyone. For example, OHR suggested that supervisors keep meetings to 50 minutes so that staff would have time to transition from one meeting to another. For DocuSign to work, staff in units across campus had to integrate it into their signature processes and design the forms to use. When we shifted to remote operations, DoIT and OHR worked collaboratively to develop and deploy a new solution for secure online payroll processing.

In April we turned our attention to online teaching. A conversation between Provost Philip Rous and Vice President Jack Suess led to the identification of funds to scale quickly a training program for faculty in online teaching into a broad program that would provide the opportunity for training to all faculty. Developed and deployed by our Division of Professional Studies, the program, which we called PIVOT, trained over 400 faculty in late spring and summer. Complementing this effort, our Faculty Development Center offered faculty the opportunity to take pedagogical training that would improve their teaching techniques both generally and in the online space. DoIT scaled our virtual computer lab solutions so that more faculty could use them in their courses and developed an approach for using technology to manage online exams, including access, testing, and compliance. Our academic advising team worked with DoIT to rethink first-year orientation using a variety of technologies, leading to the highest level of student satisfaction they have ever had.

Meanwhile, the campus moved ahead with the deployment of other digital solutions designed to improve our work to support strategic initiatives, regardless of whether we were in a pandemic. For example, a work group of the Strategic Enrollment Plan Committee, which included staff from Enrollment Management, our colleges, the graduate school, marketing, and DoIT, implemented Salesforce's CRM system, tailoring it to our needs so that staff across the university could engage more effectively with prospective and current students. Enrollment management uses the CRM system to bring together in one place a range of data that enhances communications and interactions with students throughout the recruitment, application, admission, and enrollment process.

Not everything went as well as it might have. Some higher education institutions, such as liberal arts colleges, brought nearly all of their students back to their residential campuses for fall 2020 and designed systems to test them for COVID-19 and train them for on-campus work and living under the circumstances. At UMBC, most of our students were off campus and still taking classes remotely that fall. Yet we offered a limited number of in-person or hybrid classes. Students living on campus in a reduced capacity residential environment participated in these, but so did students living off campus who would come to UMBC only one or two days per week.

We had the digital tools to provide COVID-19 training and testing for these students in place by the summer of 2020, but we had one hangup: what to do with students in hybrid classes? Some hybrid classes were almost all online, and others were nearly all in person. For some courses, the on-campus component only involved picking up and returning equipment. For others, the in-person sessions were concentrated in the second half of the semester. DoIT staff worked with the colleges and departments and mined campus data sources to identify those students in hybrid classes who would be on campus regularly and, therefore, had to engage in weekly COVID-19 testing. DoIT finally accomplished this in October 2020, a little later than planned.

One of the key lessons learned from our experience is that we have to adapt strategically as well as technologically. The question for leaders now is not whether to continue this digital transformation, but what has and has not worked, what solutions should endure, which new tools to adopt at what pace, and how should our campus adapt to or incorporate new digital tools. For example, neither our recent strategic plan nor an ongoing classroom scheduling initiative has recognized the extent to which we would need to expand online and hybrid teaching, not just in the short run while our physical campus was closed, but in the long run as we emerged from the worst of the pandemic and returned to a new normal. Similarly, our planning has not taken into account how the experience of remote work would shape faculty and staff work preferences and options, as many now have the desire and tools to work remotely, at least some of the time. We have changed our thinking about how work, facilities, and technology fit together, and this will shape our planning as we continue our digital transformation.

A second key lesson learned is the centrality of collaboration to the development of digital infrastructure. Technology is a means rather than an end. It does not deploy itself. Our DoIT staff alone do not make it work. It takes cross-unit teams composed of those who own business processes and those in IT working together to develop applications, integrate them into or redesign business processes, and then deploy them, working out bugs as they go.

A final lesson learned is that it is helpful to have a robust digital infrastructure in place when crises hit, rather than having to develop them from scratch. We do not have crystal balls that will tell us what crises are coming and what our needs might be in their midst. Yet, robust investment in digital tools, deployment with colleagues across the campus, and training to support staff and faculty who use these tools will provide a solid foundation for our operations in both quiet times and crises. These resources support our resilience.

Financial Sustainability in Higher Education
Trends

Colleges and universities are complex, multi-mission organizations with complicated financial and budget structures. They provide educational programs, career services, residential life, dining, parking, mental health counseling, recreation and athletic opportunities, and student organizations. The extent to which they do so depends on funding.

The funding model for public higher education has changed over the past quarter-century, as shown in figure 2 from the State Higher

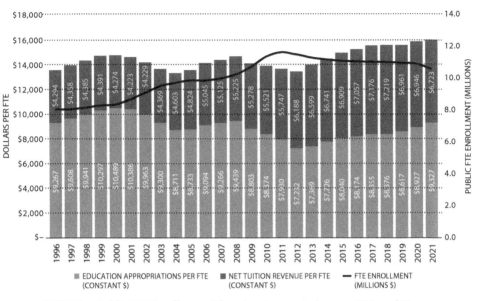

FIGURE 2. Public FTE Enrollment, Education Appropriations per FTE, and Net Tuition Revenue Per FTE, United States, FY 1996–2021 (constant dollars)
Source: https://shef.sheeo.org/wp-content/uploads/2022/06/SHEEO_SHEF_FY21_Report.pdf.

Education Executive Officers Association (SHEEO). During this time, states have cut their average higher education appropriations per student (constant dollars per FTE). The trend line looks like a roller coaster. Appropriations peaked in FY 2000 at $10,207. Many states cut their appropriations during the recession that followed, reaching a low point in 2004 at an average $8,475 per student. As the economy recovered, states overall increased spending for higher education reaching another peak in 2008 at $9,189, though still at a level lower than 2001. The Great Recession produced further cuts starting in 2009, hitting a new low point of $7,039 in 2012. Again, most states increased funding during the recovery and for 2020 reached $8,636, though at a level below both 2008 and 2001.[29]

During this time, a majority of public colleges and universities increased tuition, mainly to compensate for state appropriation cuts and increased demands for services. (Private, nonprofit institutions also increased tuition in constant dollars, to cover increased costs, new services or amenities, and financial aid.) In 2001 average net tuition revenue per FTE at public colleges and universities was $4,159, and total educational revenues (appropriations plus net tuition) was $14,366. In 2014 net tuition revenue per FTE had increased to $6,522, but total educational revenues, at $14,049, were still comparable to those in 2001. Since then, both state appropriations and net tuition have increased so that total educational revenue per FTE peaked in 2020 at $15,362.

While this amount is about $1,000 per student higher than in 2001, demands for services from colleges and universities and inflation have brought upward pressure on costs. For example, investments in technology have been substantial over the past two decades, enhancing educational technology, automating business processes, and providing the ubiquitous connectivity we all now expect. Demand for other services, such as mental health counseling, has also increased. Meanwhile, the 2020 total revenue level was short lived and perhaps even a mirage, as many states cut higher education funding during the 2020 fiscal year and other revenue sources declined.

This shift in university revenue sources from state appropriation toward net tuition has had important consequences. For one, it has shifted the burden of payment for higher education from state tax revenues to students and their families, who then finance this increase through their income, their assets, financial aid, and debt. For another, although Congress has increased the maximum Pell Grant over time, it has not kept up with increases in net tuition and student debt has grown. These shifts have elevated student debt as a political and policy issue. By making higher education as much a private as a public good, they have also elevated the question of value (return on investment) for many students and their families. For a third, it has placed even more pressure on colleges and universities to be both more efficient and more accountable.

Higher education has struggled for years with expenses increasing beyond inflation and pressures to hold down the cost of atten-

dance. Public higher education has also faced great variation in ability and willingness of states to support them.

These forces were magnified during the pandemic. There was
pressure to hold tuition rates flat or even to cut them in response
to the pandemic's financial toll on students and their families. We
shut down most of our auxiliary services, which resulted in the loss
of previously reliable revenue, and many institutions refunded fees
and charges that students had already paid. States suffered loss of
tax revenues due to business shutdowns and unemployment, resulting in appropriations reductions for higher education in most
states. Enrollment targets were not met due to many factors, including barriers for international students, preference not to attend remote courses, and loss of family income. It is within this
budgetary context that university leaders and administrators, already dealing with issues of value, affordability, and sources of revenue, unexpectedly found themselves in the spring of 2020 when a
new recession and round of budget cuts hit.

But this was not our first rodeo.

In our early years as a young university, UMBC stretched its resources to build a campus that reflected the vision of its early leaders,
faculty, and staff. That meant spending nearly every dollar brought in
to establish quality programs, hire necessary faculty and staff, and
create the infrastructure to support students, faculty, and staff.
Around 2005 it became clear that UMBC needed to create a model
that could more reliably sustain the university. The arrival of a new
VP of Administration and Finance, Lynne Schaefer, provided an opportunity to assess current financial strategies and make changes to
create that more sustainable model.

The role of the chief business officer (CBO) or chief financial officer (CFO) has evolved in recent decades to become that of strategic partner to the president and provost, financial educator to the
campus at large, and creative problem solver amid revenue scarcity,
competition, and complex business models. The president, provost,
and CBO must be on the same page in setting the tone for budget

discussions and in establishing expectations and accountability. A successful CBO/CFO should promote transparency in financial information, help other leaders interpret that information, and make sure the financial decision-making process is fair and inclusive. Holding to these practices under normal circumstances helps to build the trust needed to weather challenges and crises.

One of the first steps Schaefer took as our CBO was to implement a more formal, disciplined budget process that relied on more conservative revenue and cost estimates, established priorities, and used a multiyear approach when investing in new initiatives. We avoided or delayed many desirable capital projects, investing only in those of the highest priority, to reduce our debt load. The ability to achieve consensus on top priorities—what we will fund and what we will delay or eliminate—is a key attribute in a strategic financial plan. We also launched a multifaceted campaign to make the case for UMBC's value and financial needs to state and legislative officials, board members, and university system leaders.

Our progress in building financial strength was slow but steady. We began actively reporting on our key financial ratios for the FY 2005 year-end, when our primary reserve ratio (expendable net assets divided by total expenses) was a mere 0.13, meaning we had reserves to cover our normal expenses for just over 1.5 months in a disaster when no revenue came in (e.g., Hurricane Katrina in Louisiana and Mississippi). Sharing those ratios was a key part of gaining buy-in from senior leaders for the necessary belt-tightening. By 2019 the primary reserve ratio had more than tripled to 0.41, giving coverage for nearly 5 months, and getting us to the NACUBO Standard.[30] Shared governance leaders on campus were very important partners and were regularly briefed during these steps.

By the beginning of the great recession late in 2008, UMBC had been able to set aside a modest cushion against unforeseen events, and confidence had grown in the reliability of the annual budget. When the state began a series of cuts in October 2008, we were better prepared.

The Great Recession

While there continues to be debate over the causes of the great recession that followed the collapse of Lehman Brothers and the ensuing turmoil in the global financial sector, there is no doubt about its consequences. State and local revenues (not including federal grants) declined by about $100 billion in real terms between 2007 and 2009. As most states require balanced budgets, they account for revenue declines by raising taxes, cutting expenditures, or drawing on reserves. Given the steep declines in revenue, most states cut spending and they tended to do so primarily in so-called discretionary areas, such as education, health care, and social services.[31]

At UMBC, we felt the impact of the great recession almost immediately, with revenue cuts arriving in October 2008 for the 2009 fiscal year we were already in. The impact continued for several years as the state of Maryland cut public higher education funding in each of fiscal years 2009, 2010, and 2011. Meanwhile, the Board of Regents, our governing body, held tuition flat or approved tuition increases at or below the rate of inflation, thereby reducing our ability to compensate for cuts through this mechanism. This shift from prior practice of raising tuition rates to offset financial challenges reflected political negotiations amid changing attitudes about the cost and value of higher education. So, we decreased spending and drew down reserves to account for the state cuts in our funding.

As we dealt with these painful cuts, UMBC's leadership agreed to guiding principles and then worked to enhance our long-term finances. First, in fall 2008, knowing that we were facing extended financial challenges, our leadership agreed to the principles that would inform our budget deliberations and decisions and that we continue to use:

- First, protect the quality of the academic program. We would not implement across-the-board budget reductions, but rather differential budget reductions that allowed our

educational programs to continue largely as normal. Moreover, we would continue to invest in strategic initiatives as
possible.
- Second, we would support the members of our community.
Our mantra was to "put people first." We would use layoffs to
reduce funding only as a last resort when all other options
were exhausted.

While we did not resort to the widespread layoffs seen on other
campuses across the country, the state did require that we furlough
or implement temporary salary reductions for staff and faculty in
fiscal years 2009, 2010, and 2011. In these three years, the number
of furlough days given to each employee, or the percentage of temporary salary reductions, were differentially applied, with those at
the lower end of the pay scale taking fewer days or a smaller percent
salary reduction.

In addition, employees received no salary increases in fiscal years
2010 through 2013. Of the total $24 million in state appropriation
cuts and reversions over this period, our ongoing base appropriation was reduced by only $5 million. Furlough and temporary sal-
ary reductions were not carried forward permanently but accounted
for another $6.2 million of the reductions taken during that pe-
riod. Of course, these actions were very unfortunate for faculty
and staff but positive for our long-term sustainability. There was,
however, widespread appreciation that people kept their jobs,
when many across the country did not. The remaining $13 million
was taken as one-time cash contributions to the state from our un-
restricted net assets.

The Pandemic Recession

In spring 2020 most states—including Maryland—imposed public health restrictions that amounted to a "lockdown" to bring the
pandemic under control and most colleges and universities—
including UMBC—shut down their physical campuses and moved

teaching and operations online. These two consequences of the COVID-19 pandemic had a deep and immediate impact on university finances. In the middle of fiscal year 2020, states cut appropriations for higher education institutions. In the middle of academic year 2020–2021, many institutions refunded fees (e.g., residential, dining, and parking fees) to students for services they would not get in March, April, and May.

This was the right thing to do, but it cost institutions significant revenues. Other institutions found themselves in different circumstances than we did, and their leaders made different decisions that were certainly difficult. At UMBC we stuck to the guiding principles we agreed to in 2008 as we confronted the difficult choices of 2020. During the pandemic, we continued to "put people first" by supporting the people who make up our community and protecting the quality of our academic programs.

What was different about the 2020 recession was how unexpected it was and potentially steep the revenue cuts appeared at first. The uncertainty and worst-case scenarios around the potential revenue shortfalls took our individual and collective breaths away. They presented us with challenging choices and deliberations that tested our values.

First, we had to account for state cuts in our appropriations. In summer 2020 the state imposed a $13 million cut in our appropriation for FY 2021.

Second, in 2020 the state cut was compounded by anticipated enormous decreases in auxiliary revenues. Our initial worst-case estimate was an $80 million loss from our planned FY 2021 budget, an overwhelming number in a $500 million total budget. Overall, our auxiliary revenue losses at UMBC—initially estimated at over $50 million in a $70 million auxiliary budget—were so significant and much greater than the average for a number of reasons. We reduced capacity in our residence halls, we minimized the number of faculty and staff on campus, which meant decreased revenues from parking and food, we did not charge many student fees, and those fees we did charge were frozen at the prior year rates. In addition, the USM Board of Regents froze tuition rates for 2020–2021 at the 2019–2020 levels.

We were able to suspend many planned investments and implemented strategies to reduce that figure to $65 million. Then we went to work to reduce that amount to the absolute minimum while staying true to our values.

We deliberated in March over how to handle student fees already paid for that semester. On the one hand, it seemed fair to refund to students (and their families) fees for services they were not going to get (e.g., housing, dining, parking, athletics, and recreation). On the other hand, we relied on these revenues to provide a quality educational experience. We decided to provide the refund both because it was fair and because it provided financial support to many when the pandemic lockdown impacted them economically (e.g., lost jobs). Most campuses across the country decided to issue refunds. We provided the refunds for the 2019–2020 academic year. We also made the difficult decision not to charge most fees for the 2020–2021 academic year, making the decision on a semester-by-semester basis as we determined to remain remote in the fall and spring with most services unavailable to students.

Our expenditures changed in terms of composition and levels. During the pandemic, we increased funding for activities designed to manage or fight COVID-19. This included COVID-19 testing, PPE, and additional instructional technology. During the height of the pandemic, some spending also naturally decreased, including expenditures for travel and supplies. For the rest of the budget, we implemented differential reductions based on our principles and goals. Our colleges took lower percentage cuts than the remainder of the university. In addition, we deferred lower-priority capital projects yet sustained key initiatives and investments, such as those to implement our strategic enrollment plan and to invest in remote teaching quality and technology.

Again, we put people first. We committed to no layoffs of regular faculty and staff and kept most student employees on the payroll until the end of the spring 2020 semester. While we did not layoff or furlough people, we knew we had to reduce our salary expenses. We started with a hiring freeze, anticipating at least an additional 1 percent salary savings. We eliminated a number of vacant positions. This still was not enough, so we resorted to a temporary salary reduction (TSR) plan. We applied the TSR only to those who made over $100,000 per year and did so in a progressive approach that increased the TSR as salaries increased. We had significant positive support for the TSR and the progressive approach we took to it.

The recession that stemmed from the pandemic shutdown hit university budgets hard, yet we had resources to draw on in the short term that eased what would otherwise have been more painful. We had been building our financial reserves over years of discipline and collective commitment, providing us a budgetary cushion. We had also developed a budget process that had included vice presidents and deans who were, therefore, already knowledgeable about both budgeting and UMBC's budget. This has established a sense of shared responsibility and accountability for the university's finances. They were, therefore, colleagues in the work rather than potential obstacles to developing a fair and balanced budget. There was no pushback when we discussed the need for spending cuts.

4

Courage

Courage for Leaders

Merriam-Webster Dictionary defines "courage" as "the mental or moral strength to venture, persevere, and withstand danger, fear, or difficulty."[1] Institutional courage is a special kind of resilience, "venturing" despite difficulty to attain a moral goal. Institutional leaders create this courage when they lead with integrity, guided by their personal and institutional values and principles, as they make and communicate difficult decisions.

Creating an empowered university, for example, takes institutional courage. It takes courage when leaders empower their community members to look in the mirror, be honest about what is seen, listen to others, and have difficult conversations. If we leaders want others to lean in and speak up, we must courageously model integrity and openness. By doing so, one creates an environment in which people feel safe to speak up. Leaders, therefore, must engage in active listening that provides the time and space for safe, if difficult, conversations.

Active listening and staying engaged are not easy. People with competing agendas, claims, and perspectives contest most important decisions. People will disagree. Some are not and will not be happy. Leaders must create opportunities to hear from everyone involved, nonetheless, because a campus is enriched and empowered by such conversations. These conversations allow us to move forward, considering a fuller range of information and ideas.

Sometimes difficult issues struggle to surface, because they have the potential to embarrass people or create costly solutions. Jennifer Freyd, an expert on "institutional courage," asks us to "cherish the whistleblower" who brings these issues forward. Very often, institutions punish them when they should reward them instead for their concern about the institution, their willingness to raise issues, their determination that we should do the right thing.[2]

We all have the ability to be courageous. We learn it through experience, working through a challenging problem or difficult situation, talking with peers and mentors to understand a situation and the options for moving forward, and taking the risks.

Courage involves doing what is right even when there is pushback, an easier route, or a less costly course of action. It is often much easier to take the path of least resistance, but that is not real leadership. Courage usually involves risk, but leaders can temper that risk and be effective, through patience, information gathering, and an ability to assess risk before proceeding.

Leaders often succeed or fail depending on how well they manage a short-term issue or crisis so that it leads to long-term, sustainable change. Leaders experience a tension between tackling the urgent phase of a crisis ("putting out fires") and laying the foundation for work over a sufficient period to ensure implementation and sustainability. This requires buy-in from key stakeholders, the work of change agents, and a sustained commitment of resources.

How students perform depends on all that happens in the intricate web of a student's life, in and out of the classroom, so we must broaden our perspectives. What pieces of this web take courage for institutions to strengthen? In this chapter, we examine the role that courage plays as we tackle such challenges as ensuring health and safety during a pandemic, rebuilding a Title IX program, supporting diversity and inclusion, and enabling the well-being of community members.

Courage during COVID-19

In the midst of the great recession, UMBC's leadership team determined that we needed to develop a set of principles that would guide our decisions as we responded to the financial challenges faced by our university. We developed these guiding principles in consultation with shared governance and communicated them to the campus community. Put simply, these guidelines articulated our shared values of "putting people first and protecting our academic programs."

These simple, but powerful, principles continued to guide our work together after the end of the great recession and, in the midst of the COVID-19 pandemic, we relied on them as we faced an even more challenging situation in 2020. Our leadership team discussed the trade-offs we faced in depth and decided we would challenge ourselves to do what we perceived to be the "right thing" rather than easiest, most popular, or least costly.

First, we took a cautious approach to public health and protecting the health and safety of our community, which of course had significant collateral impacts on almost all aspects of how our university operated. It meant that in-person and on-campus experiences were limited. Graduations were online rather than in person. We had masking and vaccination mandates. We delayed the general return to campus until the summer and fall of 2021. While most supported our approach, there were many who did not, but we listened to scientific and public health guidance and did what we believed was right for our campus and consistent with our mission.

Our decision to hold a virtual rather than in-person commencement was relatively easy in spring 2020. However, in the face of fierce advocacy for a return to an in-person commencement on the part of some students and their families, we also determined that it would not be safe or feasible for our community to bring so many people to campus in December 2020 or in spring 2021. Vaccines were not yet widely available. It took courage to hold onto this decision, which we based on our best judgment about the health and safety of our campus community and stakeholders, even though many were upset and let us know it.

Early in 2021, our campus had begun setting the schedule of courses for fall 2021, which would be our first after COVID-19 vaccinations would be widely available. Campus leaders strongly suggested that the colleges and their faculty bring as many classes back to in person as possible by then. However, it soon became apparent that the balance between remote and in-person classes was not shifting as much toward in person as we had hoped. The provost and deans sent the scheduling teams across our colleges back to the drawing board to bring more courses to campus by fall. With the flexibility we granted, each college dean used an approach that fit their style and the culture of their college. Nonetheless, faculty and staff resisted revisiting the work already done, some faculty voiced anxiety about returning to in-person classes, and many expressed uncertainty about what the pandemic would look like by fall. Others, however, argued that students were not making adequate academic progress in online settings and that the number of students who would enroll in the fall might decline if our university would be mainly online while nearby institutions were in person. We continued our conversations, persuading more faculty to return to in person teaching, though a significant number declined and remained online that fall.

Another opportunity to test our courage arrived in fall 2021, when we returned to a largely in-person campus with new requirements for frequent COVID-19 testing and the imposition of a vaccine mandate for students, faculty, and staff. Our campus culture has been deliberately lenient on most issues, without harsh disciplinary actions, but COVID-19 brought serious health concerns and, therefore, required us to confront how we would hold each person accountable for doing what was required. We wanted to keep students in classes. We wanted people to keep their jobs. In the end, we balanced those factors with our overarching goal of keeping the campus community as a whole safe and healthy.

We took several steps to monitor and enforce compliance. As a very important first step, we established databases and reporting mechanisms that would provide us with the tracking information needed. We first focused student compliance with testing and vaccines on those residing on campus but then also held commuting students to the same vaccine requirements. (Commuting students had the highest rate of disenrollment during this period.) For on-campus residents, we achieved compliance through a progressive scale that included isolation, quarantine, temporary suspension of housing access, and finally very rarely removal from on-campus housing. We also negotiated with campus labor unions to get to agreement on a progressive disciplinary process for noncompliance, which included warning, suspension, and termination. Once we had good data and reporting, which was not easy, our compliance strategy worked. By the beginning of the fall semester, we had achieved nearly 100 percent compliance with the vaccine mandate for all those who had not been granted a medical or religious exemption. We maintained a very low campus positivity rate throughout the 2020–2021 and 2021–2022 academic years.

Second, we took a people-centered approach to our budget. We decided to provide our students with refunds of housing, dining, and other fees in spring 2020, which resulted in a loss of revenue that exceeded $18 million. We then also decided that we would not charge students certain fees during academic year 2020–2021, even when other institutions reinstated those fees. We experienced large reductions in auxiliary revenue in the areas of residential life and dining due to the very low occupancy we allowed in our residence halls during the 2020–2021 academic year. We were not the only ones to experience lost revenues. Many residential campuses faced similar losses.

Salaries and benefits account for a large proportion of our budget, as they do for most colleges and universities. So, to stabilize our budget we had to address salary costs. While some institutions resorted to layoffs, our principle of putting people first meant that we sought to avoid these actions. We discussed our options among the leadership team and consulted with shared governance about the problem and possible solutions. We agreed to institute a temporary salary reduction plan that would reduce our salary expenses. We sought to minimize the impact of these reductions through a progressive plan, under which we reduced the salaries only of those earning $100,000 and above, and we increased the percentage reduction for each higher salary band. We believed this the fairest approach. Our campus did, too, as we heard supportive comments and almost no complaints.

By contrast, over objections from some staff, we eliminated nearly 50 vacant positions during our hiring freeze to balance the budget in the wake of cuts in state appropriations and static enrollment. We believed the state was not likely to restore its funding cuts; therefore, we had reduced operating expenses all we dared. We had decided we would not lay off current employees; this seemed the fairest and most sensible way forward. However, as on most campuses, many on our campus believed these positions were still necessary, even when vacant for lengthy periods. It took courage on the part of our senior leadership to face reality and agree to this plan, despite objections.

Other college and university leaders made their own decisions with regard to these same questions. This is not to say that our way was the best or only way, but as "budgets are moral documents," we decided that our steps were right for us. Our institution may have been better off in the short run if we had not taken any of these steps and relied more heavily on cash reserves. However, we concluded that we would set ourselves on a better long-term path of sustainability if we had the courage to put fairness and the needs of people ahead of short-term institutional financial pressures.

What one campus might consider the right action, another might not. It all depends on the context. If a campus is used to a top-down leadership style, then campus community members might take certain actions as given. If a campus has a culture of shared governance, inclusive leadership, and broad discussion, however, then taking an unpopular and/or resisted position takes more courage as it will require tough conversations, persuasion, and resolve.

Title IX

"Whatever we wear, wherever we go, Yes means yes, and no means no!" More than a slogan, this chant aimed at sexual consent provides an example of what we mean by finding the courage to initiate culture change. Changing culture is challenging because it requires a change in perceptions, beliefs, power relations, and outcomes. The steps an organization must take to change its culture, programs, processes, and outcomes with regard to Title IX and sexual misconduct are very difficult. The emotionally charged challenge of sexual assault and misconduct necessitates change management with sensitivity and respect.

On a fall day in 2018 we could hear the students chanting as they climbed the stairs to the tenth floor of the Administration Building. The *Baltimore Sun* had run a story about a legal case brought against UMBC and others for allegedly mishandling sexual assault. While the incidents in question were real and troubling, the facts in the case and as reported in the media were not accurate, and several of the accusations were false. Indeed, US District Court Judge Deborah Chasanow eventually dismissed the case, stating that the plaintiffs' lawsuit "fails to state any viable claim."[3] In the meantime, students who were understandably passionate about safety and justice had drawn conclusions and made demands. We found ourselves in the middle of a difficult protest.

As we described in *The Empowered University*, the students poured onto the tenth floor of the Administration Building, packing the President's Conference Room and overflowing into the hall. President Freeman Hrabowski invited the students to have a conversation, listened attentively and respectfully, and began a discussion that would lead to collaboration between the administration and partner organizations on campus to improve our Title IX policies and processes and address issues of safety on campus. Later in the week, we followed this impromptu meeting with a town hall, in which students, faculty, and staff spoke about issues of and experiences with sexual harassment and misconduct. Many of the stories we heard that day were very painful. We thought we had done all that we needed to comply with Title IX, but after this week of difficult and challenging conversations, we were determined to do more.

Was this a crisis? Title IX had been of heightened concern on our campus and nationally for some time. In response to the Obama administration's "Dear Colleague" Letter of 2011, we had revisited our Title IX policies and procedures and hired new staff. We were in the process of providing more substantive training to a broader number of staff and faculty. Indeed, the day the story broke in the *Sun*, two Title IX experts led an all-day training on Title IX for about 200 members of our community. We were taking the issue seriously.

Yet here we were in the midst of what was undeniably a crisis. On our campus, reaction to the news story was immediate and deep. It touched a nerve, especially for survivors, allies, and others who did not believe we were doing enough. Students, faculty, and staff were upset. They had made their case, feelings, and demands known through social media, campus protest, and formal communications. The events were in the print media and discussed on social media. Jobs were on the line.

Student activism and protest have played a vital role in the history of our campuses, cultural movements, and our politics, often pushing all of us to have the courage to be our best selves as people and institutions. In the 1960s and 1970s students protested US involvement in the war in Vietnam. They led sit-ins for civil rights, joined the Freedom Riders, and held protests aimed to improve Black student life and success on US campuses. Students at the University of Georgia protested for women's rights in 1968. Students played leadership roles in the Free Speech movement at Berkeley, the movement for an end to apartheid through divestment in South Africa, and environmental activism from Earth Day to Sunrise.

Protests are such a staple of college life that the producers of *The Chair* included a protest as a central scene in their series. They can be powerful. As campus leaders, we need the courage to acknowledge the rights of students to protest, raise difficult issues, and make their needs known and to support them in the process.

More recently, students have led demonstrations against sexual assault and demanded institutional responsibility and action for a vigorous Title IX program. At Columbia University, beginning September 2014, Emma Sulkowicz carried a 50-pound mattress with her on campus as a demonstration against Columbia's handling of their sexual assault case and as a general demonstration against sexual assault. In October 2014 a student group called No Red Tape stacked 28 mattresses on the doorstep of the home of President Lee Bollinger, an act in support of Sulkowicz.[4]

As the #MeToo movement emerged, there were more protests. For example, in February 2021 the University Survivors Movement staged demonstrations against sexual assault at 17 campuses. Signs at these demonstrations accused universities of having "a rape problem" or "a problem with consent."[5] In October 2021 a coalition of survivor support and advocacy groups—End Rape on Campus, It's On Us, Know Your IX, The National Women's Law Center, and Equal Rights Advocates—delivered the ED Act Now petition with 50,000 signatures to Education Secretary Miguel Cardona and Assistant Secretary for Civil Rights Suzanne Goldberg. The petition called on the Education Department to shorten the time they were planning to take to review and replace Trump administration rules for Title IX, a demand that Goldberg said the department would not meet. *Inside Higher Ed* quoted a rally participant as saying, "I should be in class, not begging for basic civil rights. But I can't stand by anymore as I watch my university blatantly violate the rights of survivors." There were further protests that fall at the University of Massachusetts Amherst, Auburn University, and the University of Kansas.[6]

Whenever we are making decisions under such challenging situations as the protest on our campus in fall 2018, we feel tremendous responsibility, stress, and pressure. When there are issues of trust, the pressure increases. Leaders who have been through this will never forget it. Despite the pressure, we must practice what we want to see in others. Useful habits of mind include remaining calm, civil, respectful, and transparent. People watch leaders to see how they react, whether they get defensive, or whether they are willing to apologize, if needed. People also feel a strong need to be heard and taken seriously. We must listen first and convey care. If we come off as being defensive, we erode trust further. It is really easy to get upset, but anger is counterproductive.

The discussions we had in fall 2018 were difficult because of the subject matter and also because people were drawing conclusions and presenting demands based on misinformation, some of which we could correct but some of which we could not because we had a responsibility to protect the confidentiality of individuals. We were aware that some might perceive an effort to correct misinformation that was circulating as a ploy on the part of leadership to deny the "facts." We were also aware that some believed that the public had the right to know the details of Title IX cases then under investigation, despite legal and privacy requirements. When we took time to properly investigate these cases, some assumed that we either were doing nothing or did not care, because the public did not have the facts. We were navigating our way through a challenging situation, in which many did not know whom to trust.

We began, therefore, by working to rebuild trust. When Hrabowski met with protesting students, he created a space for dialogue by saying, "I am sorry we have come to this place. Clearly, we need to do more." We set aside time to reflect and consider the long-term issues. We were able to establish enough of a rapport during the first week of the crisis to move forward. We took the time to listen and to communicate the fact that we were taking the issue very seriously both in terms of short-term and longer-term responses. We took immediate steps based on shared information while we developed a collaborative process for the longer term.

One immediate step we refused to take, though, was to agree to the demands of protesters to fire specific staff. As we wrote in *The*

Empowered University: "One of the demands was that I [Freeman Hrabowski] immediately fire several colleagues involved in the Title IX process. The students wanted to see immediate action, and if I agreed to do that there would not have been a protest on Monday. However, I made it clear that no one would be made a scapegoat and that we would not make impulsive personnel decisions, particularly if they would be based on claims that were not true."[7] For difficult conversations to be successful, they require authentic engagement that involves active listening and being honest about a situation. We do not reject all or accept all. We work to connect, listening for truth and sharing truth, and building trust with a shared view of problems and solutions.

Eventually, we were able to regain a significant degree of trust and develop a collaborative, long-term approach for genuinely improving and restructuring our Title IX program and processes. We accomplished this through listening, inclusive information-gathering and deliberation processes, and then planning for major reforms. The initiatives that we could implement immediately we did, both to improve what we were doing and to signal further to our campus partners (students, faculty, and staff) that our intentions to change were authentic. One example was the implementation of a new and mandated in-person Title IX training program for all faculty and staff that was completed by all responsible employees within three months. We also regained trust by implementing a process that would lead us to deeper reforms, making this work a highly visible institutional priority, and investing significant new resources in the effort. When we shared our intentions to do this with campus leaders—vice presidents, deans, and senates—there was no pushback at all. Everyone understood that the issue was important and that, to be true to our values, we had to do this work.

As we got underway, we noticed the work of Jennifer Freyd at the University of Oregon on what she called "institutional courage." She and her colleagues have since created an independent nonprofit called the Center for Institutional Courage, which defines the concept in this way:[8]

- "It is an institution's commitment to seek the truth and engage in moral action, despite unpleasantness, risk, and short-term cost.
- "It is a pledge to protect and care for those who depend on the institution.
- "It is a compass oriented toward the common good of individuals, institutions, and the world.
- "It is a force that transforms institutions into more accountable, equitable, effective places for everyone."

They contrast institutional courage with the notion of "institutional betrayal," through which institutions can make lives worse rather than better as they cause harm to people who depend on them. Institutions betray the people who depend on them when, for example, they put institutional concerns (profits, revenues, reputation, self-protection) above the needs and rights of individuals. In the process, institutions may show an indifference to, retaliate against, or punish victims. To illuminate the process that institutions often engage in to deflect accusations, Freyd coined the term DARVO, which stands for "Deny the behavior, Attack the individual doing the confronting, and Reverse the roles of Victim and Offender."[9]

Freyd outlined steps that institutions can take to display courage with regard to sexual assault.[10] These steps include ensuring that leaders are educated about sexual violence and related trauma. They also include complying with criminal laws and civil rights codes and responding to victim disclosures with sensitivity. Courageous institutions, moreover, bear witness and apologize. They conduct surveys and self-assessments of campus climate and procedures, and they are transparent about policy and data. They "cherish the whistleblower." Freyd writes there are two key actions: First, act like "a good friend or another supportive person: listen well."[11] Second, "Commit resources.""

Courage happens when institutions take proactive steps "to be more accountable, transparent, and supportive of people who depend on them."[12] We were so inspired by this notion of institutional courage that we decided to call our Title IX reform initiative "Retriever Courage." A small implementation team led this effort at first, identifying initiatives that it could get started right away and developing a process for gathering broad input and making recommendations. Those immediate steps included creating a new student ID card with crisis and emergency response contact information on the back, conducting a lighting tour with students to identify dark areas on campus and light fixtures in need of repair (and then quickly repairing them), and establishing a Retriever Courage Implementation Team (IT).

We brought together campus experts, student organizations, and shared governance leaders on the IT and charged them with identifying and overseeing implementation of needed changes. Lynne Schaefer, vice president for administration and finance, and Nancy Young, vice president for student affairs, co-chaired the IT, which also engaged an outside consulting team to conduct an independent evaluation of all aspects of our efforts to address Title IX and sexual misconduct. The team also sought broad input through a Student Advisory Committee (SAC) and a Faculty and Staff Advisory Committee (FASAC) that, along with the consultants, would investigate and consider the issues and present a report to the IT with findings and recommendations.

The IT began its work in the fall of 2018 and then met weekly over the next year, overseeing the implementation of short-term initiatives and longer-term investigations. It hired Grand River Solutions as consultants in January 2019 and followed with a request for reports from the SAC and FASAC. The three groups presented reports in the spring of 2019. In the summer of 2019 the IT created subgroups to work through and prioritize the recommendations from the three reports. The IT then presented the findings and recommendations to the University Steering Committee (a group of leaders from shared governance groups—the Student Government Association, the Graduate Student Association, the Faculty Senate, the Professional Staff Senate, and the Non-Exempt

Staff Senate) and to university leadership, who gave the green light to proceed.

From the fall of 2018 to fall 2019, while we waited for the three reports to move through this process, the campus, Retriever Courage, and our partners implemented projects based on early UMBC community suggestions. We added three new staff members in the Counseling Center. We improved campus lighting. We issued the requested new campus ID cards. Retriever Courage created displays with brochures. We presented in-person Title IX/sexual misconduct prevention training to more than 2,000 community members and piloted training to 200 students.

While their reports varied in length, the consultants, students, and faculty/staff made a series of recommendations that had a great deal of similarity. They found that UMBC's Title IX office was neither adequately tracking cases nor handling cases in a consistent manner. They argued that UMBC's Title IX and Sexual Assault training for students, faculty, and staff was inadequate. They also found that the location of the Title IX office in the General Counsel's Office presented the potential for institutional conflicts of interest.

Our campus leadership decided that immediate action would begin by moving the Office of Human Relations from the Office of General Counsel to the Office of the President, rename it the Office of Equity and Inclusion (OEI), and reorganize its work. We tasked OEI with promoting the university's core values of equity and inclusion and managing UMBC's work on Title IX and civil rights, including discrimination, bias, harassment, and hate. We agreed to a structure for OEI that would address the issues of case tracking; consistent case handling, investigation, and adjudication; and mandatory training. In January 2020 we established the new OEI with Candace Dodson-Reed, as chief of staff, serving as the executive director. She in turn hired six new staff members for OEI, including a director of equity and inclusion, a Title IX coordinator, and a training and case manager, as well as two civil rights investigators to fill existing positions that were vacant.[13]

In its first year, drawing on increased institutional funding, OEI staff worked to build a foundation to grow on. They summarized and shared findings from a campus climate survey. They launched a new website, with policies, frequently asked questions, and more. To address tracking concerns, they created a confidential online reporting/referral form and implemented new case management software that assisted in collecting, tracing, and responding to complaints. In a major step forward, OEI redesigned and launched annual mandatory training for students and responsible employees. The office processed 427 total cases of sexual misconduct and discrimination. OEI also established an Inclusion Council, consisting of students, faculty, and staff, to provide OEI and the UMBC community with advice and recommendations regarding our work to increase diversity, enhance equity, and promote inclusion.

Success is never final. We have more work to do and so do the nation's higher education institutions. The National Academies of Sciences, Engineering, and Medicine issued a powerful report in 2018 entitled *Sexual Harassment of Women: Climate, Culture, and Consequences in Academic Science, Engineering, and Medicine.*[14] This report made waves when the Academies issued it. The report argued that higher education institutions must change their cultures and climates to effectively reduce sexual harassment. The report also led the Academies, in 2019, to establish The Action Collaborative on Preventing Sexual Harassment in Higher Education in partnership with about 60 colleges, universities, and research institutions.[15] The Collaborative provides a forum in which the partners "take a leading role in preventing harassment by devoting time and resources to collaboratively identify, develop, implement, and research efforts that address and prevent harassment through changing the organizational climates and cultures, and through considering the long-term implications of current actions on organizational climate."[16]

In October 2021 the Association of American Universities issued principles for preventing sexual harassment in higher education. The discussions that led to these principles began in October 2019 with an AAU advisory board chaired by University of Southern California President Carol Folt and University of Kansas Chancellor Douglas Girod. Folt said, "This unprecedented effort demonstrates the tremendous capacity for doing good that exists within the AAU when member institutions work to address a systemic challenge."[17] The eight principles focus on fostering a climate in which sexual misconduct is unacceptable and implementing policies and practices that support a harassment-free learning, living, and working environment. They include training for all members of the campus community about acceptable behavior and how to report sexual misconduct. They also include supporting those who report, holding those found responsible accountable in a fair and equitable manner, and completing investigations even when the respondent has left the campus.[18]

Are guidelines enough? Tracey Vitchers, president of It's On Us, responded to the guidelines, saying, "When you look at the tone of the protests currently happening, students are truly demanding that schools do more than just provide survivor support. It is unacceptable to students today that schools are simply taking the approach of reacting to sexual violence after it has occurred, rather than taking proactive steps to prevent it. And you're seeing that in the protest signs and in the demands from students." Vitchers also remarked, "For AAU to come forward and say that it is the responsibility of their institutions to create a climate where sexual misconduct is unacceptable, that's going to require AAU—if they're really going to enforce these principles—to hold their institutions who are part of their network accountable for doing comprehensive prevention education."[19]

If they are not held accountable by AAU, these institutions will have to find the "institutional courage" to hold themselves accountable. At UMBC, we are holding ourselves accountable, in part, through the work of our Inclusion Council. The Council has recently issued a report with recommendations for further improving both OEI in general and our Title IX organization in particular. Their recommendations regarding sexual misconduct, harassment, and interpersonal violence include hiring a survivor advocate, establishing a respondent services coordination team, creating a peer education/advocacy group, and expanding training, education, and awareness. The survivor advocate would support survivors and be involved in student training, establishing a social media presence, coordinating a yearly consent campaign, and supporting the peer advocacy program. The respondent services coordination team would support respondents and make resources available. We already engage in mandatory training for students, faculty, and staff. The report recommends outreach specific to graduate students and to vulnerable and historically marginalized populations (i.e., students of color, LGBTQ+ students, international students, religiously affiliated survivors, and others).[20] Our campus leadership will consider these recommendations as we have further dialogue about the way forward.

Title IX is now 50 years old. While it has become a political football, with regulations shifting with each change in federal administration, the law has nonetheless made a difference. We all have more work to do to support survivors, make sure our Title IX processes are reasonable and objective, and ensure that resources enable timely and fair investigations.

Race

On April 19, 2015, Freddie Gray, Jr., died from injuries sustained a week earlier while in police custody in Baltimore City. Over the next week, demonstrators gathered to protest Gray's death. On April 27, 2015, the day of Gray's funeral, rioters looted stores and set fires in several neighborhoods across Baltimore City. Maryland Governor Hogan declared a state of emergency and sent state troopers and National Guard soldiers to the city. The governor lifted the state of emergency after a week.

Although our campus is located in suburban Baltimore County, our community felt these events in the city quite deeply. Some community members participated in nonviolent protests in downtown Baltimore. We held a town hall to discuss structural racism, racial discrimination, and segregation in Baltimore and the nation, placing current events in historical context. That fall, UMBC hosted the Imagining America conference and used that event to engage scholars, activists, and community members in dialogue about the interaction of culture, the arts, history, race, and social justice.

Our experiences at the time of the tragic death of Freddie Gray remind us that the issue of structural racism had already come to our campuses long before the tragic deaths of Ahmaud Arbery, Breonna Taylor, and George Floyd in 2020. In fact, we forget—and need to recall—that there were Black student protests on our campuses in 2014 and 2015 that echoed still earlier Black student protests in the 1960s. Indeed, our nation's troubled history with race, slavery, Jim Crow, and structural racism dates back centuries, and Blacks have resisted or rebelled against these in myriad ways, from escaping slavery in the antebellum South to mounting legal cases against Jim Crow laws to the boycotts, marches, and sit-ins of the modern Civil Rights movement.

What was different and unexpected about the death of George Floyd was that, unlike the death of Freddie Gray, there was video for all to see, and the "knee on the neck" sparked a nationwide movement composed of people of all backgrounds. Protests over Floyd's death began in Minneapolis and spread quickly across the nation and even to cities around the world. They accelerated conversations about structural racism, police reform, and health disparities laid bare by COVID-19. They also led to discussions on campuses nationwide, including ours, about improving race relations and creating genuinely welcoming, inclusive, and equitable environments.

Two of us, Freeman Hrabowski and Peter Henderson, along with our colleague Kate Tracy, wrote an article for *The Atlantic* on the ways higher education could lead the effort to dismantle structural racism. In this article, we argued

> channeling the growing public and private support for meaningful
> change into action requires Americans, in every sector, to engage in
> difficult conversations, and to be honest about our problems and

deliberate in developing solutions, and we in higher education are no exception. Those of us in this field have an obligation to engage in this work because we have become more central than ever to our students' American dreams. We hold out to our students the promise of an enriched life and social mobility, and yet we often fall short in providing these to all who arrive on our campuses.[21]

We then noted that UC Berkeley Professor David Kirp had recently called out higher education for its six-year graduation rate of 60 percent for full-time freshmen at bachelor's degree-granting institutions, which he called "the college dropout scandal." We asked, "If 60 percent is a 'scandal,' what do we call the rate for Blacks, which is 40 percent? It would be simplistic—and wrong—to conclude that our students of color are failing. Instead, we must admit that higher education is failing them."

In the 1980s we had a difficult racial climate at UMBC. There were people who were racist and tried their best to upset Black students on campus. As vice provost, Freeman Hrabowski had conversations with President Michael Hooker and Provost Adam Yarmolinsky about the racial environment on campus. He took them to see racist graffiti in restrooms, which he told them was unacceptable. When one suggested that they remove the graffiti, Freeman said, "No. We need to call the police." Several racial incidents, mainly in residence halls, also led to Black student protests about race relations and racism.

Meanwhile, when the University System of Maryland Board of Regents appointed Freeman Hrabowski president of UMBC in 1993, he was the first Black president of a predominantly white university in the Baltimore region. Some people disparaged the appointment, saying, "He was hired because he's Black," or "He is window dressing," or "He won't last a year."

The outcome, however, has defied the early naysayers. The campus gave Hrabowski a chance, and together they made significant progress over three decades. In 2022 he retired after 30 years as president. Indeed, the conditions were right to build a diverse, inclusive, multicultural campus in the Baltimore-Washington corridor. Built at the same time as and near UMBC, Columbia, Maryland, in Howard County, has been a racially progressive town since its inception. UMBC grew in a symbiotic relationship with Columbia, and the diversity of the one began to reflect the diversity of the other. In addition, the culture of UMBC shifted slowly over time, and now we are in a new place. We have strong relationships among colleagues from different backgrounds. We can talk about race, when others still struggle with these conversations.

Indeed, we have worked hard over three decades to create a campus culture that supports all students. Our student population has changed from predominantly white to highly diverse and multicultural. We developed and implemented a program that supported high-achieving Black people in the natural sciences and engineering that changed perceptions on our campus about who could succeed at UMBC. We have doubled the six-year completion rate for first-time freshmen and closed the completion gap between white and Black students. We are the number one undergraduate institution for Black students who continue on to earn PhDs in the natural sciences and engineering as well as MD-PhDs.

Yet, as the social unrest in the wake of George Floyd's death gave urgency to conversations about equity and inclusion nationally, they did so as well on our campus. We found that students, faculty, staff, and alumni wanted to talk. They sent us emails and met us for conversations, sharing their experiences on our campus with racial insensitivity, discrimination, implicit bias, hostile departmental cultures, and structural impediments for underrepresented minorities, including Blacks. Despite our progress and despite being a "model campus" for supporting Black students, we still had deep-rooted concerns about racial challenges on campus. All of this was happening, moreover, at a time when we were also seeing an increase in harassment and threats toward Asians, Asian-Americans, and Pacific Islanders.

Our dean of engineering and information technology hosted a meeting with campus leaders and staff from the OEI to discuss comments made to him by alumni, now in graduate school, about their experiences in the College of Engineering and Information Technology. These alumni conveyed that they had received a solid education at UMBC and many faculty cared and were supportive. However, they believed that they, individually and collectively, were not as supported as majority students were and related that some faculty had treated them in biased and disrespectful ways. UMBC's chapter of the National Society of Black Engineers (NSBE) also expressed concern that they were not receiving the same level of support as other engineering organizations.

We made the choice to do more, as we had with Title IX. First, we listened. We had conversations and held town halls as we had with Retriever Courage. Those who raised issues with us wanted to feel that we were taking them and their concerns seriously—paying as much attention to this issue as we had to issues of sexual assault. We listened attentively in our conversations. Second, we considered how we allocated resources. For example, we provided more support for our NSBE chapter. Third, we required training on race and bias for faculty and staff in targeted departments.

In the process of establishing our OEI, we created an Inclusion Council to help us take a more holistic and empathetic approach to Title IX. By the time we launched it on June 30, 2020, however, we expected it to also help us with issues of structural racism and implicit bias. The Inclusion Council is now addressing inclusion for people of all backgrounds, including race and ethnicity, gender, gender identity, sexual orientation, religion, national origin, disability, and more.

The National Association of Diversity Officers in Higher Education (NADOHE) recently issued a report, "A Framework for Advancing Anti-Racism Strategy on Campus," that outlines steps colleges and universities can implement to address structural racism and provide equity in their operations and academic mission. President Paulette Granberry Russell defines "equity" as "Fairness and the ability to participate fully with no artificial barriers to one's success as a student, faculty, or staff member."[22] The report sees opportunities for institutions to enact equity through the appointment of senior level diversity officers and the resources they are provided.

Through its report, NADOHE also suggests work for colleges and universities across all of their units and activities. There is work to do in the areas of institutional vision, culture and climate assessment, communications, and data collection and analysis. The report focuses on the work needed to enhance antiracism training, bias reporting, and discrimination and harassment procedures. The report emphasizes the need for continued work around access and student success including admissions, financial aid, scholarship and internship opportunities, articulation agreements, transfer student pathways, and curriculum and pedagogy reform. It notes the importance as well of equity and inclusion in faculty diversity initiatives, shared governance committee selection, staff hiring and advancement, supplier diversity programs, and campus and community policing.[23]

At UMBC, we have empowered our Inclusion Council to work with leaders across campus who are responsible for improving our climate, policies, and outcomes. The Council has issued a report that presents a comprehensive list of potential actions for us to consider, many similar to the list detailed by NADOHE.[24] Among others, the report includes the following recommendations with regard to DEI:

- Training, workshops, and awareness campaigns on diversity, equity, and inclusion (DEI); bias and microaggressions; and intercultural competence
- Expanded student recruitment in heavily minority geographic areas and new strategies for recruiting Latinx students
- Review of admissions policies and practices, including making admissions permanently test-optional
- Review of UMBC's curriculum and courses to promote inclusive instructional pedagogy and course content
- Inclusion of DEI work in faculty promotion and tenure review

- Revised human resources policies and processes to include bias and DEI standards, promote salary equity, and improve processes for job reclassifications
- Greater transparency in policing and wider adoption of restorative justice practices

We created an Implementation Team for these recommendations that we modeled on our Retriever Courage work. The work of the Implementation Team is not top down but rather led by those across our community. The team has faculty and staff co-chairs and includes representatives from the Inclusion Council, Shared Governance leaders, and subject matter experts. It is reviewing the Council report's recommendations and developing long-range plans.[25] The team is prioritizing recommendations, engaging departments and divisions as partners, and creating a plan of work with a timeline for completion. This empowered work includes both broad leadership and accountability.

New UMBC President Valerie Sheares Ashby has lifted up this work. She has created the new position at UMBC of vice president for institutional equity and chief diversity officer to lead a university-wide effort to take our work on racial inclusion to the next level. Together, the Inclusion Council and its report, the Implementation Team and its planning, and the new president and her focus on institutional diversity and equity provide fertile ground for a future harvest. Playing the long game means taking intentional steps that are sustainable.

This is not a new endeavor for us, although we have more work to do. Since the late 1980s, the Meyerhoff Scholars Program, now a national model, has supported underrepresented minority undergraduates who continue on to earn PhDs and MD-PhDs in the natural sciences and engineering. We have worked with the Howard Hughes Medical Institute (HHMI) to support the replication of the Meyerhoff program at the University of North Carolina Chapel Hill (Chancellor's Science Scholars) and Pennsylvania State University (Millennium Scholars). HHMI has recently committed up to $500 million through the Driving Change Program to support 24 research universities that establish programs designed to achieve outcomes similar to those of our Meyerhoff program.[26] It has also committed $1.5 billion to support 150 early-career faculty who are committed to DEI through a new Freeman Hrabowski Scholars Program.[27]

UMBC is now also collaborating with Johns Hopkins University (JHU) to increase diversity in graduate education. JHU is in the midst of its own DEI initiative and has recently published "Realizing Our Promise: The Second JHU Roadmap on Diversity, Equity, and Inclusion."[28] JHU has outlined 24 goals for the institution, undergraduates, graduate students, staff, faculty, alumni, and the Baltimore community. Goal 1 for graduate students is "Successfully build the Vivien Thomas Scholars Initiative to advance STEM PhD diversity."

Bloomberg Philanthropies provided JHU with a $150 million grant to support this scholars program, which will create 100 new positions in JHU's 30 STEM PhD programs. JHU is partnering with UMBC along with five HBCUs (Howard, Morehouse, Spelman, Prairie View, and Morgan State) in this program. The partner schools will be "providing expertise, advice and collaboration across multiple key components for program success, including identifying effective outreach strategies, providing guidance on essential program components, and guiding the creation of collaborative structures at partner institutions and JHU alike to support students and excite them about graduate STEM careers."[29]

UMBC's Division of Student Affairs also promotes inclusion through I3B, which stands for Initiatives for Identity, Inclusion, and Belonging. I3B's programs and spaces provide support to students and cultural education opportunities. Mosaic (The Center for Culture and Diversity) is a student-centered space dedicated to cross-cultural education, identity development, and the development of community among students who are culturally conscious and informed. The Pride Center provides an LGBTQ+-centered space for socializing, study, student group meetings, and connections to the LGBTQ+ community. The Gathering Space for Spiritual Well-Being provides a spirituality-centered space where students may explore holistic well-being as connected to spiritual and religious identities.

UMBC's Office of the Provost also has programs to support faculty diversity. As we described in *The Empowered University*, we used an ADVANCE grant from the National Science Foundation to support the recruitment, hiring, and advancement of women in our science and engineering faculty. We then used the lessons learned from that work to extend our work in diversifying the faculty to increase the recruitment and hiring of faculty from underrepresented racial and ethnic groups. This work encompassed the development of new policies and practices, including departmental hiring plans that the provost reviews and approves. It has included implicit bias training and a program we call STRIDE, which uses faculty fellows who have in-depth conversations with faculty search committees about broadening the pool of applicants, reducing implicit bias, and developing a welcoming and inclusive departmental culture.

The National Institutes of Health recently announced a new program that will help create a more diverse pool of principal investigators (PIs). This program established a new class within the R01 research grant program that would extend funding to new and at-risk investigators who score well in peer review but whose score falls just outside the funding cutoff. "At-risk" is defined for purposes of this program as those investigators who would have no NIH funding if their high-scoring proposal were not funded. The hope is that this approach will increase the number and percent of underrepresented minorities whom NIH funds.[30]

Despite the strategies for increasing faculty diversity that we detailed in *The Empowered University*, there is more to do. In 2020 we promoted three Black faculty members to full professor. Since then, two have left UMBC for positions at other institutions, and we promoted the third to dean. Is this a failure? Or, is this the natural progression of things, as individuals seek new, higher-level positions? One left to become a dean, another for rich research opportunities at NIH, and a third to head research with a nonprofit. We have stayed connected to those who have left, helping them in their new positions, because the advancement of Black faculty is bigger than one institution.

UMBC has more work to do. So do other colleges and universities. For example, when Hrabowski recently spoke to the board of trustees of a prominent public research university engaged in a search for a new president, it came as a surprise to many board members to learn that there was a 20-percentage point difference in the six-year graduation rate for white and Black students on their main campus. They were not even aware of this problem, much less engaged in discussions about how to address it. Meanwhile, the *Washington Post* published an article at about the same time noting how Black faculty on this same campus were now engaged in raising the issue of faculty diversity, which they argued was sorely lacking there.[31]

Rather than wait to react when protest comes again—which it surely will when there is another Freddie Gray or George Floyd tragedy—college and university leaders can work proactively now to address these critically important issues for our campuses and society. A November 2020 study by EAB found that 82 percent of higher education institutions they surveyed had released statements following the death of George Floyd. Of these statements, however, 60 percent included short-term actions and just 39 percent included long-term actions. The most common short-term actions included celebrating Juneteenth, conducting a campus listening tour, and establishing an antiracism task force. Longer-term actions included antiracism trainings, advancing recruitment and retention of faculty of color, expanding resources for Black, Indigenous, and People of Color (BIPOC) students, staff, and faculty, and improving partnerships with local and regional communities.[32]

EAB[33] and *The Chronicle of Higher Education*[34] have reported the following examples of institutions that have implemented initiatives to address structural racism on their campuses:

- Roanoke College established a Center for Studying Structures of Race to study the legacies of racism in modern society.

- Adelphi University required its schools and colleges to develop unit-level strategic diversity plans.
- Framingham State University developed a resource center for educational materials on antiracism.
- The University of Tennessee at Knoxville pledged to increase faculty diversity, recruit more students of color, and improve its relationship with law enforcement agencies.
- Vermont State Colleges system adopted an antiracism pledge, which includes providing safe spaces, support, and wellness resources for students of color and their allies.
- University of California Berkeley reorganized its police department to include mental health professionals.

These represent just a small sample of initiatives that others can emulate.

Meanwhile, some institutions have investigated past ties to slavery and outlined steps to redress them. Brown University, one of the leaders in this area, has released the second edition of "Report of the Brown University Steering Committee on Slavery and Justice." Amherst College is investigating its ties to slavery as part of an antiracism plan. The College of William and Mary is building a memorial that recognizes the history of slavery at the college. Harvard University has issued a report detailing its ties to slavery, and the President and Fellows of Harvard College (The Harvard Corporation) has committed $100 million for initiatives "in response to the profound harm documented."[35]

Among the initial steps that colleges and universities have taken since the summer of 2020, one of the most frequent has been hiring a chief diversity officer (CDO). As NADOHE has asserted in its report noted previously, if leaders signal to campus that addressing DEI is a priority and they grant CDOs the power and resources they need, these leaders can make a difference. However, structural racism is a complex societal problem, and CDOs alone cannot change the culture and practices of an institution. They are helpful but not sufficient. Senior leaders must make DEI a priority, even to the extent that they consider such work part of everyone's job description. Leaders must communicate this priority strongly and consistently, though not in such a way that people tune out. They must commit the resources necessary for work that is productive and sustainable.[36]

Not only is there much work for us in higher education to do, but we are also mindful that there are those who contest and undermine this work. In September 2020, late in his term as president, Donald Trump issued an "Executive Order on Combatting Race and Sex Stereotyping." This executive order (EO) stated, "It shall be the policy of the United States not to promote race or sex stereotyping or scapegoating in the Federal workforce or in the Uniformed Services, and not to allow grant funds to be used for these purposes. In addition, Federal contractors will not be permitted to inculcate such views in their employees."[37] NPR reported in October 2020 that, while several organizations had filed lawsuits challenging the EO, it had nonetheless "had a widespread chilling effect as federal agencies, the military, government contractors and grant recipients scramble to figure out how to comply."[38] Given its definitions, the EO immediately created an environment that chilled speech and led many contractors, including colleges and universities, to suspend diversity training until President Biden later revoked the EO on his first day in office, January 20, 2021.

In 2021 the effort to constrain the discussion of race and racism gathered steam. Legislators in various states introduced legislation that would ban or inhibit the teaching or discussion of race, racism, critical race theory, and/or the 1619 project begun by the *New York Times* to understand the history and effects of slavery in the United States. Legislation has passed in multiple states, though the outcomes were often undetermined at the time. Governors vetoed the legislation in some states, and organizations filed and received injunctions against enforcement of legislation in others.[39]

While this effort to muzzle the discussion of race in schools and higher education institutions has proceeded, a similar effort is underway to ban books, particularly those focused on race, gender, and sexuality.[40] Legislators in many states have recently written bills undermining progress we have made in supporting those who are LGBTQ+. In 2023 they are writing bills aiming at rolling back progress in supporting people who are transgender. We may see this as a wedge issue in the 2024 elections.

Meanwhile, elected officials and candidates for office have further politicized debate on structural racism. For example, in his successful 2021 bid for governor in Virginia, Glenn Youngkin, former co-CEO of the Carlyle Group, vowed to ban schools from allowing teachers to instruct their students in "critical race theory," even though teachers in Virginia public schools were not actually doing so. Once in office, Youngkin issued an EO on his first day as governor enacting the ban. He has since taken aim at the word "equity," a concept his predecessor, Ralph Northam, turned to extensively in his effort to address racism in the wake of his blackface scandal. *The Washington Post* reported in March 2022:[41] "It was hard to miss the thread running through the race-related policies Gov. Youngkin purged from the Virginia education system last week for being 'divisive.' Almost all featured the word 'equity.' 'Resource equity'—gone. 'Responsibility to advance racial, social, and economic equity'—gone. 'Virginia's Equity Audit Tool'—gone. The effort echoed Youngkin's push to rename the Office of Diversity, Equity, and Inclusion as the Office of Diversity, Opportunity, and Inclusion, which the General Assembly rejected." The *Post* noted that shortly after the death of George Floyd, Youngkin and Kewsong Lee, co-CEOs of the Carlyle Group, "hired a chief diversity officer and put out a strongly worded statement condemning 'racism and injustice.'"[42] That was 2020; this was 2022.

Across the Potomac in Maryland, by contrast, Wes Moore, an African American Rhodes Scholar, won the race for governor in 2022, promising to "leave no one behind." His agenda includes ending child poverty, providing universal pre-kindergarten, subsidizing childcare, raising teacher pay,[43] and reducing systemic barriers to Black families' pursuit of work, wages, and wealth.[44] He has pledged to fully fund Maryland's "Blueprint for Education," which seeks to reduce inequities among schools and students. He plans to set "clear benchmarks for institutions of higher education and community colleges to produce 40,000 new STEM graduates each year and utilize incentives like tuition assistance and loan forgiveness to drive students into STEM programs and reward institutions for achieving their benchmarks."[45]

In 2023 we find ourselves at a crossroads.

We have made progress in higher education, but we have more work to do. On the one hand, the percentage of Blacks over 24 with a bachelor's degree has increased since the 1960s, from 4 percent to 28 percent. On the other hand, though, the proportion today varies by racial and ethnic group: Hispanics at 20 percent, Blacks at 28 percent, whites at 41 percent, and Asians at 61 percent (though some Asians, like Filipinos, and Pacific Islanders are underrepresented).

These outcome differences stem from many factors. Just to note one set of factors regarding Blacks, recent data from Gallup and Lumina show that while "21 percent of Black students said they feel discriminated against frequently or occasionally in their program of study . . . Only 15 percent of other students said they feel the same." In addition, "36 percent of Black bachelor's students have caregiving responsibilities or full-time jobs, double the 18 percent of all other students with those responsibilities."[46]

There is good news. In December 2022 Claudine Gay was elected the thirtieth president of Harvard University, the first African American to hold the position. A new report from the National Academies of Sciences, Engineering, and Medicine recommends responsibilities for DEI at STEM institutions, including colleges and universities, should be included in leadership role descriptions and requirements for advancement into management.[47] Inside Higher Ed reported that "between 2020 and 2022, in the aftermath of George Floyd's murder by Minneapolis police, membership in the National Association of Diversity Officers in Higher Education increased by 60 percent."[48]

Much still concerns us. The US Supreme Court has overturned affirmative action, leading to questions about how universities may sustain efforts to increase diversity. Elected officials in many states continue to take steps that threaten DEI or the ability of faculty to teach the history of race relations in the United States. Meanwhile, we cannot yet clearly see whether new members of NADOHE will be well supported in their work.

On February 1, 2023, historian Heather Cox Richardson noted in her daily blog, "Letters from an American," that the date held an important national story for us. It was, at once, the anniversary of Congressional passage of the Thirteenth Amendment abolishing slavery in 1865, the anniversary of a sit-in in 1960 at Woolworth's by Black students protesting segregation, and the day that Tyre Nichol's parents buried their son in Memphis, Tennessee, after his death from a severe beating by police officers. Dr. Richardson also noted that the College Board released that day the official curriculum for a new Advanced Placement course in African American studies. She observed, "In January, right-wing Florida governor Ron DeSantis complained that the draft course was 'indoctrination' and 'lacks educational value and is contrary to Florida law,' and he said he would ban it. The version released today has been stripped of information about Black feminism, the queer experience, incarceration, and the Black Lives Matter movement."[49]

The *Chronicle of Higher Education* reported on additional concerning developments:

> In January, the Manhattan and Goldwater Institutes, both conservative think tanks, unveiled model state legislation targeting public colleges. The legislation would prevent them from employing diversity, equity, and inclusion officers; end mandatory diversity training; prohibit colleges from requiring diversity statements; and ban preferences for admission or employment based on characteristics such as race or sex.
>
> Calling the DEI office "the nerve center of woke ideology on university campuses," the authors write that "DEI officers form a kind of revolutionary vanguard on campuses; their livelihood can only be justified by discovering—i.e., manufacturing—new inequities to be remedied."[50]

Within days of that *Chronicle* report, however, *Inside Higher Ed* reported that, while demand for DEI officials has increased at higher education institutions, so has turnover. The main reasons that DEI administrators and staffers leave their positions are complex, although isolation, burnout, and lack of support from institutional leadership are at the top of the list. The article noted that "[s]ome campuses are invested in [DEI] work and take it seriously; others are merely looking for someone to mediate conflict with students and faculty of color."[51]

Apparently, one governor was directly inspired by the model legislation the Manhattan Institute put forward to attack DEI efforts. *The Washington Post* reported in late January that "Florida Gov. Ron DeSantis on Tuesday called for diversity programs to be dismantled at the state colleges and universities." The *Post* went on to describe how the governor and his administration were taking action. "Hours later, trustees at New College of Florida, six of whom DeSantis recently appointed, replaced the school's president and directed staff to draft a policy that would shutter diversity offices at the public liberal arts institution."[52]

In February, a bill was introduced into the Florida legislature that would enact the educational vision of Governor DeSantis, a candidate for president in 2024. *The Chronicle* chronicled as follows: "House Bill 999 takes up almost every bullet-pointed goal that DeSantis included for public higher education in a press release last month. It would prohibit public colleges from funding any projects that 'espouse diversity, equity, and inclusion or Critical Race Theory rhetoric,' no matter the funding source; allow boards of trustees to conduct a post-tenure review of faculty members at any time for any cause; and put faculty hiring into the hands of trustees."[53]

Elected officials in other states, such as Texas, South Carolina, and Oklahoma, followed Florida's lead.[54] Meanwhile, the University of North Carolina Board of Trustees voted to ban the use of diversity statements in admissions and hiring.[55] In March 2023 the *Chronicle of Higher Education* reported that legislators have introduced

21 bills in 13 states designed to "restrict college DEI efforts." Bills in six states seek to restrict DEI offices and staff; bills in seven states seek to restrict or eliminate mandatory DEI training; and bills in nine states target the use of diversity statements and/or identity-based preferences in admissions or hiring.[56]

The stakes for fairness and equity are high. The stakes are also high for our nation, which will only prosper at its level of potential if we find and nurture talent wherever it exists among our population. Which path will we choose as a nation and a people? Will we roll back DEI initiatives or will we continue the effort to close gaps in higher education?

We can expect to live in contentious times in a heavily divided society, but we must encourage the conversations on and off our campuses about structural racism and other forms of discrimination. A leader who is self-assured and willing to be vulnerable can set up these conversations so that, if uncomfortable, they can be civil and productive, resulting in shared understanding and collective action.

How can this be achieved? A few tools were enumerated by Stone, Patton, and Heen in *Difficult Conversations: How to Discuss What Matters Most* and were summarized by the Office of Human Resources at Ohio State University:[57]

1. Make it safe to talk: Embrace a mutual purpose. Offer mutual respect.
2. Adopt the "Yes, And . . ." stance: recognize that the way each person sees and feels things matters.
3. Listen: Seek first to understand and then to be understood. Ask open-ended questions such as "Can you tell me more . . ." or "help me understand . . ."

We add the following suggestions:[58]

- Be clear about the purpose and focus of a conversation.
- Set ground rules. Ask that everyone listen respectfully. Allow everyone to speak and ask hard questions. Request that all responses criticize ideas, not individuals.

- Start with a centering thought. Remind students and colleagues that those who are angry do not bring their best thinking to a problem or issue.
- Be humble. Come prepared to be vulnerable, acknowledge that you are prepared to learn, and listen as well as share.
- Avoid terms that have become politicized or inflammatory. They separate people with different opinions, while our challenge is to bring people together.
- Focus on evidence. People should support their claims with facts and data.
- Focus on fairness. Ask people to think about what works for people of all backgrounds and for those who are most disadvantaged.

The goal of our conversations is to help us hear a range of perspectives and think critically about problems and solutions. Once these conversations take place on campus, then further conversations can happen more productively in the public sphere.

Several governors are now testing what many consider extreme approaches to undermining diversity and inclusion in higher education as they prepare for possible runs for the presidency in 2024. Some fear that it is possible that the extreme actions of some of these states could be replicated at the federal level, depending on the outcomes of upcoming elections.

Colleges and universities must be active participants in democracy, encouraging students and others to vote—not telling them whom to vote for, but encouraging their participation. We must make sure they have the critical skills to understand the impact of voting decisions and election outcomes on our lives every day. We must teach students how to think about what Henry David Thoreau referred to as "the whole vote"—which means not just showing up on election day but taking the time to learn about candidates and their policies, engage others in conversation about issues, and seek to understand how policies would affect their lives and society as a whole.[59] Elections have consequences.

It would be easy to be discouraged. After the Civil War, we saw tremendous progress under Reconstruction only to see gains dissolve in the era of Jim Crow. People were discouraged at that time but did not give up hope. Here we are again. The Rev. Dr. Martin Luther King, paraphrasing Theodore Parker, said, "The arc of the moral universe is long, but it bends toward justice."[60] We now add, "but it does so only if we make it." We should never forget history. We must be inspired by the generations before us who never gave up hope, who believed in a better future for their children and grandchildren, and who organized. We must continue to hope and do the work.

LGBTQ+

College and university campuses have been, with some exceptions, inclusive spaces for those who identify as LGBTQ+. Kristen Renn notes, "Higher education has historically been and remains a positive location for students' identity development. For some students, increased independence from their home community and family creates a space for exploring sexuality and gender in privacy and safety." She also relates that most LGBTQ+ students report that the climate in college is better than they experienced in high school.[61]

From the Stonewall riots in 1969 to the AIDS epidemic of the 1980s and 1990s to *Obergefell v Hodges* in 2015, US LGBTQ+ residents have shaped and reshaped their lives and rights. Similarly, LGBTQ+ members of our campuses and the groups they have formed have been the lead actors changing the culture of our universities to make them more welcoming and inclusive. They have created and shaped the spaces that allow newcomers to explore their sexuality and gender in a safe environment.

At UMBC, students, faculty, and staff who are lesbian, gay, bisexual, transgender, nonbinary, queer, intersex, asexual, and/or other gender or sexual minorities have worked with and pushed the university leadership to be welcoming and inclusive for LGBTQ+ members of our community. Through a combination of individual and institutional courage, we have made a lot of progress. When we think we are welcoming enough already, though, there is more we are called to do, and that call often begins with difficult conversations.

Students have been leaders in this work at UMBC. They formed the Freedom Alliance in 1995, and Queers United Mobilized and Bringing Change (QUMBC) in 2009. Today the LGBTQ Student Union and the Queer and Trans People of Color (QPOC) community represent LGBTQ+ students. The LGBTQ Student Union is an organization of LGBTQ+ students and their allies established "for the purpose of providing a fun and safe queer community for LGBTQIA+ students at UMBC." They host many events, including Coming Out Day, which dates back to 1995, and the annual drag show, which dates from 2004.[62] QPOC is "a student organization created by queer people of color for queer people of color." Their goal is "to create a safe, secure, and welcoming community on UMBC's campus for all students who identify as queer and people of color. We are dedicated to ensuring everyone is respected and celebrated for who they are."[63]

LGBTQ+ students have established physical spaces to gather, build community, and support one another. The Freedom Alliance created the Freedom Alliance Lounge in 1995 with permission from university leaders. They later renamed it the Queer Student Lounge. In 2010, working with the Freedom Alliance and QUMBC, the university established the Pride Center, which continues today. The space includes a meeting area and an interior office open during the fall and spring semesters. Students use the space for socializing, group study, and student organization meetings.[64]

The Women's Center at UMBC has played an important supportive role for LGBTQ+ students. In 2012 the Women's Center organized Between Women, a group for LGBTQ+ identified women students. The following year, the Center organized Spectrum, a group for transgender and gender-nonconforming students. One faculty member related that the Women's Center "carries a lot of student trauma."

Staff and faculty, meanwhile, have also formed organizations or networks to provide mutual support and advocate for issues of importance to the LGBTQ+ community. The first LGB staff and faculty group formed in the 1990s. Later, LGBT staff and faculty created the Lavender List as a way to communicate among themselves. In 2012 faculty searching for a group to represent their interests formed a new LGBT Faculty and Staff Association (FSA), which they later renamed the LGBTQ FSA. Unlike other such faculty affinity groups on our campus, this FSA deliberately included faculty and staff members and individuals from all colleges.

Difficult conversations are central to culture change, and sometimes they happen within a community. When the LGBTQ FSA changed its name, for example, this was a big deal. One professor had objected to adding "Q" to the name of the group when they formed in 2012 because people had called him "queer" as a pejorative term in his younger days. In the meantime, though, younger people had embraced the term queer to describe themselves. When the older professor retired, the FSA decided to add the "Q" to raise up the many people who identified that way, even though the change let one person down.

Susan McDonough, associate professor of history, suggested that the university also provide a public webpage titled the OutList, on which faculty and staff can choose to post their names, pronouns, and photos. The site, which has been up since 2013, states as its purpose to promote "greater visibility of the LGBTQ community and reflects the commitment to diversity and inclusivity at UMBC." Today, the OutList includes about 30 staff and 20 faculty members. Among faculty, their fields remain concentrated in the College of Arts, Humanities, and Social Sciences. They include just one faculty member in each of the College of Natural and Mathematical Sciences, the College of Engineering and Information Technology, and the School of Social Work. Manil Suri, Distinguished University Professor in UMBC's department of Mathematics and Statistics, wrote a 2015 piece for the *New York Times*, "Why Is Science So Straight?" His point is that being "out" appears to happen less frequently in the natural sciences and engineering fields than it does in other academic fields.[65]

It is affirming for those who identify as LGBTQ+ to see their experiences included in the curriculum, providing students opportunities to learn about and engage in these issues.[66] Carole McCann, professor in what is now gender, women's and sexuality studies (GWST), offered the first course on an LGBTQ topic in 1988. This course focused on AIDS. GWST offered the first queer studies class in 1997. Today, faculty in GWST and other departments offer courses with an LGBTQ+ focus or topics that include Introduction to Critical Sexuality Studies, Human Sexuality in Sociological Perspective, Psychology of Sexual Orientation and Gender Identity, Sexual Diversity, and Sexuality and Queer Theory. They also offer History and Politics of Sexuality, Sexuality and Reproduction in the U.S., Queer Representations in Film and TV, Black, Queer and Feminist Film, and Gender, Sexuality and Theatrical Performance. GWST offers most of these courses, but there are many joint classes with the history, economics, political science, sociology, psychology, and other departments.

We have seen progress on policy issues decided at the state or system level, generally in reaction to advocacy from the LGBTQ+ community. In 1996 the University System of Maryland Board of Regents held hearings about a policy of nondiscrimination for sexual orientation. System faculty and staff testified in favor of such a policy, as did UMBC president Freeman Hrabowski, the only USM president to do so. The USM Regents instituted the policy the next year. In 2012 they added a policy of nondiscrimination on the basis of gender identity.

A key issue for LGBTQ+ community members is the availability of covered healthcare that meets their specific needs. A decade ago, health insurance for same-sex partners was available but only as a taxable benefit. State health insurance supported neither reproductive technology for same-sex couples nor gender-affirming care for transgender individuals. After passage of marriage equality in Maryland in 2012, spearheaded by Equality Maryland and then-state senators Rich Madaleno and Jamie Raskin, health insurance became available for all employee spouses whether opposite sex or same sex. Such health insurance was no longer taxable, but an employee could only receive it if married.

Marriage equality was not enough to provide full health insurance coverage for LGBTQ+ employees and their partners—the Maryland General Assembly had to act on reproductive technology as well. Health insurance for state employees had only covered reproductive technology for a woman using "the sperm of her husband." After marriage equality became law, the Assembly passed legislation that covered such technology for all married couples (same-sex or opposite-sex), including when the sperm came from a nonspouse male.

The Assembly also took action to cover gender-affirming care for transgender community members. This was a big deal for the Trans community. Previously, one had to obtain a diagnosis of "gender dysphoria"—essentially be diagnosed with a "mental illness"—and then live as a person of the gender one is transitioning to for a year before getting appropriate gender-affirming care. Now, state employees and their dependents could receive coverage for this care without such prerequisites.

While LGBTQ+ people have been key actors in creating an accepting and supporting culture on our campus, the university has played a role as well, though often in a reactive rather than proactive way. University leaders granted the Freedom Alliance the space in Sherman Hall that they turned into their lounge in 1995. The university allowed all-gender housing starting in the Walker Avenue Apartments in 2006 and took a big step forward with all-gender restrooms beginning in 2016. In 2017 we hired Keith Bowman, an openly gay man, as dean of our College of Engineering and Information Technology. Bowman came to us from San Francisco State, where he had been dean of science and engineering, and is likely the first openly gay man to lead a public research university's engineering college.[67] We have very recently established a policy and process for allowing students to change their names and genders in our university records.

Dean Bowman says that *courage* is his favorite word, and it does take both individual and institutional courage to create a welcoming and inclusive climate for LGBTQ+ students, faculty, and staff. Individual courage is critical. Keith notes that people have spat at and assaulted him, vandalized his car, and threatened his employment for being gay. During dean searches he has, on the one hand, been asked about his wife by well-intentioned but heteronormative people involved in the search, and, on the other, been asked to "describe my personal life," specifically in a bid to "out" him. These remain typical incidents for many LGBTQ+ faculty.

The story of all-gender restrooms at UMBC shows how activism, as in the case of Title IX, can lead to an act of institutional courage that expands inclusivity. Students began the effort to obtain all-gender restrooms at UMBC. In an effort to be inclusive of transgender and nonbinary community members, the university relabeled all single-room restrooms as "all gender" in 2016. That was easy but insufficient. Students pushed for more, though, leading to a collaborative effort of students, staff, and faculty that pressured the administration into creating multiuser, all-gender restrooms over several years. It took significant work.

When students who led the movement floated the idea of multiuser, all-gender restrooms, there were many who shook their heads. Some departments approved, while others were uncomfortable or opposed. Some administrators in positions of authority argued that such facilities could result in problems with harassment and liability. Others in facilities management said that it was physically impossible to create multiuser, all-gender restrooms because of plumbing configurations.

Staff continued to push, despite their fears of repercussions, until the university took action. When leaders argued that we already had all-gender restrooms, staff who were leading the advocacy effort had to present evidence that all of these were single-user restrooms and not distributed in a way to create equal access. (Having to wait in line when one really needs a restroom after a class is a maddening experience.) Indeed, the standoff was frustrating and demoralizing. "We were 'this close' to organizing a protest," recalls a staff leader in the LGBTQ+ FSA. Eventually, President Hrabowski, with support of the provost and vice president for administration and finance, said, "I want this to happen, and I want it to happen now." This was the breakthrough. As one staff member related, "Upper administration listened to us and fought with us to ensure folks across campus were doing their jobs."

Shelly Wiechelt, associate dean of social work, and Keith Bowman, dean of engineering, co-chaired the committee that oversaw the identification of feasible locations for multiuser, all-gender restrooms, with the first opening in 2019. Cael Mulcahy, director of operations in our College of Arts, Humanities, and Social Sciences, was essential to this work. They brought expertise in UMBC building management, knowledge of the affected community, and connections with both that community and the facilities management team. Eventually, they were the most involved person in the all-gender restroom implementation. We now have multiuser, all-gender bathrooms in our library, Commons, life sciences building, the Event Center, residence halls, the performing arts building, and most buildings on campus. We do not yet have them in some of the older buildings, though, such as engineering.

When we officially opened the first multiuser, all-gender restrooms, there was so much joy. Notably, this win for the LGBTQ+ community did not stem from tragedy (as it too often does), but rather from collaborative, persistent advocacy. It was a huge symbolic and practical success, demonstrating strong community support for this initiative, which sought to make our campus more welcoming and inclusive. Over 30 people attended the celebration for the first such restroom, including many students, faculty, staff, and administrators, as well as the provost and president. Staff brought a rainbow arch of balloons that festooned the entrance to the restroom. LGBTQ+ students cut the ribbon; the celebration included perusal of the new facilities, some refreshments, and rainbow balloons.

Our commitment to DEI goes further. When Keith Bowman interviews faculty candidates for the college of engineering and information technology, he tells them, "We don't just talk about equity and inclusion, we believe in justice and doing right by people." In doing so, he is signaling that UMBC is supportive of all people, regardless of race, gender, gender identity, sexual orientation, and so on. We have made large strides, yet there is always more that we can do.

As an institution, we can do more to ensure that our community is consistently welcoming and inclusive. In his 2015 editorial, Suri wrote that UMBC is "very gay friendly." While that may be true generally, how friendly depends on one's role, department, major, or classes. LGBTQ+ faculty have different comfort levels, depending on the department they work in or whether they are tenured or contingent. LGBTQ+ staff have different experiences depending on their unit or co-workers. LGBTQ+ students may have a supportive experience or a hostile one, depending on how they present themselves and whom they encounter in the classroom, in administrative offices, or among their peers.

We begin by remembering that, despite progress, this can still be a hostile world for LGBTQ+ members of our community. Some state and national politicians continue to focus on transgender issues, particularly bathroom access and sports, as cultural wedge issues. At the federal level, the Supreme Court ruled in 2020 that employment discrimination based on sexual orientation or gender identity is illegal under Title VII of the Civil Rights Act. However, 16 states still do not have laws on the books prohibiting employment discrimination based on sexual orientation and gender identity, and one state prohibits such discrimination for sexual orientation, but not gender identity.[68] Meanwhile, in his concurring opinion in *Dobbs v Jackson Women's Health Organization*, Associate Justice Clarence Thomas suggested that the court revisit the 2015 *Obergefell* decision among others.

Some of the work we, as university leaders, can do going forward includes messaging and action. We can conduct routine climate surveys that include LGBTQ+ as well as other issues around race and gender, for example. These surveys are helpful in gauging where we are, what we need to do, and what we can do. We can provide consistent and frequent messaging regarding our values, specifically regarding a welcoming and inclusive culture and environment. We can continue to encourage this in all of our colleges and divisions, departments, and administrative units. We can also require training on LGBTQ+ issues.

With regard to climate, training remains an important tool that colleges and universities have not yet universally adopted. Our OEI has offered training on pronoun use. Our Mosaic Center offers SafeZone: LGBTQ+ Allyship Development Training to help students, staff, faculty, and alumni to create a more welcoming, affirmative atmosphere at UMBC for LGBTQ+ members. This offering for community members at all levels of knowledge and comfort with LGBTQ+ culture and concerns, includes basic terminology, core concepts, LGBTQ+ intersections, pronoun usage, and allyship development.[69]

We have not yet made this training mandatory but should consider this. As some LGBTQ+ staff have noted, there are people on our campus who need to learn "how to work with your co-workers who are different from you." As some LGBTQ+ students have related, there are faculty who refuse to use their clearly stated preferred names and pronouns. Training can include orientation sessions for new students, faculty, and staff, as well as periodic training for faculty and staff about fundamental rights and current issues. We could potentially use our staff performance, promotion and tenure, and contract review processes to enforce this.

We also need to do more to help students one day navigate a world that might not be as friendly and supportive as our campus. Only 22 states offer a resilient set of employment and housing protections for the LGBTQ+ community.[70] It was just a decade ago that the federal government changed its policies so that one could not be fired from a national security job for being gay, lesbian, bisexual, or transgender. In the current political climate, it is reasonable to be concerned that advances could be overturned. Meanwhile, UMBC engineering dean Keith Bowman has related that undergraduate and graduate students still approach him to discuss whether they should scrub their social media, LinkedIn profiles, and the rest of their presence on the internet before they apply for jobs.

While we have nondiscrimination policies in place, our climate is not always healthy for everyone, and retention remains a problem. As a general matter, several prominent LGBTQ+ staff have recently left UMBC. Some turnover is expected, but we have seen further departures that raise concerns. People notice, for example, when the one queer, Latina staff member and the one nonbinary, Black faculty member leave. We need to pay closer attention to intersectionality and think about how to create work environments that are more inclusive and supportive of people with intersecting marginalized identities.

We have also had challenges in retaining staff in counseling. This has been a general problem for us, as it has been for other colleges and universities at a time when we all seek to expand our staff in this area. It is also a more specific problem for LGBTQ+ counseling. Such counselors are frequently exhausted and experience burnout. We lost one counselor who focused on LGBTQ+ issues just before the pandemic, and their replacement just left as well.

Mental Health

Mental health challenges span a large set of issues, so there is no one-size-fits-all approach that will help every community member. Some experience academic stress or grieve the loss of a loved one. Others have serious episodes of anxiety, depression, bipolar disorder, or schizophrenia. Counseling or wellness centers also treat those who are on the autism spectrum or are struggling with substance abuse or eating disorders.

Further complicating the mental health landscape, campuses may have different distributions of issues. The students who commute to a community college will have a different set of issues than those attending a residential liberal arts college. Undergraduates and graduate students face different challenges. Community members who identify as LGBTQIA may have identity issues or relationships that are challenged by coming out. Those from racial and ethnic minority groups may have personal or social experiences that are traumatic and/or intensify other mental health issues.

In every case, the campus approach to well-being and mental health must be culturally responsive, and trauma informed. Beyond that, these various challenges generally require different approaches for support. Some community members may benefit from individual counseling, others from group counseling. Some may benefit from peer counseling, while others require psychiatric support. Some may benefit from a referral to an outside provider.

While we often see mental health as an issue of individual or collective resilience, we have included it in this chapter rather than the previous, because it takes institutional courage to, once again, challenge a campus to change its culture to tackle an issue. In this case, we are challenging campuses to both understand that mental health is critical to student success and see that addressing mental health is the work of everyone, not just the counseling department (just as diversity is the work of everyone and not just that of the office of DEI).

The Soul of Our Nation

Thomas Insel, former director of the National Institute of Mental Health, argues, "Mental health has become a measure of the soul of our nation."[71] So, how is our "soul" faring, then? The data reveal a grim picture.

In general:[72]

- 21 percent of Americans experienced a mental illness over the past year
- 5.6 percent of Americans experienced a serious mental illness (SMI), which the NIH defines as a "[d]isorder resulting in serious functional impairment, which substantially limits or interferes with one or more major life activities."
  - Women (7.0 percent) had a higher SMI rate than men (4.2 percent) did.
  - Young adults aged 18–25 had the highest SMI rate (9.7 percent) among adults.

During the pandemic[73]

- 20 percent of Americans reported that the pandemic had a significant negative impact on their mental health
- 45 percent of those Americans with any mental illness reported a significant negative impact
- 55 percent of those with an SMI reported a significant negative impact

Compared to other high-income countries[74]

- More US adults have received mental health diagnoses than adults in other high-income countries (Canada, Australia, New Zealand, Norway, Sweden, United Kingdom, France, Switzerland, and Germany)
- Self-reported emotional distress rates are highest in Canada and the United States among these countries
- The United States has the highest suicide rate, and the rate has increased every year since 2000, while this rate has declined significantly in France, Norway, and Sweden

These data are alarming but perhaps not surprising to the extent that one's environment affects individual mental health. As a nation, since 2000, we have experienced a major terrorist attack, two long wars in the Middle East, a "great recession," and increased political polarization and animosity. Cable news and social media exacerbate our divisions and create challenges for political discourse. While social media have their benefits, research shows that it can also increase mental health challenges. All of these have landed in the midst of longer-term social and economic change, some of it wrenching, due to globalization, the offshoring of manufacturing, technological change, and shifting demographics. We continue to experience discord and unrest over race relations, gender, LGBTQIA+ identity, abortion, and gun rights. We experienced an assault on the US Capitol, an event never seen before even during the US Civil War. Finally, as if these events were not enough, we have now lived since March 2020 with the fear, uncertainty, grief, and discord of COVID-19 in its pandemic and endemic phases. It is no wonder we are wound up and on edge.

The pandemic and the restrictions enacted to combat it were of course, the stressors at the forefront as we contemplated how to support the mental well-being of those in our community. In March 2020 the State of Maryland imposed restrictions on its citizens to help bring the spread of COVID-19 under control—to "flatten the curve"—to protect the health of Marylanders and to reduce pressure on healthcare staff and resources. While this was the right path to take under the circumstances, the pandemic and the response to it were both traumatic events.

First, we experienced the trauma of the disease. We feared catching COVID-19. We were afraid for the health and safety of our loved ones, friends, and colleagues. In some instances, we lost them to the disease. Moreover, the disease affected certain communities disproportionately—the elderly, those with health vulnerabilities, frontline workers, and communities of color.

Uncertainty made the fear worse. In the early days, we knew very little about the virus and how it spread. Doctors confronted with this new disease scrambled to understand what might work to treat patients with it. What information we did get about the disease and its spread was often contested or in flux. At any given time, various authorities communicated different, even contradictory, theories and information. Meanwhile, as time went on, experts learned more, drew new conclusions, and changed their information or recommended guidelines.

Second, we experienced the trauma of the "lockdown." As places of employment moved their work online and most businesses except for those providing essentials closed, we felt isolation and uncertainty. Some of us lost jobs, at least temporarily, while others continued their jobs in high-risk environments. We all wondered when life could return to "normal," a question that soon became contentious and politicized, adding rancor to our fear, uncertainty, and grief.

It is no surprise then that as US residents we have been experiencing what some have called a "mental health pandemic." The percent of adults in the United States who reported symptoms of anxiety disorder or depression disorder in the previous seven days increased from 11 percent in 2019 to 41 percent in 2021.[75] Many people in the United States have sought therapy or medication. Therapists and psychiatrists have reported a significant increase in demand for their services and found their practices and schedules full.

Students

We all experience stress in a world that is dangerous or demanding. The college experience is rewarding for students but also stressful academically, financially, socially, and psychologically. Academically, students encounter new ideas that change knowledge and worldviews. They have assignments, essay deadlines, examinations, and pressure to do well or meet the expectations of self and others. Financially, some may be balancing work and study, worrying about student debt, or stressing about internships and careers. Socially, students are often away from home for the first time and encountering new relationships and opportunities for self-exploration that may be exciting but also unsettling. Psychologically, many students are at sea about majors, careers, and identities, creating uncertainty and fear. Some experience higher levels of stress in these situations, pushing them further along the anxiety spectrum.

Sometimes the result is the diagnosis of a depressive or anxiety disorder.

Wendy Fleischman and Howard Gardner have argued that increased concern about mental health predates the pandemic and that the chief driver of anxiety and depression for students is academic pressure. The authors observe that faculty and administrators tend to ascribe the rise in student mental health issues to their being away from home, experiencing financial pressures, or balancing a workload. Fleischman and Gardner found that their survey respondents, however, felt a mounting, and sometimes overwhelming, pressure to earn good grades, get internships, and find jobs after graduation. They argue that most students focus mainly on themselves and their careers rather than expanding their minds and learning new things. The majority of students have a "transactional view" of college, according to the authors, and only a minority view college as a time primarily for exploration or transformation.[76]

Whether college students have an exploratory or transactional relationship (or both) with the college experience, they are journeying through a challenging period in their lives, made more stressful by college, social challenges, and the pandemic. Young adults aged 18 to 25 are more susceptible to mental illness than older adults are. According to the National Alliance on Mental Illness, one in three young adults reported any mental illness compared to one in five adults overall, and one in ten reported an SMI compared to one in twenty overall.[77] The January 2022 Student Voice Survey by *Inside Higher Ed* and College Pulse found 35 percent of college students have struggled a "fair amount" recently with depression or anxiety and another 33 percent have struggled with these "a great deal."[78]

Within the broader context of student mental health, we also need to pay close attention to the more specific mental health concerns of students from marginalized groups. Olivia Sanchez has reported the following in *The Hechinger Report*:

> While grappling with pandemic-related challenges and typical college student woes, Black students may be dealing with increased public

attention on police brutality and distress in their communities, for example. Latino students may be grappling with heated debates on immigration policy that affect their loved ones, or the challenges of straddling two different cultures. LGBTQ+ students may face questions about gender, sexuality, identity and acceptance. . . . Research shows mental health treatment is more effective when it's in line with the client's culture and when clients perceive their therapist to be culturally competent. But many colleges are still figuring out how exactly to care for students from underserved groups.[79]

While the Student Voice Survey found that 33 percent of college students have recently struggled with depression and anxiety "a great deal," still-higher percentages of those who identify as female (38 percent), as having had an adverse childhood event/trauma (43 percent), as LGBTQIA+ (49 percent), or as part of a lower socioeconomic class (50 percent) report struggling a great deal.[80]

Students experienced a range of added stressors during the pandemic. Academically, undergraduate and graduate students had to adjust to virtual learning. Even though our faculty worked hard to learn the technological and pedagogical skills associated with online teaching, there remained issues that affected students. Some faculty were better than others at online course delivery (some had experience, while others had none). Some students had technological issues—access to laptops or Wi-Fi—that affected their ability to connect. Some students said there were benefits to online instruction, including the availability of asynchronous lectures and resources. Others, though, felt that in-person learning was better and missed this aspect of their education. Graduate students found their research and degree progress disrupted. To release some pressure for those dealing with the anxiety of the abrupt shift to online learning, we allowed students to take courses pass/fail during the spring 2020 semester.

Students experienced the same fears of disease and uncertainties of life that staff and faculty experienced. Some had the stress of isolation from friends and faculty, while others went home to stressful environments. Some experienced the loss of loved ones. Many lost the opportunity to participate in on-campus experiences, events, activities, and groups. At UMBC, we held no in-person graduations since campus shut down until December 2021, meaning many students and their families were not able to experience directly this rite of passage.

Trauma can change the brain, including the trauma of living through the most threatening public health crisis of our lifetimes. As more of one's brain is dedicated to processing trauma, there is less available for other activities—including learning. Here is where "trauma-informed pedagogy" can be helpful. UMBC's Faculty Development Center has provided faculty with training that brings this practice into their teaching.[81]

Loss of the on-campus experience can significantly affect students. Athletes and other students often find their identity, belonging, fun, and outlet in their sports team or student group. Shutting down athletics during the early months of the pandemic meant that athletes lost this experience, the bonding with their teammates, and the athletic competition. One can imagine that this might also have been true for students in other student groups that could not readily move online, though UMBC's Mock Trial Team thrived in the 2021 national championship that was held virtually, winning it over Yale University in the final.

Economically, many students and their families experienced financial challenges due to the recession of 2020. We allowed student workers at UMBC to stay on the payroll through spring 2020, but many students lost jobs. Additionally, other family members whom students relied on—parents and others—for financial support also lost jobs. In addition, many students also struggled with food insecurity. Retriever Essentials is our student food pantry that gathers and provides food to students who are experiencing homelessness or food insecurity. During the past two years, student use of Retriever Essentials has increased.

During the first year of the pandemic, we reduced the number of students in our residence halls out of concern about COVID-19 transmission. However, we let some students remain in our resi-dence halls for a variety of reasons, among them that they did not have a home they could safely return to, whether the result of neg-ative or abusive environments, international travel restrictions, or other reasons. In some cases, students who had come out in college as LGBTQ+ were no longer welcome at home.

While concern about trends in student mental health predates the pandemic, it is not surprising given the above experiences that rates of depression and anxiety increased during it. The Healthy Minds Network reported an increase in depression among students from 25 percent in 2015–2016 to 36 percent in 2018–2019 and a fur-ther increase to 41 percent during the pandemic. They also reported an increase in anxiety disorders among students from 21 percent in 2015–2016 to 31 percent in 2018–2019, with a further increase dur-ing the pandemic to 34 percent.[82]

National Reports Provide Guidance

Since college can be a demanding, mind-stretching, and stress-ful experience for students, creating a culture of well-being and a plan to support it will also support student success. The pandemic has brought well-being and mental health to the forefront as never before. In 2020 the American Council on Education, with support from Active Minds, the Healthy Minds Network, the Jed Founda-tion, the Steve Fund, and the American College Health Associa-tion, published a statement, *Mental Health, Higher Education, and COVID-19: Strategies for Leaders to Support Campus Well-Being*.[83] This report focused on what campus leaders should do during the COVID-19 crisis to enhance communication and support. In 2021 the National Academies of Sciences, Engineering, and Medicine (NASEM) published *Mental Health, Substance Abuse, and Wellbeing in Higher Education: Supporting the Whole Student*. This report pro-vides a framework that colleges and universities can use to im-prove their overall approaches to mental health and student well-being.[84]

The study committee that authored the NASEM report describes a "holistic" understanding of what it means to support students. They write, "Wellbeing is a holistic concept referring to both physical and mental health. It includes a sense of personal safety and security, emotional support and connection, mechanisms to cope with stressors, and access to services when appropriate for short- and long-term care."[85] Given this, the committee recommended a "multipronged approach" that includes "a focus on prevention, identification of high-risk students in a thoughtful way, effective community-based approaches, treatment services for identified cases, and relapse prevention and post-treatment support."[86] In addition, it is critical for a college or university to cultivate "an institutional culture of acceptance and support," the NASEM Committee argues. Such a culture normalizes the occurrence of mental illness and the use of resources to address mental health challenges and thus "is critical in helping those who need support to overcome the ongoing obstacle that stigma plays in access to counseling."[87]

It takes institutional courage to change institutional culture. As we discussed in *The Empowered University*, changing institutional culture takes substantial and sustained effort. It can begin with the president and other leaders signaling that an issue, such as addressing mental health, is a campus priority. To be successful, though, there must be broader buy-in and leadership within the community. Campus conversations that draw in community members to discuss an issue; review, digest, and analyze data about that issue; and draw conclusions about the nature of a problem, possible solutions, and who should act are a great place to start. Change happens when others buy in and take a leadership role. These leaders help shift the culture—values, attitudes, and behaviors—and lead change over time.

For leaders, it takes courage to be vulnerable and to model for others that being vulnerable is okay for everyone. Some asked former UMBC President Hrabowski, "How can you always be so optimistic? How can you always urge us to 'keep hope alive'?" Hrabowski did not sugar-coat his response to make a point. Instead, he related that he, too, has his moments of doubt and concern. What helps him get through these moments is the support of colleagues and students who tell him "we can get through this," just as he conveys the same message to the campus at large. It takes a team to stay strong, have resolve, and display the courage to move ahead. It takes a community to support students, faculty, and staff as they face mental health challenges of any sort.

The shared governance leadership on our campus asked President Hrabowski to speak about mental health in our community as part of our 2022 Mental Health Awareness Day. It takes courage for a leader to share authentically challenges experienced during the pandemic and tools used to increase personal resilience. Hrabowski noted that the pandemic has been stressful for all of us, that depression and anxiety are real concerns, and that if we harness the power of the human spirit, we can go beyond what we think we can do. Of course, we have to be realistic about the challenges that the pandemic has created, but we can approach those challenges with hope and optimism, with a feeling that we are all in this together, and that we will get through this as we have gotten through other challenges before.

Personally, Hrabowski noted how he and his wife have persevered by turning to faith and prayer, laughter and gratitude, and breathing and mindfulness. Exercise is important. His wife does Pilates and he walks and runs. They both engage in meditation, tai chi, and acupuncture. They both watch what they eat, as certain foods—such as those with too much sugar—can affect energy and mood. Hrabowski also noted that he uses the Calm app daily, listening to short, guided meditations that help him center and re-energize.

We should include mental health in our strategic planning and/or create a strategic plan specifically for mental health that focuses on students, faculty, and staff.[88] A campus strategy for mental health could look like this. First, the campus should collect data to understand mental health and illness, substance abuse, and well-being among community members. The NASEM committee maintains, "The collected data must be disaggregated by unit, program level, and student identities, and compared to similar data from peer institutions."[89] Second, the assessment should examine the strategies and resources the campus currently has in place to address these issues and what new strategies and funds would be necessary to more adequately address the task.[90] Third, a campus mental health strategy should use evidence-based strategies, interventions, and initiatives. They should also create a coordinated approach among all those who engage with students to maximize resources.[91]

Training for all community members is central to a successful mental health strategy. The NASEM report urges institutions to "encourage students to seek resources, join groups, and seek counseling." More specifically, they recommend:

- As part of formal orientation to college life, all students should participate in structured opportunities to learn about individual well-being and the cultivation of a healthy, respectful campus climate.
- This orientation should include material on how to develop resilience in the face of inevitable challenges they will experience both in college and in life.
- The training should acknowledge how behaviors such as sleep, nutrition, exercise, social media, and work can both enhance and be affected by one's level of wellbeing.
- The training should also include information on how to recognize and address implicit bias, and about the role that students themselves play in creating a community that supports each other's well-being.[92]

The options available to students for support are broad. These include peer support groups, faculty and staff, and counselors. Some students will reach out to peers before seeking professional support, so this can be a critical component of a comprehensive plan. Our experience with telehealth during the pandemic suggests that we should continue this as an option. Many appreciate in-person counseling, but telehealth may facilitate engagement by those who may not otherwise visit the counseling center, including those who are off campus or deeply depressed. Its convenience can also help reduce the incidence of individuals dropping out of care before it is effective. Providing other wellness options can also reduce stress and prevent issues that are more serious. These may include meditation, mindfulness, or yoga practices.

ACE recommends that, as a long-term strategy, institutions should provide "gatekeeper skills training" to faculty. This training helps faculty "notice, intervene, and refer those students and colleagues who are in distress." Similarly, the NASEM report found that counseling centers are necessary but not sufficient. Supporting student well-being requires an "all hands" approach. In particular, training faculty on how to identify and speak to students in distress is an important part of a comprehensive strategy.[93]

At UMBC: Students

Before the pandemic, we increased our counseling staff at UMBC and planned for the construction of a new Center for Wellbeing. Despite the severe pressure the pandemic and the recession placed on our resources, we pushed ahead with staffing and this new facility during the pandemic. The Center houses Retriever Integrated Health, gathering space for spiritual practices, and our program focused on student conduct and community standards. The Integrated Health Center combines University Health Services, University Counseling, and the Office of Health Promotion. We brought these three centers together so that healthcare professionals could more easily refer students experiencing mental health challenges to counseling with the programs interconnected and co-located.

During the pandemic, we took further steps to support students. We worked to maintain staffing levels in counseling despite turnover. We allowed students to take a pass/fail grading option for spring 2020. We provided contact information for counseling services whenever we issued campus communications regarding the pandemic and challenging social issues. We also posted notices across campus that provide information to campus members who suspect that a colleague or student is struggling with mental health challenges. The information provides guidance on what one should notice and whom to contact.

A particular challenge that we have faced, likely along with other higher education institutions, is turnover among our counseling staff. As noted in the previous chapter, we have not experienced a "great resignation" among our staff except in pockets. One of these pockets has been counseling. Among units in our Division of Student Affairs, counseling experienced significantly higher separations, ranging from 27 to 33 percent annually over the past three years. It is our understanding that there is high demand for professional counseling staff, so many depart when other offers come along. This disrupts our ability to provide the kind of counseling support that we wish to provide to students, staff, and faculty. We have addressed this by hiring new staff in counseling to replace those who have left, yet this is a short-term action, not necessarily a sustainable one if conditions continue to motivate turnover.

We continue to cultivate a culture in which members of our community can acknowledge struggles with mental health and seek help. The first step in dealing with an issue is to name the problem. For those experiencing mental health challenges, our message is that it is okay to let others know and seek help. The second step is to provide appropriate support. Our counseling center provides individual counseling for mental health and alcohol and substance abuse, groups that students may join, and referrals to external providers. It provides access to togetherall, an online peer-to-peer community in which students can anonymously discuss their challenges and get support, as well as to Well Track, which provides online tools and resources, including assessments for anxiety and depression, and opportunities to practice mindfulness.

We also seek to cultivate a culture in which we all have a responsibility to support those who are experiencing mental health challenges. Our counselors consult with faculty who are concerned about a student. We provide access to Mental Health First Aid, a training program that helps participants understand how to identify and support those in crisis, and to kognito, a program that allows people to learn and practice how to have conversations with those in crisis. When there are challenges, people who are concerned about someone in our community can reach out to the Behavioral Risk Assessment and Consultation Team (BRACT), which can intervene and steer a person in crisis to the support they need.

At UMBC: Faculty and Staff

For students to thrive, they depend on faculty and staff who thrive.

When we closed our physical campus in March 2020, we had much to deal with as institutions, as leaders, and as people suddenly caught in a public health crisis that was about to be compounded by an economic recession. It was a jarring time. The COVID-19 "lockdown" of 2020 affected members of the UMBC community— administrators, staff, faculty, and students—as it did others in our state. Many on our tight-knit campus felt the loss of community, a collective loss, as this sense of community is important to who we are as an institution.

The president of our faculty senate described the transition to online teaching as an "existential crisis" for some faculty. Their jobs and the skills needed to do them had changed overnight. One of our college deans described her role as "grief leadership" similar to what any leader has to provide in a time of emergency, crisis, or uncertainty.

US Senator Elizabeth Warren recently reminded us, "The COVID-19 pandemic has showed us what working families already know: childcare is critical infrastructure."[94] Many faculty and staff working remotely found themselves in caregiving roles for children, partners, or parents. Issues of work-life balance that were previously on our institutional radar now became a more urgent concern during the pandemic when the boundary between work and home blurred. This was a particular challenge for those who had children participating in school from home. Parents often found themselves supervising this schooling.

This issue of caregiving was more often a challenge for women, though many men also had significant caregiving responsibilities as well.[95] As Jessica Colace, an associate professor of sociology at Indiana University, put it in an interview with the *Chronicle of Higher Education*:

> Back in December and into January of 2021, we surveyed about 350 faculty, staff, and graduate students. Across the board, even if they also had increased caregiving responsibilities at home, they weren't slacking off on their core tasks for the university. What was getting cut instead was research. There was also stress. We saw that those with caregiving responsibilities—who were disproportionately women and especially women of color—had amplified stress during the pandemic. Burning the candle at both ends, waking up at three or four in the morning to work for a couple of hours, before the kids woke, then staying up until midnight.[96]

Several women on our staff offered that they were proud of all they did for their families while also taking care of work. One talked about the birth of her first child during the pandemic. Another spoke happily about toilet training her daughter while working from home. Faculty, however, found their creative activity, research, and writing disrupted by the pandemic. Research has shown that, nationally, women faculty have decreased their submissions to academic journals due to increased caregiving responsibilities during the pandemic.[97] "We are all in the same storm, but not in the same boat," wrote Cassidy Sugimoto, professor of informatics at Indiana University, with her colleagues. "The scientific workforce has moved *en masse* into the home, where male faculty are four times more likely to have a partner engaged in full domestic care than their female colleagues."[98]

When we closed our physical campus, faculty and their students lost access to dance studios, performance spaces, archives, the library, laboratories, research equipment, and more. Those faculty with significant caregiving responsibilities found that they were able to tend to these only at the expense of their research and writing. In response, the provost's office, working with department chairs, helped maintain faculty career progression by revising promotion and tenure protocols and procedures.

At UMBC, faculty experienced further challenges and stressors during academic year 2020–2021.

- Very few department chairs had any training in crisis management. The provost's office and deans helped chairs deal with the pandemic crisis with particular emphasis on support and communication with faculty, staff, and students working under diverse circumstances.
- Communication with faculty about how to handle courses during the pandemic was an additional challenge. Faculty wanted to know who had the power to determine whether a course would be held in person or online and when decisions would be made. Many underestimated the complexities and logistics of class scheduling.
- Many faculty were concerned about their health and safety once leadership decided to reopen our campus more fully in fall 2021 and move much more of the instruction back to in-person teaching.

To get a sense of how their employees were faring emotionally during the pandemic, the University of Wisconsin at Milwaukee surveyed its employees in late 2021. About 10 percent of employees (631 out of 6700) responded. When the university shared their results, *The Chronicle of Higher Education* wrote, "Among the 631 university employees who responded, 73 percent reported having one symptom of post-traumatic stress disorder caused by the pandemic. Nearly 40 percent reported having three or more symptoms." James (Dmitri) Topitzes, a professor of social work at UWM said, "For many people, the pandemic is not just an irritant. It really destabilized folks."[99]

Strategies to counter mental health symptoms included spending time with family, friends, or pets, or spending time outdoors. Work was a stressor during the pandemic, particularly when staff adjusted to remote work, balanced work and caregiving, and took on additional work when colleagues left during a hiring freeze, but work could also be an antidote to stress when it involved interacting with others and focused on work that was particularly meaningful.[100]

During National Health Education Week in fall 2021, the USM Training Committee provided six health education workshops with a focus on mental health. The topics were:[101]

- Tools to handle stress
- Managing worry and anxiety
- Healthy food choices on the go
- Living with change
- Running on "E": Adding energy and fun to your life
- Mindfulness: Being present in your work and life

The committee chose this focus because of the increases in stress and anxiety stemming from the COVID pandemic.

At UMBC we addressed these many concerns through a series of interventions. We held town halls about mental health. We provided guidance to supervisors about telework policies (e.g., limiting interactions to work hours, length of meetings). We instituted new policies around caregiving and worked with departments to temporarily change promotion and tenure review policies (e.g., a delay in the promotion and tenure clock for caregivers). We let faculty decide the modality of their courses, even if we were suggesting more in-person course delivery.

We held a UMBC Mental Health Awareness Day on April 7, 2022. Our shared governance leadership—faculty senate, staff senates, and student governments—developed this idea, which they based on similar events at other institutions. The day included sessions focused on mental health awareness, behaviors of concern, graduate student mental health, faculty mental well-being, and grief and healing. The day also included walks, fitness, connecting with nature, and cultivating mindfulness and resilience.

Going Forward

We live in challenging times, to be sure, yet leaders must provide their institutions with opportunities to be the best they can for all students. Leaders should have the courage to face truths, make courageous decisions based on guiding principles that do not change, and then develop the community buy-in to realize goals in a sustainable way. We must have the courage to push ourselves to be inclusive on our campuses in a way that reflects our multicultural society and supports success for all students. Taking action requires the will to do more, the will to tackle tough issues, and the will to have tough conversations with colleagues—including those who are friends. It also means being proactive rather than reactive, and continuing important work even when the pressure is off because it is the right thing to do.

5

Passion

A Quiet Passion

We in higher education do not typically use the word "passion" to describe our work. When we focus on scholarship, our aim is to be detached, objective, and dispassionate. When we focus on teaching, our aim is to calmly transmit knowledge to students and patiently build their skills. Yet, beneath this calm, dispassionate surface, we pursue excellence with an intensity, a quiet passion. This passion is for the pursuit of our fundamental educational mission: that by promoting successful student learning and ensuring a high-quality student experience, we make a profound difference in the lives of our students, our communities and, by extension, the future of our country.

Leaders at all higher education institutions and at all levels within them have the potential to affect deeply the quality of the student experience by harnessing the passion and care they have about their work. We do this most effectively when we pay close attention to our students, understand their backgrounds, align institutional culture and resources with the goal of student success, and dedicate ourselves to positive outcomes for students from all backgrounds—whether they are working for postsecondary certificates, associate's degrees, or bachelor's degrees.

As at other times in the long history of higher education, we have seen this passion become more visible in a time of crisis. When COVID-19 upended our personal and professional lives and profoundly disrupted the operations of our institutions, it was the passion and commitment of our staff, faculty, and students that made this work. While this transition was by necessity imperfect, it was a remarkable collective achievement in the face of great uncertainty.

The National Survey of Student Engagement (NSSE) found that 73 percent of students believed that faculty and staff at their institution did "a good job" in managing this unprecedented crisis. Faculty opinion was consistent with this observation, with 86 percent of faculty reporting that, despite the many challenges, they were able to keep their commitment to educating their students well and helping them adapt. Jillian Kinzie, interim co-director of NSSE, remarked, "The fact that those stats are high across the board, and pretty close, suggests that there's been a lot of grace afforded to each other and appreciation for what faculty and staff did to help students adapt, and that faculty were really intentional about their efforts."[1]

Of course, while we cannot expect perfection in an environment of uncertainty and disruption, we are heartened by the dedication and passion that our campus communities displayed to help us move safely forward in a challenging, potentially overwhelming, period. *Inside Higher Ed* reported that Kate Drezek McConnell, vice president for curricular and pedagogical innovation at the Association of American Colleges and Universities, remarked, "What faculty and institutions were able to achieve in pivoting to an all-virtual environment is a concrete repudiation of the old trope that higher education cannot change or innovate quickly, and I am sure that the majority of faculty worked diligently to help students adapt."[2]

McConnell went on to note another critical lesson from the pandemic, saying, "The pivot, however, also illustrated the limited effectiveness of some traditional approaches to college teaching, like the stand and deliver lecture, and raised challenges to some of our traditional means for assessments, like tests."[3] It is notable that the transition away from traditional methods of pedagogy within our institutions began well before the pandemic and is largely based upon evidence-based concepts of the cognitive science of learning. The pandemic has perhaps accelerated that existing trend.

While we applaud our faculty, staff, and students for their incredible work during the pandemic, we agree that there is more to do to ensure student success. The pandemic, economic challenges, political upheaval, social unrest, and shifts in course delivery have all contributed to our awareness of the need for deeper thinking and intentionality with regard to our academic program—what we teach, how we teach, and how we support student success and learning. Passion is critical not just for institutions and their staff and faculty but also for our students. Passion among students is linked to greater academic motivation, particularly in individualistic societies like the United States, according to research by Xingyu Li at Stanford University. Li and colleagues found that academic achievement in reading, mathematics, and science was correlated with enjoyment, interest, identity and efficacy.[4]

How do we nurture a passion for learning in our students? At UMBC, we used to say, "It is cool to be smart." Over time, though, we began to understand how this reinforced the notion of a "fixed mindset," that we were already as smart as we would ever be. We then changed our approach by focusing on "grit," the notion that we can all grow, we can all learn, if we work hard. High expectations fuel this "growth mindset," which is reinforced when we have a passion for our work.

Motivation is critical. It can be internal, that is a student can arrive with a driving interest or ambition, that "fire in the belly" that can lead to success. Motivation can be external in origin and transformed into internal motivation. This can occur when we design empowering settings that support high expectations. These settings allow students to learn how to learn, achieve success, and develop a sense of efficacy. We can design courses and experiences to create empowering settings through active learning and team-based learning. We can help students build their own empowering settings as they create community, find a sense of belonging, and engage in group work.[5]

Student success is multidimensional. Relationships that students have with other students, faculty, and staff are critical to supporting student success and the student experience. In *How College Works*, Daniel Chambliss and Christopher Takacs, both of Hamilton College, argue that a student's success in college often hinges on whether they have at least one close student relationship and one close faculty relationship.[6] Peter Felten, John Gardner, and their colleagues have made a clear case that, in addition to relationships and high expectations, student learning is supported by institutional policies. Leaders must articulate goals for student learning, align budgets and resources with those goals, and insist on assessment of policies and initiatives to understand what is working, what is not, and what needs to be changed.[7]

"Many institutions talk about supporting all students and about being mission driven," writes Freeman Hrabowski. "However, institutions that are most effective are those that foster broad agreement on priorities, allow people to ask questions and act upon their own initiative, and offer incentives and rewards to those who innovate."[8] This is how we create the passionate university. We will focus here on how passion can drive student success by exploring enrollment and student support; the knowledge and skills students need for life, careers, and civic engagement; pedagogy and course design; digital support for teaching and learning; and the modalities of course delivery.

Enrollment

"Enrollment! Enrollment! Enrollment! It's all about enrollment!," former UMBC president Hrabowski often declared as we sought to maintain enrollment numbers during the pandemic.

As our pandemic response wore on, the extra energy it demanded of our community did not relent. We discussed which long-term tasks we should sustain and possibly accelerate while placing others

on hold. Even before COVID-19 affected our campus, we had begun
the process of developing a new strategic enrollment plan. We had
seen the national and regional enrollment projections and the demographic changes driving them. We clearly needed to create and
implement a plan that would help us sustain an enrollment level
that fit with our academic program, student support, auxiliary en-
terprises, budget goals, and facilities.

The pandemic deepened the challenge, increasing the urgency of
our work and making enrollment management a campus priority.
The recession hit many families hard, leading to declines in enrollment along with tuition revenue at a time when our state funding
and auxiliary revenue declined sharply. We breathed a sigh of relief when our fall 2020 enrollment declined by just one percentage
point. We then turned toward the task of increasing enrollment as
we worked to reopen our campus in fall 2021. We succeeded in several ways but came up short in others.

Demographic Change

Most universities had their eyes on enrollment even before the
pandemic. Birth rates, particularly among whites, had decreased
significantly beginning with the great recession of 2008–2009.
Other things remaining equal, this presaged a significant decline
in college-bound high school graduates after 2026. Nathan Grawe
has added important nuance to these projections, noting that the
challenges faced by any particular institution will vary by region, demographics, and selectivity. Indeed, some selective institutions or
universities in regions with population growth may see increases
in applications and enrollments, while the majority of institutions
nationwide compete for dwindling applicant pools.[9]

The ethnic composition of the US population has also been
changing: the fastest-growing groups are those with the lowest rate
of high school graduation and college enrollment. On a hopeful
note, the percentage of Hispanics graduating from high school has
increased. Thus, the number of students who could go on to college

may be as much as 10 percent higher in the peak year of 2026 than previously thought. Yet, that remains a peak year, and we will see subsequent declines. This downward trend could lead to what might at best be a zero-sum competition for new students, unless institutional and government policies increase the accessibility and affordability of postsecondary education.[10]

Expanding the Pie

Projections are not destiny. They show us what would happen if we project current trends out into the future given certain assumptions. We can bend the arc and change the future.

At the national level, policy changes could bring a larger proportion of high school graduates to postsecondary education. State and federal efforts could reduce the cost of community college, perhaps making it free or nearly so. Congress could significantly expand the maximum Pell grant or take steps to bring student debt under control. These actions and more could increase access and affordability and, by extension, enrollment.

At the institutional level, we can adopt recruitment practices that increase the number of first-time freshmen and transfer students from community colleges. We can also increase overall enrollment by implementing student success initiatives that increase retention and completion.

All of these efforts will mean reaching out to students from groups that are currently underrepresented in higher education, such as low-income, first-generation, racial and ethnic minorities, and others.

The Pandemic and Enrollment

The pandemic compounded demographic changes in the US population that affect our universities.[11]

First, the trends already in motion affecting the number of applicants and enrollments were further disrupted in 2020. Some students opted to sit out for a semester or year because they did not want to begin or continue their college educations online. Others were not able to begin or continue because they or a parent lost a job and the income needed to make attendance possible. As a result, there were declines in enrollment for most institutions, and deep declines for some, particularly two-year institutions.

Second, the pandemic disrupted not just the trends but also our strategies, at least temporarily. To counter the decline in enrollment likely to begin in the middle of this decade, higher education can reach out to underrepresented groups, as noted previously, to expand our applicant pools while also expanding access. During the pandemic, however, students from these groups have been the most likely to delay enrollment or seek work instead of postsecondary education. This may be a temporary phenomenon, although it raises concerns. The current labor market, characterized by the "great resignation" and the difficulty of employers finding workers, has signaled to some that immediate work may pay off better than prospective opportunities following college, at least in the short run. As institutions, we may need to return to the question of how we communicate the long-term value of a four-year degree.

Institutional Level

At the institutional level, we are all concerned about enrollment for two reasons. First, to meet our mission of serving students, families, our state, and nation, we need to recruit a critical mass of students who can succeed at our institutions. Second, the financial sustainability of our institutions depends to varying degrees on the tuition dollars that enrollment brings.

At UMBC we developed and implemented a strategic enrollment plan that sought to increase enrollment through both recruitment and retention. This work, with the support of external experts, began before the pandemic when the Strategic Enrollment Planning Steering Committee met from August 2019 to January 2020. The committee's plan established five-year targets for undergraduate and graduate enrollment headcounts by college and student type, retention rates, and graduation rates. As part of the target setting, the committee considered market forces, demographics, academic program plans, and the impact of these targets on net tuition revenue, incoming headcount, and total headcount.

An Implementation Committee co-chaired by the provost and the vice president of administration and finance then identified several near-term initiatives that would jumpstart the plan. The committee named initiative leads, identified goals and timelines, and established a structure for monitoring and supporting the efforts. The committee intended to have as big an impact as possible for fall 2020 and to build the foundation for ongoing growth. The timing was fortuitous, with the start of the pandemic early in our efforts. The work helped us to hold our fall 2020 enrollment "steady" (i.e., just a slight decrease) despite the shift to online courses. It then paved the way for substantial increases in first year and graduate enrollment and our largest incoming first-year undergraduate class by far in fall 2021. That fall, the number of first-time, first-year undergraduates at UMBC increased to 2,035, a 23 percent one-year increase and a 34 percent five-year increase. We are delighted with this outcome from our efforts. Major enhancements to student success initiatives further bolstered enrollment by impacting attrition that might have resulted in significant enrollment losses.

We built our plan around the unique characteristics, opportunities, and assets of UMBC. We started with a holistic approach to shoring up our recruitment, admissions, and marketing infrastructure. The near-term initiatives included investing in a new customer relationship management (CRM) system, enhancing our digital marketing resources, and short-term intensive actions to maximize both new fall 2020 enrollments and retention of current students. We also expanded our financial aid optimization strategies to enhance yield and retention outcomes.

To achieve our retention and graduation goals, we invested additional resources in our Student Success Center to help students perform better academically and increase retention. We hired additional academic advocates, developed an enhanced case management system for students being supported by academic advocates, and provided more support for transfer students. We also instituted a 90-credit degree audit for all students to ensure they remained on track for a degree. We created a "Finish Line" program, which allowed us to reconnect with students who had stopped out, enroll them in the courses they needed to graduate, and then support completion. We established new or updated graduate programs, including master in professional studies in software engineering and two certificate programs in industrial and organizational psychology and mechanical engineering.

Who Will Be Our Students?

Our student body continues to evolve. The students who are arriving on our campuses across the nation are more diverse, racially and ethnically, than ever. In just the past few years, UMBC has become a majority minority institution. While we have strived to support students of all backgrounds and achieve "inclusive excellence," we understand that this diversity has implications for how we support equity, inclusion, and student success. In addition, our students are now mainly from Gen Z (born 1995–2012). These students grew up with technology—laptops, smartphones, and social media—making them "digital natives" who rely on these devices more than ever. We will need to adapt to these characteristics in our students.

International students have been an important piece of the enrollment puzzle at many US higher education institutions for years. Indeed, some institutions have relied on increases in undergraduate and graduate enrollment of international students to sustain or even significantly increase enrollment. Thoughts about our ability to rely on these international students have fluctuated over time. In the late 1990s there was concern that we had allowed in too many international graduate students. After the terrorist attacks of September 11, 2001, there was a decrease in the number of international students in the United States, leading to concerns that we may actually be losing them to competition, especially from institutions in the United Kingdom, Canada, and Australia. The numbers then rebounded only to decline again during the Trump administration due to changes in visa regulations and then the pandemic, which closed our borders temporarily.

We do not have a crystal ball that will tell us what the future holds for international enrollment at our institutions. But at UMBC we have taken steps to support and grow our international student population. During the pandemic, we created a "Global Ambassadors Program" that recruited some of our international students in the United States to reach out to those who were taking classes at UMBC remotely from overseas. This effort sought to sustain our connections with overseas students and provide a sense of continued belonging to our community. Some international students were able to return to the United States, particularly in early 2021, provided they would quarantine for 14 days. Many international students found this requirement to be onerous financially. To relieve this concern, our Graduate Student Association (GSA) set aside sufficient GSA funds to rent a hotel block for use by our international students while they were in quarantine after arriving back in the United States. We have also developed a more robust infrastructure to support new and current international students.

Digital Tools for Course Delivery

During the spring of 2020, college and university administrators hastily devised plans to continue their academic programs, despite the urgent need to shut down their physical campuses. The subsequent sudden shift of courses to online instruction at most colleges made headlines. Some institutions moved to online instruction for the rest of the semester. Others, like UMBC, adopted a temporary shift to online instruction, only to make it permanent for the semester as the crisis clarified. By the fall of 2020 institutions began following diverse paths. At UMBC most of our classes remained online, though a small number met in person at least part of the term. We continued in this manner through the spring of 2021. For the fall of 2021 we moved to a mix of in-person, hybrid, and online instruction.

The dramatic shifts, first in 2020 to online instruction and then in 2021 to multimodal instruction, required urgent and then sustained work from faculty, staff, and students. For faculty, the move to online teaching was sudden, and for many it required the adoption of new technologies, course plans, pedagogical approaches, or all of the above. They then had to coach their students on how to use the technology and how to navigate a virtual course. Then, the second shift to a multimodal mix of in-person, hybrid, and online instruction proved to be just as dramatic and taxing. Faculty continued to reinvent their courses, now moving from online teaching to in-person or hybrid instruction. Regardless of which modality they formally used, many faculty also prepared content for delivery in multiple formats as students taking in-person classes who get sick have to catch up online. One faculty member asserted that, in effect, all classes are now "hybrid."

The Shift Online in 2020

As we helped faculty convert their courses to online instruction, we drew on digital resources we had invested in and deployed over the previous decade. We rolled out Blackboard, which provided faculty with functions such as a gradebook, online announcements, a discussion forum, and Collaborate video conferencing. We had also licensed Cisco's WebEx for virtual meetings that faculty could use for online classes, discussions, and meetings. Most important, DoIT and the Division of Professional Studies (DPS) had jointly developed and launched a program for training faculty who wanted to use technology for teaching a hybrid or online course. We would soon build on that. We were also in a relatively good position to roll out training because the Provost, DoIT, and DPS had partnered in 2019 to invest in instructional technology staffing and three new staff put us in a better position overall when we had to train faculty across all of our colleges.

In a short period, we were able to train faculty for teaching in the online environment. First, we rolled out short-term training in spring 2020 to help faculty successfully move their courses online in the middle of the semester. In particular, we focused on training faculty in the basic functions of using Blackboard, video conferencing, and effective online testing. Then, Sarah Shin, associate provost for academic affairs, convened a working group to develop initiatives for supporting faculty throughout the summer and into the fall of 2020. We developed and provided a comprehensive training we called Planning Instructional Variety in Online Teaching (PIVOT). In late April we began offering PIVOT training to faculty who would be teaching during the summer. In June and July we trained faculty who would be teaching in the fall. During this period, over 400 of our faculty, about 70 percent, participated in training, generally tailored to faculty in each college. Meanwhile, our Faculty Development Center (FDC) offered faculty who were transitioning to online teaching the opportunity to take pedagogical training that would improve their teaching techniques both generally and in the online space.

Faculty took our PIVOT Live training over a week through five 60-minute webinars: (1) preparing to teach online, (2) active learning strategies for online classes, (3) engaging students and building online community, (4) reconceptualizing online assessments, and (5) supporting students and monitoring progress. As an incentive to faculty to participate, we provided a stipend to those who completed all five modules. For more advanced faculty, we also offered PIVOT+, which is a self-paced course of ten modules taken over 10 days. Twenty-five PIVOT faculty mentors who had previously taken the DPS training for online teaching led faculty discipline-based learning communities across our three colleges. The administration supported this effort, compensating mentors for their time and providing stipends to faculty who took the PIVOT training course.[12]

Training faculty in instructional technology has had a positive impact:[13]

- Nearly 85 percent of faculty participants said PIVOT was helpful for their pedagogical shift to online teaching.
- For fall 2020 students gave faculty who had completed PIVOT training higher "Student Evaluation of Educational Quality" scores.
- Courses taught by PIVOT-trained instructors had increased Blackboard interactions, which indicates improved engagement.
- Faculty who participated in PIVOT Live or completed PIVOT+ were more likely to be open to alternative course delivery formats in fall 2021.

Our programs adapted to the online environment as well. The Meyerhoff Scholars Program moved its six-week summer bridge online for its fall 2020 entering cohort of freshmen. During the summer bridge, new Meyerhoff Scholars take courses in mathematics, science, and the humanities. The program engages them in meetings, lectures, and cultural events. The bridge provides an opportunity for the new Scholars to develop a sense of community and teaches them about time management, study skills, and problem solving. Since the program was virtual, staff could not offer all of the usual activities. Therefore, they innovated. For one thing, they involved alumni not in the Baltimore area in the online sessions. These alums gave talks about their experiences, careers, and practical skills such as how to work in a lab or keep a lab notebook. We may keep this innovation when the program is in person again.

The Shift to Multimodal Teaching in the 2021–2022 Academic Year

Before the pandemic, about 5 percent of our students took courses offered online, and just 1 percent took all of their courses online. The overwhelming majority of our students—95 percent—took all of their courses in person, with some minor variation by college. This was typical of a public research university with a residential campus and contrasted sharply with the University of Maryland Global Campus (UMGC), whose domestic students take almost all of their courses online.

We have had two dramatic shifts in modality in the years since. With the pandemic, of course, the 2020–2021 academic year looked very different. We offered almost all of our courses online. Then, as our campus reopened for the 2021–2022 academic year, we shifted toward a multimodal model. Most of our courses were in person for 2021–2022, but there remained a healthy mix of in-person, hybrid, and online instruction, and most students were taking at least one course fully online. For fall 2021 about 10 percent of our students took three or more courses online, about two-thirds took one or two courses fully online, and one-quarter took only in-person or hybrid courses with none fully online.

The conditions of the pandemic, including the rapid rise of the Delta variant in fall 2021 and the Omicron variant in the spring of 2022, deeply affected the 2021–2022 academic year. Some of the continued use of online and hybrid course delivery in fall 2021 was due to concerns about new variants and the possibility of break-through cases. Also, the many safety protocols we had in place con-tinued to constrain our instructional modes. For example, we still had reduced classroom capacities in effect that made it almost im-possible for faculty to offer many of our large lecture courses in person. It would have been wrong, therefore, to conclude that the mix of modalities that emerged for the 2021–2022 academic year would remain once we lifted classroom capacity constraints in ef-fect for that academic year. In fact, the improved availability of vaccines and boosters together with the high rate of vaccination among our campus community allowed the classroom constraints to be removed by the early summer of 2022, and this gave rise to a significant reduction in online courses as our larger lecture the-aters could now be fully utilized.

That said, the public health constraints do not explain the variation in modalities that we began to see in the fall of 2021. Faculty in the natural sciences, computer science, and engineering are more likely to teach in person than are their counterparts in the arts, humanities, and social sciences. Presumably, this is in part because programs and courses involving laboratory research or technology are best taught that way.

However, this does not entirely hold at the graduate level. Faculty in our College of Engineering and Information Technology continue to teach the majority of their graduate courses fully online (54 percent), particularly in information systems and computer science. The online nature of these courses reflected both the ability to offer those courses in that modality and the demand for online courses in those fields from graduate students. Students in information systems have increased demand for online sections of graduate courses, with 80 percent of graduate sections in that department now online.

In the fall of 2021, at the undergraduate level, the percentage of courses that were hybrid was very low, but 73 percent of faculty responding to a survey in October 2021 said that their biggest challenge was offering content in more than one format. At first glance, this seems anomalous, as fewer than 10 percent of courses offered were officially hybrid. However, we required our students who experienced breakthrough COVID-19 infections and their contacts to shift from in-person or hybrid to online learning in the middle of a semester. To address this, many faculty—regardless of the official modality of the course—prepared for this eventuality. The steps they took included hi-flex delivery, which involves simultaneous in-person and online course delivery. Or, they recorded lectures and posted the recordings online afterward, which, in effect, means an in-person course becomes an asynchronous hybrid. Whatever approach they take, the time they invested in course delivery increased (estimates of increased time vary from 50 to 100 percent more.

Lessons Learned

About a decade ago, many pundits predicted that technology would disrupt higher education. The media wrote articles and conference organizers brought together panels of experts to talk about how technology would change academia. We shared a particular fascination with MOOCs (massive, open, online courses) and startups—the "shiny objects" that would bring online teaching into the mainstream. Books argued that college would be "unbundled," skills outcomes would be more important than courses ("butts in seats"), and bits and bytes would replace bricks and mortar. This has not happened, at least not in the way and to the extent predicted.

We have now lived through a large, unplanned experiment in the use of technology in education. We have experienced the accelerated adoption of technology. We have seen successes and challenges. We have formed judgments about what works, what does not, and what can be used going forward, often in novel ways. Faculty are now using those technologies that work that they had not used previously or they are using them more intensively, even as they shift to hybrid or in-person teaching.

We should bear in mind that the student experience during the shift among course modalities has been mixed and uneven. On the bright side, the overwhelming majority of UMBC students (84 percent) reported that online instruction went well in spring 2020. The process of moving classes online was a human and communal process that could be quite positive. One English professor related:

> I'm very proud of my English students this semester [spring 2020]. When the hammer dropped in mid-March, they immediately stepped up with their internet knowledge, much greater than mine, and suggested ways to keep the class spirit alive. We moved online on several "platforms," and it really was a wonderful experience. An interesting effect of our online communications was that as we spoke from our homes to one another, we got to know each other much more

intimately than I ever experienced when classes met face to face. There was a sense of mutual caretaking. . . . That seminar was titled "The Discourses of Happiness," so the subject matter lent itself to thinking about big life issues requiring just that.[14]

We saw this experience repeated in other classes.

Some students found online learning convenient given their schedules or discovered benefits in online learning, such as asynchronous access to recorded lectures and other resources. Some students have even thrived in the online environment. For example, we have launched a new initiative called "Finish Line." Through this program, our enrollment management team reached out to former UMBC students who had stopped out of their studies just short of earning a bachelor's degree. Many of these students showed immediate interest and, with the right academic and financial support, re-enrolled. Because almost all of our courses were online at the time of the program launch, the Finish Line students pursued the final courses they needed remotely, which they said actually worked best for most of them as they had other work and family responsibilities.

The higher education press, however, has featured a series of articles about student disengagement during the pandemic, and some students have not thrived in the online environment. They missed the in-person learning experience or found online learning less conducive to their learning style. They had difficulty keeping pace and focus in new or stressful circumstances. They faced inconsistent practices. For example, faculty used different online tools, so students sometimes needed to learn how to use several applications or conferencing platforms.

Faculty have reported that the student transition to online learning and back to in-person classes has been challenging. There has been an increase in students who find it challenging to manage their time or complete tasks on time, have difficulty focusing in the online environment, send email messages to faculty seeking clarification of content or assignments, and request more time extensions for assignments and papers. Many students do not turn their cameras on for online instruction. One faculty member, responding to an open-ended question in a faculty workload survey, wrote, "I had to prepare for online versions of the courses. I had to answer a lot more emails. So many students submitted assignments late. Workload increased during shutdowns . . . Much of the increased load hasn't gone away with the return to campus—it just became the new normal. The administrative load is massive and my inbox is full of students with Situations."[15]

Here are some lessons learned for the future about use of digital tools in higher education to create positive experiences and outcomes for both students and faculty.[16]

First, the rapid transition from in-person to online teaching and the subsequent transition from online to a mix of modalities has produced failures we should discard and innovations that we should keep. For example, teaching a single course in multiple modes—commonly called hi-flex—is very hard to accomplish effectively. Hi-flex requires advanced technology and training and contradicts what many acknowledge to be some of the components of good pedagogical practice. Some faculty are finding instead that other types of hybrid courses, such as holding one class per week in person and another online, are more practical and effective. This is similar to the existing pedagogical practice of the flipped classroom, and faculty can use it effectively if done right. We continue to innovate. We have new efforts underway in asynchronous lecture capture and the development of new approaches to online testing.

Second, we should judge the effectiveness of courses based on their student learning outcomes not just their deployment of technology. Faculty can enhance teaching and learning through the design of their courses, regardless of the way they deliver them (in person, hybrid, online). Faculty who learn to use technology for course delivery often find themselves reflecting on course design as well as digital tools. As John Fritz, associate vice president for instructional technology, has observed, "To be intentional about the use of technology is to think critically about one's teaching assumptions and practice, and if or how they can or should be changed to help students learn." UMBC has a strong history of course redesign that has enhanced student outcomes, and this latest period of innovation may advance our work further.

Third, we must continue to think about ways to improve the student experience. UMBC's Fostering Online Learning Improvement and Opportunity (FOLIO) working group comprising students, staff, and faculty provided training and support to students encountering new modes of instruction. For example, the FOLIO group established a website with available services and resources in one place and tools to help faculty promote effective engagement in their online classes. They also provided students with tips for online learning, such as participation, asking questions, connecting with the instructor, teaching assistant (TA), or other students, staying engaged with asynchronous courses, and avoiding multitasking during class time.[17]

Fourth, we benefited from a culture of collaboration in our deployment of technology and our transitions among modalities of course delivery. Partnerships among the provost's office, DoIT, and DPS provided a strong foundation from which to build during a crisis: digital tools, instructional technology staff, and a training program. The willingness of DoIT to work with faculty led to a cadre of faculty trained in instructional technology who, in a moment of urgent online transition, served as liaisons between their faculty colleagues and the staff who supported the transition to online teaching.

Fifth, most faculty teach the way they were taught. Most older faculty were not likely taught with technology, so providing training to faculty online let them experience online learning for themselves and understand how their students would experience their courses in an online format. While faculty may learn from any instructor, they may feel more comfortable learning about technology from other faculty (particularly in their own department) who understand the specifics of course delivery in their field.

Sixth, at this point in the transition away from fully online instruction, we are finding that "hybrid" courses take many different shapes. Some of the permutations we have seen include the follow-ing: two course meetings per week, with one in-person and a second online; course lectures online, with discussion sections in person (or the reverse); the first two weeks of course meetings online and the rest of the semester in person; hi-flex mode, in which a course is offered simultaneously in person and online, or in person with recorded lectures posted afterward for asynchronous viewing; two sections of a course, one held in person and one held online; and flipped classes with prerecorded lectures posted in advance of in-person sessions. Surely, there are other variations.

Similarly, while the above discussion of course modality focuses on whether class meetings are in person or online or some of each, professors and instructors use technology for course delivery in other ways as well. Tools now available and in use include the following:

- Learning management systems (LMS) (Blackboard, Google Classroom, etc.)
- Online gradebooks (Blackboard, Google Classroom, etc.)
- Virtual meeting platforms (Blackboard Collaborate, WebEx, Zoom, Discord, etc.)
- Video (Vimeo, YouTube, etc., for lecture recordings, docu-mentaries, and so on)
- Clickers and Survey applications (Slido, etc.)
- Lecture slides (PowerPoint, Google Slides)
- Virtual laboratories, GPS applications, software development tools, online games
- Statistical applications (R, Stata, SPSS, SPS, etc.)
- Online datasets (ICPSR, Dataverse, US Census, Vital Rec-ords, etc.)
- Digital articles, books, archives, census records, exhibits, and more
- Email, texting, announcements, discussion/message forums (Blackboard, Slack, etc.)
- Wikis, blogs
- Testing applications

When instructors post syllabi, grades, announcements, assignments, discussion questions, recorded lectures, PowerPoint slides,
digital tools and resources, and tests and exams, or responds to discussions, emails, and texts, they have used technology to enhance
course delivery.

Student Success

Both faculty and staff play critical roles in student success.
When faculty improve their teaching and course delivery, they are
more successful in transferring knowledge and skills. When staff
have the tools necessary to engage students who are struggling,
they are more successful in providing the just in time resources
and guidance that support student retention and progress.

Course Design

Course delivery is as critical as course content when it comes to
teaching and learning, and we should pay more attention to this in
all of its dimensions.[18] The quality of instruction affects learning,
grades, inclusion and equity, persistence and completion, and student aspirations. It is a given that faculty must have subject matter
knowledge to provide quality instruction, but they must also have
general and discipline-specific teaching skills.

We now have considerable research on how students learn, with
tested examples of pedagogical and course innovations that work.
Peter Felten, John Gardner, and their colleagues have shared that research on learning has established that certain pedagogies and
practices are effective with both struggling undergraduates and all
students. Beth McMurtrie, writing in *The Chronicle of Higher Education*, echoes this, noting, "Scholarship on teaching and learning has
grown exponentially over the decades, encompassing thousands of
experiments, stacks of books and journal articles, and major initiatives to bring the science of learning to the classroom. Yet many
faculty members are untouched by this work, unsure how to apply

it to their teaching, or skeptical of its value."[19] "Our challenge," Felten and Gardner write, "is no longer simply to ascertain what it is we need to do; our challenge now is to do it."[20]

We have tools for improving teaching and learning. At the graduate level, we can incorporate training on pedagogy and teaching in doctoral programs and ensure doctoral students have preservice training and experience. We can establish professional development programs for faculty that provide insights on how people learn, pedagogical training, and mentoring on course redesign.[21]

It is not a new insight that, while our doctoral students often go on to positions in which they teach, our graduate programs do not always include explicit instruction in pedagogy and teaching. In 1993 the Council of Graduate Schools and the Association of American Colleges and Universities launched the Preparing Future Faculty (PFF) program to prepare graduate students for research, teaching, and service. Yet, change in higher education can be slow. In 2019 Cathy Davidson, professor of English at the City University of New York's Graduate Center, crowdsourced a list of programs that offer pedagogical instruction for graduate students. The list had a considerable number of programs, "humanities heavy," and Davidson said that the next step was to ask programs not on the list why they are not. "It seems irresponsible not to require some form of pedagogical training, whether a course or some other intensive training, for your own graduate students who are teaching your own undergraduates."[22]

At best, we expect graduate students to pick up teaching methods and skills by observing their professors and serving as teaching assistants. Colleen Flaherty has written that it is understood that graduate students will go on to teach, but that "graduate education has historically treated this fact as a kind of inconvenient truth, overlooking or flat out ignoring students' need for pedagogical training. That's explicit pedagogical training, not the sink-or-swim method adopted by so many programs that throw their graduate student instructors into teaching undergraduates with no real preparation."[23] We can do better.

The field of cognitive science has provided useful insights since the 1990s on how students learn. Formal courses for graduate students that provide general knowledge of how people learn, pedagogical skills, and discipline-specific teaching insights are now available and an imperative as we focus on helping students succeed. "A graduate seminar on teaching and pedagogy doesn't, and . . . perhaps shouldn't, be treated as 'professional training,' as the scholarship on teaching and learning provides ample space for [disciplinary] discussions and contributions," write Jessey Wright and Melissa Jacquart.[24]

Inside Higher Ed has provided two examples of programs that require pedagogical instruction for graduate students. The School of Economics at Georgia Tech requires all teaching assistants to take a two-course sequence in teaching fundamentals and course design. Berkeley requires graduate instructors to take a pedagogy course and participate in a daylong teaching conference.[25]

At UMBC, we have taken steps to support graduate student pedagogical training. As part of the August graduate student orientation activities, we have a daylong preparation for TAs that is required of new TAs and open to continuing TAs. Participants get a broad introduction to pedagogy, information about our systems and available resources, and time to spend with experienced TAs who offer insider information on lab management, grading, and so forth.

We have also joined NSF's Center for the Integration of Research, Teaching, and Learning (CIRTL) network and established a center on our campus. NSF established CIRTL to improve undergraduate STEM education by improving faculty teaching. CIRTL has mainly focused on graduate students and postdoctorate fellows, with a few early career faculty in the mix. Through workshops and courses on our campus and access to the national CIRTL network, our graduate students and postdocs access knowledge and skills about teaching and learning that enhance the student experience. We provide a learning community, share best practice, and award certifications.[26]

The movement to disseminate new approaches to teaching and learning and new models for course design is now more than two decades old, yet we in higher education are still in the process of convincing faculty to adopt new techniques. We must do more to support our faculty as they learn about and adopt new approaches to teaching across disciplines, particularly for introductory courses. The list of techniques that faculty can use to support student learning has grown to include flipped classrooms, active learning, problem-based learning, group- or team-based learning, experiential learning, interactive lectures, and asynchronous lectures and resources. UMBC's Faculty Development Center has provided faculty the space and time to develop their pedagogical skills and redesign their courses. The Center administers the Hrabowski Innovation Fund, which provides funding and advice to faculty engaged in course innovation activities.

These approaches support not only knowledge acquisition but also a range of skills. Using them, faculty can teach their students how to listen actively and constructively, think independently, and have difficult conversations. They can develop their research methods, understanding and use of evidence, and ability to communicate orally and in writing. Excellent teachers also find ways to promote interaction among students who are diverse (as we do in our Chemistry Discovery Center, which randomly assigns students to four-person study groups). They also engage students, not just in class, but also by pulling students into their research and creative projects.

During the pandemic, faculty and students experienced changes in course delivery, financial insecurity, COVID anxiety, family deaths and episodes of isolation, stress, and exhaustion. Cumulative stress has placed strains on our minds and bodies, affecting behavior, including teaching and learning. Beth McMurtrie, writing in the *Chronicle of Higher Education*, relates how many students today are disconnected from their courses and college experience. Students turn their cameras off for online courses, they frequently miss classes online or in-person, they miss assignment due dates or fail to hand them in at all, and they are retaining less of what they are taught. A sizeable number of students are struggling.[27]

We may be seeing a disturbing divergence in student outcomes at this juncture. Stephanie Riegg Cellini of Brookings reviewed recent literature on performance in online courses and concluded, "Online coursework generally yields worse student performance than in-person coursework. The negative effects of online course-taking are particularly pronounced for less-academically prepared students and for students pursuing bachelor's degrees."[28] Students who normally do well tend to perform well or better in online courses, but those who do not do as well to begin with—those who are less academically prepared, for example—tend to perform worse. If you recruit your student population from the top 10 percent of high school graduates, then this may not be much of an issue. For those institutions whose students are diverse in their academic preparation and motivation, this may be of great concern.

What are faculty doing to help students reconnect, increase their motivation, and learn? Faculty are beginning by creating opportunities for students to build relationships and a sense of community. Group projects, team-based learning, and study groups provide opportunities for students to connect with each other. Faculty are also using active learning to help students stay interested and focused. Shorter lectures, more activities, field trips, and podcasts allow students to learn in digestible chunks of time and through active, problem-based, or "real world" experiences that provide meaning and interest.[29]

David Asai, Bruce Alberts, and Janet Coffey have suggested another reason to redesign courses, in particular Introduction to Biology: broader appreciation for science, the scientific method, and scientific evidence. A large fraction of the US population have rejected COVID-19 vaccines, resulting in many preventable deaths. This fact, they argue, is evidence of a "shocking failure of science to produce citizens who understand and respect scientific evidence." They note that each year 1 million college students enroll in introductory biology, providing an opportunity to address this situation. Many of these courses have been taught as "weed out" courses. Faculty could redesign these courses, offering a "powerful way to nurture a widespread respect for science, as well as for diversifying the academic profession." They continue, "The restructured courses should empower their students through active learning pedagogies and replace their standard 'cookbook' laboratories with course-based research experiences—such as those from Tiny Earth, the Genomics Education Partnership, and Phage Hunters Advancing Genomics and Evolutionary Science."[30]

Faculty are including empowerment and agency in courses. For example, the difference between your grandfather's civics class and your daughter's is that the former focused on teaching what the political system looks like and how it operates while the latter not only teaches that but also empowers students to take ownership of the system and change it.[31] As another example, a multidisciplinary team on our campus, funded by a Hrabowski Innovation Grant, has developed "Preventing Gender-Based Harm at UMBC," a 3-credit first-year seminar "educating undergraduate students about gender-based harm at all levels of society, and empowering them to create change. In addition to traditional academic content . . . on gender-based harm and its impact, students will learn healthy relationship practices and skills through evidence-based prevention models and will exercise the knowledge they glean over the course of the semester through hands-on projects encouraging civic engagement and community activism."[32]

This work is critical. Freeman Hrabowski has urged, "Student success is not only passing a course, but also passing the next one that requires it." That is, faculty must teach students in such a way that they learn, retain, and build on the material in their class. This requires faculty to teach students how to learn. Hermann Ebbinghaus, an early pioneer in the study of memory, created what he called the learning curve and the forgetting curve, both exponential. The learning curve suggests that there are steep increases in knowledge at first and that over time, the acquisition of knowledge levels out. The less well-known forgetting curve postulates that with the passage of time, we forget what we learn, with the drop in retention steepest in the first day. The insight suggests that rote memorization and cramming for a test do not lead to substantial long-term gains in knowledge. "Spaced practice," which uses regular, repetitive, smaller study and practice, promotes long-term proficiency.[33] Beth McMurtrie writes, "Learning and other evidence-based practices, such as building more small assignments, or scaffolding, into the syllabus, have been shown to close performance gaps and help all students succeed."[34]

The pandemic has been one motivator for course redesign. During the pandemic, our Faculty Development Center also offered faculty who were pivoting to online teaching a complementary course in pedagogical approaches to the online environment. This proved popular as the switch in modalities brought the issue of pedagogy to the fore. Indeed, faculty have shared that they are now more aware of the pedagogical aspects of teaching in whatever modality they are working.

Services Supporting Student Success

While the shift to online instruction grabbed the headlines during the pandemic, institutions have continued the long-term work of supporting student academic success. For example, Steven Mintz, professor of history at the University of Texas and former director of the University of Texas System's Institute for Transformational Learning, has outlined "common sense student success strategies" to support persistence and completion. He urges institutions to simplify degree pathways, identify and remove curricular bottlenecks, support the transfer process, connect students to opportunities that foster a sense of belonging, and address academic inequities through summer bridge programs or peer-led study groups. He also encourages institutions to "support departments that want to reimagine and reengineer degree pathways" and to "reimagine advising and support services."[35]

When we improve advising and student support services, we engage struggling students with the people, programs, and resources that can make a difference in their retention, completion, and life outcomes. Mintz suggests "working with faculty to identify students at risk of failure; incorporating time management and study skills strategies into lower division courses; reaching out to students who shift majors or transfer in; creating one-stop access assistance with finances, registration, and other support services; instituting a tiered approach to academic support that includes supplemental instruction, peer-led study groups, and peer-tutoring, especially in bottleneck courses; and have a 'graduation concierge to help near completers cross the finish line.'"[36]

With 125 members, the Association of Public and Land-grant Universities (APLU) has created the "Powered by Publics" Initiative. This program focuses on affordability, teaching and learning, and holistic student support.[37]

At UMBC we continued to push forward with other innovations to support student success in our academic program. We had already accomplished much at UMBC over the past 30 years, as we have previously discussed in *The Empowered University*. Through a series of innovations, we supported both high-achieving students and those who were struggling. We simultaneously doubled our 6-year completion rate for all students (from 35 percent in the late-1980s to 70 percent today) and implemented initiatives that made us the undergraduate institution that sends more Black undergraduates on to earn PhDs in the natural sciences and engineering than any other. Our innovations included robust programming for the first-year experience, the formation of living-learning communities, the creation of an Honors College and discipline-focused scholars programs, the Meyerhoff Scholars Program for diversity in STEM, and the redesign of introductory courses across our three colleges.

At the end of a three-year process, UMBC's Strategic Planning Committee issued a final report in December 2015 that addressed four areas: the Student Experience; Curriculum and Pedagogy; Research, Scholarship and Creative Achievement; and Community and Extended Connections. We set the following as the primary goal for the student experience: "Create vibrant, exceptional, and comprehensive undergraduate and graduate student experiences that integrate in- and out-of-classroom learning to prepare graduates for meaningful careers and civic and personal lives." To realize this overarching goal, we set further specific goals: increasing degree completion, improving advising, providing more applied learning experiences, and enabling students to obtain cultural and global competencies.[38]

We began implementing initiatives to achieve these goals in 2016 and were still in the midst of this work in early 2020 when the COVID-19 public health crisis arrived and might have derailed our efforts. Despite the distraction, we continued this work during our pandemic response as it remained important in its own right. We also supported a complementary initiative, the strategic enrollment plan (SEP). The SEP focused on achieving enrollment goals through enhancements to marketing, recruitment, admissions, and retention, the last of which intersects with our work to increase student success. To increase student success—as measured by retention and completion—we focused on academic progress and advising. We also enhanced programs for students at risk for failing or leaving.

Regarding advising, the strategic planning group that focused on the student experience reported:

> Stakeholders say that advising and mentoring of students is uneven. Some areas of the advising community get high marks, such as orientation advising. Some academic departments reportedly do an excellent job of curricular advising and mentoring of students headed to graduate school, into the job market or participating in research. However, other academic departments have a reputation for doing poorly in these vital areas. Not all units embrace and/or utilize online advising tools. In short, the quality of advising and mentoring seems to vary widely by unit, as well as by individual.[39]

At UMBC our Office of Academic and Pre-professional Advising provides academic advising to students who have not yet declared a major or have decided they will go on to a professional school. Our colleges and their departments provide advising to those students who have declared a major. During our strategic planning process, we learned that the quality of advising and mentoring was uneven across these organizations and departments. In *The Empowered University*, we discussed how we had discovered the same sort of unevenness across departments for both promotion and tenure guidelines and parental leave, so this unevenness was not a surprise. In response, we formed an Advising Task Force in 2016 that assessed previous work in this area and provided new recommendations in 2018. We then implemented a series of innovations to improve both the advising offered and student understanding of college planning.

Regarding academic progress, the strategic planning group that focused on the student experience also reported:

> Stakeholders observe that it can be difficult to meet curriculum requirements and make steady progress through their degree programs. Roughly 80% of students say that they have been unable to register for required courses because they are either full or not offered. About 40% of students have not been able to take a course because of the time it is offered. Some 20% of incoming students say they are neutral, dissatisfied, or very dissatisfied with their academic schedule. Undergraduate program directors report problems scheduling classes because of the interdependency of curricula, conflicts between required courses, and limited classroom availability.[40]

We have crunched the data to understand better the academic progress of our students. We are now restarting prepandemic conversations about interventions to improve course availability and scheduling.

We have implemented a range of innovations from 2016 to the present to improve student success.[41] We established an Undergraduate Student Success and Persistence Committee (USSPC) charged with identifying interventions to support persistence and completion. We developed and implemented a new MATH 104 pathway for non-STEM majors and a plan to better align study abroad opportunities with major course requirements. We launched "The Major

Event" in fall 2018 to help students learn about programs across UMBC and a "Finish 15" campaign that encourages students to take at least 15 credits per semester, the minimum needed on average to complete in four years. We have increased student participation in the summer bridge program that gives students a head start on the first year. Inspired by our success with this, we have also implemented a new winter bridge for students who start in the spring semester. We now require first-year students to take a mandatory first year experience course and for all students we now require a 90-hour degree audit check.

At the graduate level, we have implemented efforts to help students along their paths as well. First, we joined the PhD Career Pathways Project of the Council of Graduate Schools and the Coalition for Next Generation Life Science. We promoted use of student progression data by graduate program directors. We conducted alumni and graduate student surveys and briefed faculty on survey outcomes. On the graduate school website, we have posted enrollment, graduation, and career outcomes data for biomedical sciences programs.

During the pandemic, the university took additional steps to support graduate students. We allowed master's and doctoral students to defend their theses online. We helped students whose research and degree progress were disrupted by the pandemic. When the department supported it, we granted time extensions. We allocated increased funding so that we could offer a higher number of dissertation fellowships. Some departments reduced the number of admitted students so that they could have enough support for continuing students whose progress slowed when the pandemic disrupted research. Emeritus Professor Bill Rothstein endowed a graduate student emergency fund that was augmented through other gifts.

The Graduate School lets each program decide whether to require the GRE and how to use it in admissions. During the pandemic, those graduate programs that required the GRE had waived it. Campus-wide discussion of the future use of GRE scores in graduate admissions now focuses on the extent to which the use of GREs in admissions affects diversity, equity, and inclusion.

We also improved our advising program in several ways to better support students. We enhanced advising staff capacity by better defining expectations and revising standards. We implemented training for both new and continuing advisors and created an academic advisor career ladder. We also developed online tools to support advising: an advising dashboard providing advisors with an overview of the student's background, major, and goals; dashboards for colleges to track student progression; the student advising planner, a tool to support student advising and academic planning; the visual degree audit, a tool that allows students and faculty to quickly determine whether students are on track to complete degree and certificate requirements; and a co-curricular dashboard, to track co-curricular engagement and target interventions for "non-engaged" students who are at higher risk for dropping out.

Our enrollment and financial aid offices implemented initiatives to support retention and completion. For example, our efforts to help students in special circumstances, such as a registration hold due to an unpaid bill, students whose family income is just above Pell eligibility, and transfer students who have already used all of their available federal aid, to overcome financial challenges that impede persistence.

Today, we remain focused on improving our student success work. We recently joined the University Innovation Alliance (UIA), a group of public research universities dedicated to increasing the number and diversity of college graduates. The UIA is an alliance that shares best practices focused on supporting first-generation, underrepresented, and low-income students, with a goal of increasing graduation rates for these and other students.[42]

In addition to the work described above designed to support all students, we have recently established the Academic Success Center (ASC) to support students who may be at risk of failure or dropping out based on certain indicators. The ASC, under the Dean of Undergraduate Academic Affairs, coordinates academic support services, including policy, support, advocacy, and tutoring. It includes the Office of Academic Advocacy, which is staffed with academic advocates who work proactively with at-risk students. To implement our strategic plan goals, we have increased the number of advocates. Before the pandemic, these advocates implemented a university-wide intervention to meet with all students who have four or more course repeats. During the pandemic, they met virtually with students, discovering that more students will go online to meet with advocates than will come in to the office to meet with them. So, having learned this lesson, we will continue to offer virtual meetings.

Going forward, our academic success effort will continue its broad work while also focusing on particular groups we have identified as needing further support. To increase retention from the first to second year, our advisors and advocates will focus on first-years who have not declared a major (3 to 4 percent of students, 20 percent of attrition) or who are on probation due to low GPAs (3 percent of students, 20 percent of attrition). To support the success of transfer students, advisors will make a focused effort to extend to transfer students the enhanced support they have implemented for students in general. While Black first-year students have completion rates at or above the median rate for all first-year students, Black transfer students have a lower completion rate than other transfer students. We will extend special support to this group to further boost retention and completion. Unlike most institutions, UMBC has more men than women in its student population, and those men have a lower six-year completion rate than for women. We will investigate why this is and design interventions to help correct course.

Last, we also focus attention on the preK-12 pathway to college. The Sherman Family Foundation recently gave UMBC its largest gift to date of $21 million to establish the Betsy & George Sherman Center to advance excellence in urban schools. This funding will allow us to expand and integrate our work in teacher preparation, in developing partnerships with local schools, and applying the outcomes of educational research to improve both early childhood education and student learning outcomes.[43] This work complements other work at UMBC also funded by the Shermans to improve science and mathematics education in challenging urban school environments.[44]

Data Analytics

We can also use data analytics to understand whether students are progressing and, if not, why and how to intervene. Nationally, more than 1,400 colleges and universities are using predictive analytics to address issues like student retention and low graduation rates.[45] Institutions can use their data to shape programs and courses or to intervene with specific students who are at risk of dropping out or who would benefit from advice on anything from what majors they might enjoy and succeed in to how to find tutoring to support learning in a particular course.

Purdue University is deploying data analytics in this manner. Brent Drake, chief data officer at Purdue, recently described how they nudge students by showing them comparative data about their behaviors.

> We can look at malleable behaviors predictive of success on campus, then send messages to the students about them. Factors that can help with their success in class, like providing GPA comparisons to students who have been successful in their majors in the past; whether they're attending class; whether they have a high Internet usage rate while they're in class, which would imply that they're not paying attention to the lectures; their tardiness to class; whether they're logging in to the learning management system proportionately to their class requirements; and whether they're using the discussion board topics in the class. We provide information about the historical relationship between those behaviors and their ultimate success on campus. Then, when they log in, they see their individual data points in relation to

other students in their course or in their major or across the university.[46]

Providing these data, Drake believes, helps account for recent increases in Purdue's student retention and completion rates.

At UMBC we have a long tradition of using assessment and evaluation to understand how well our initiatives are working. For example, we built evaluation into our Meyerhoff Scholars Program from its inception using a mixed-methods approach that combines quantitative analysis with qualitative methods. We have used institutional data, survey data, focus groups, and interviews to understand how students fare in their programs and afterward. For Meyerhoff, we used the evaluation to look at student progress, outcomes (GPAs, test scores), commitment to a PhD, identification as a scientist, self-efficacy as a researcher, and outcomes from doctoral education. We have also deployed evaluation to understand other initiatives, such as our work funded by grants from NIH's BUILD program and NSF's i-Cubed program. This type of evaluation is critical both for program improvement and for proof of concept, which can establish a program as a national model.

For more than a decade, we have built on this experience with program evaluation to create data analytic tools that help us understand and improve our academic program more generally. Long before most other universities, DoIT, the office of enrollment management, and the Office of Institutional Research, Analysis, and Decision Support pioneered the development of a data warehouse that brought into one database information from data sources across the campus. This warehouse, nicknamed REX, has provided us the opportunity to understand student learning, persistence, and completion across colleges, departments, and programs and to analyze how specific cohorts of students were faring.

We have more recently augmented these resources by creating a data analytics unit the Analytics, Business Intelligence, and Student Success Technologies Group—within the office of the provost, led by economist Bob Carpenter, a former president of the faculty senate. This group is highly collaborative in nature, working with campus partners in nearly all of their work. They worked with Enrollment Management and many others on the development and use of a new customer relationship management (CRM) system. They worked with Undergraduate Academic Affairs on the development of an Academic Advocates Case Management System. During the COVID-19 pandemic, they supported campus efforts to track COVID-19 testing and created reports and resources for faculty showing whether and how students were engaging in online courses. The group has also recently invested in HelioCampus, a robust tool for data analytics and visualization.

With regard to academic success, the Analytics group has taken the initiative on several promising projects. They developed a model for predicting the probability that new freshmen will graduate within six years. This model informs staff in our Academic Success Center with plans for academic retention efforts, based on specific student characteristics. To support the Undergraduate Student Success and Persistence Committee (USSPC) charged with identifying interventions to support persistence and completion, the Analytics group has explored student progression at UMBC. Specifically, they have studied how degree pathways and course scheduling affect time to degree, retention, and graduation, identifying bottlenecks in course planning, classroom availability, and scheduling.

The Analytics group has also provided analytics mini-grants to five faculty that allow them to identify and exchange effective practices in the use of data to inform teaching. They partner with the faculty grant recipients to collect, analyze, and use data in course assessment. Tara Carpenter, principal lecturer in our Department of Chemistry, is one of the recipients of a mini-grant. She is examining practices that support deeper learning by moving students along the continuum from memorization to understanding, application, analysis, evaluation, and creation.[47]

We base our vision for data analytics on the notion that information is both a strategic and a tactical asset. If we can get the right information to the right person at the right time, we can provide "intelligent" advice. However, according to Bob Carpenter, the Analytics group needs to curate information strategically, quickly filter that information to meet faculty needs, and present information in a way that reveals patterns that faculty and staff can understand and act on.[48]

Curriculum (Or What Students Need to Know)

Student support, course design, and content delivery all matter. So does the content. Indeed, the social, economic, and political upheaval of this period has pushed us to think more deeply about what it means to be educated in the twenty-first century.

In November 2017 the American Academy of Arts & Sciences (AAA&S) released "The Future of Undergraduate Education: The Future of America." The report asserted that students should "graduate with skills and credentials that help them to succeed personally and professionally, and to navigate the challenges that they will face in their work, families, and communities."[49] How do we prepare students to navigate a world shaped by globalization, technological change, demographic shifts, terrorism and war, a pandemic, and climate change? How do we set them up for success in a world of increasing uncertainty?

We begin by creating opportunities for students to acquire scholarly knowledge and practical skills in broad areas of inquiry. Most, though not all, of our institutions have general education programs to ensure our students, in the liberal arts tradition, are broadly educated beyond the deep knowledge of a particular discipline they get from their majors. These requirements engage our students in the arts and humanities, to give them experience with analyzing texts, artistic works, and historical artifacts, and with producing creative works of writing, art, and history. They require engagement with languages, other cultures, and inter-cultural communication. They involve studies in the social sciences so that they better understand individuals, groups, and institutions, the development and implementation of public policy, and social science research methods. They oblige students to take quantitative courses that develop problem solving, logical reasoning, and mathematical concepts and techniques. They expect students to take courses in the natural sciences to develop an understanding of the natural world, to learn scientific methods, and to discern the difference between science and pseudo-science.[50]

As part of this broad liberal education, we expect our faculty to engage students in the development of a range of skills central to leading productive and meaningful lives. These functional competencies include oral and written communication, critical analysis and reasoning, scientific and quantitative reasoning, and facility with technology. Our students should have the capacity to analyze media, information, and evidence. They should have the ability to compose and persuasively convey arguments.[51]

Complementing this, we should work to help our students develop the habits of mind necessary to navigate a complicated, uncertain, and changing world. Our courses and co-curricular experiences should cultivate the following in our students: the ability to ask good questions, marshal evidence, and think critically; an aptitude for lifelong learning and the ability to adapt to change; and skills in communication, negotiation, teamwork, and leadership. With these, we hope our graduates will be open minded, and will work, live, and interact comfortably with diverse people. We expect them to be resilient, with the flexibility, agility, and willingness to learn that will be critical for personal and professional success in a changing world.[52]

The liberal arts will be as important as ever for the current generation of students as we help them develop the critical thinking skills and knowledge to understand our society, with its opportunities and its problems. Generation Z students (born 1997–2012) have arrived on our campuses. They are digital natives whose expectations and use of technology have been shaped by growing up with laptops, smartphones, Wi-Fi, the internet, and social media. Grant Thornton argues that as this group has daily experience with technology and the internet, and they have developed the ability to sift through high volumes of data and multitask. Their attention spans are short, however, leaving their critical thinking skills underdeveloped. It is our job, therefore, to address this deficiency. Strategies for working with these students will include understanding their concerns, building on their strengths, supporting the development of critical thinking, and providing them with new knowledge and ideas.[53]

We cannot overstate the need for critical thinking in a world of misinformation and disinformation. Carl Bergstrom and Jevin West of the University of Wisconsin argue, "Misinformation has reached crisis proportions. It poses a risk to international peace, interferes with democratic decision-making, endangers the well-being of the planet, and threatens public health."[54] Our students need to understand the sources of information, assess the reliability of those sources, ask whether the information and claims are supported by evidence, place that information in context, weigh its importance, and ask, "What else do I need to know?" to make sense of it all.

The American Academy of Arts and Sciences Commission on the Practice of Democratic Citizenship wrote

> As we approach the 250th anniversary of our nation's founding, civic education must do more than teach names and dates, or even impart hands-on experience. The American citizen today must be prepared to acknowledge our nation's mistakes, to recognize that we have grappled over time to improve our imperfect union, to find pride in those struggles, and to recognize that at our best, everyone is included. We suggest that citizens today must be able to deal with ongoing debate and argument, be able to engage in that debate, find compromise, and from it all find their own love of country.[55]

In other words, we can only have the difficult, productive conversations about divisions in our society if we all have common knowledge about our history, politics, and government.

While Gen Z students have lived experience with the great recession, growth of student debt, school shootings, and now the pandemic and racial unrest, they may be short on historical context that allows them to understand current affairs. In *What Universities Owe Democracy*, Ron Daniels, president of Johns Hopkins University, and his coauthors argue that we have "blithely assumed our students have an understanding of democracy that they did not in fact have."[56] As educators, we are compelled, therefore, to help our students understand our complex society and our contested political institutions.

Daniels argues that we need to do more to ensure our students are prepared to participate in liberal democracy, which is under attack around the world. Daniels defines the central characteristics of liberal democracy as freedom of thought and speech, tolerance for heterodoxy and dissent, the free flow of information and ideas, and shared and distributed authority. He outlines four skills that educated citizens must have to be effective: (1) civic knowledge: theory and history of democracy and the structures of government, (2) civic skills: critical reasoning, understanding the importance of evidence, the ability to discern the truth, and the ability to translate ideas into action; (3) civic values: a commitment to ideals of tolerance and equality; and (4) civic aspiration: the ability to cooperate with others and engage in collective action.[57]

Daniels makes a persuasive case that we should reexamine our curriculum and consider adding "a democracy requirement" for our students. Research has shown that civics courses help students develop greater political knowledge and motivation and even to get students from disengaged families to become engaged.[58] We agree and call for a greater focus on civics education—US history and politics—albeit an updated one that is in tune with our diverse society, helps students understand, and develops agency in the political process.

Daniels acknowledges that his own institution, Johns Hopkins, does not currently have a democracy requirement. "This can be explained," writes Daniels," by the same historical forces that I have traced . . . the demise of the classical curriculum, the rise of science, the specialization of disciplines and faculty, and the migration of civics to community service." He notes the recent establishment of the SNF Agora Institute at Hopkins, which "has infused our curriculum with a suite of democracy-themed courses and programming throughout our university." These courses cover such topics as polarization, disinformation, and populism.[59]

We are all rethinking how we educate our students to be informed citizens. Institutions can choose from models that colleges and universities have already adopted or develop one of their own. One size does not fit all—each institution should adopt a model (course, program, and/or center) that fits its needs and those of its students and faculty.

For example, at the undergraduate level, Stanford University has recently created a new course for first-year students entitled "Citizenship for the 21st Century." This course seeks to provide students with political and ethical aspects of citizenship from a range of perspectives.[60] The University of Virginia (UVA) recently established the Karsh Institute for Democracy, endowed with a $50 million grant from the Karsh Family. Led by Melody Barnes, former director of the Domestic Policy Council in the Obama administration, the Karsh center will "highlight the critical role of higher education in strengthening democracy and UVA's aspiration and intention to lead nationally on this front," according to UVA president, Jim Ryan.[61] The Karsh Institute will work with UVA's Batten School of Leadership and Public Policy, Miller Center for Public Affairs, the Democracy Initiative, and other centers to "prepare citizen leaders."

At UMBC our Center for Democracy and Civic Life works with students, faculty, and staff to help students establish civic purpose and find agency through actions they take on campus or in the community. The Center has a range of programs that foster dialogue or facilitate student work with community partners. For example, the Center held a forum on the 2020 presidential election, providing a space in which students could express and hear a range of perspectives on the candidates, their policies, and the election outcomes.

It also works to support electoral engagement. Historically, young adults have voted at lower rates than older adults have, so efforts by higher-education institutions to increase registration and turnout among their students could have a significant impact. Through the Center, UMBC participates in the "All In Campus Democracy Challenge," in which we encourage students to vote. Because elections have consequences, each of us should make our vote count. Voting is one dimension of broader civic action that we should all engage in. To support voting further, we participate in the National Study of Learning, Voting, and Engagement at Tufts University to benchmark our efforts to increase student electoral participation.[62]

There is a need for more in our curriculum beyond a democracy requirement and electoral engagement. The deep issues of structural racism provide just one example of why our students should obtain a deeper understanding of US history. If we do not know where we have come from, we cannot understand where we are and make informed decisions about where we want to go and how. In the wake of the death of Freddie Gray and the Baltimore Uprising, we curated a list of our courses across disciplines that focused on racial and social justice and made that list widely available to students.[63] In the wake of the murder of George Floyd, the Harvard Kennedy School now requires a two-week intensive course entitled "Race and Racism in the Making of the United States as a Global Power" as part of its master in public policy curriculum. This course covers the history of racism in the United States from slavery to the present. It also examines the contemporary challenges of structural racism, including the ways it has affected and continues to influence public policy.[64]

As our student bodies become increasingly diverse in race/ethnicity, gender/identity, sexual orientation, nationality, religion, ability/disability, veteran status, and more, we will have more work to do. On the one hand, we should adjust our curricula to meet the demand for a wider range of courses in history, cultures, identities, and languages. On the other, we must also find ways to provide an academic community of shared learning experiences that unite our students and faculty through knowledge, dialogue, and experience.

At UMBC we have been developing a range of ideas on how to foster inclusion further in our curriculum and co-curricular programming.

- We have established a task force to review our general education program that is considering general education requirements.
- We are supporting community-engaged scholarship and learning and have made changes to our promotion and tenure process to support this.
- With funding from the Mellon Foundation, we have established the Inclusion Imperative. In partnership with Bowie State University, Coppin State University, and Howard University, UMBC is supporting and expanding community-engaged humanities research, teaching, and learning focused on issues of equity, inclusion, and justice. This center has developed a diversity teaching network, a visiting faculty fellowship program, and the Humanities teaching labs that bring together interdisciplinary scholarship, digital tools, and community engagement.[65]
- Outside of the classroom, we continue to support equity and inclusion work through our Women's Center; Initiatives for Identity, Inclusion, and Belonging (i3b) in Student Affairs; the Center for Democracy and Civic Life; and the Shriver Center, which involves students in the community through service learning and civic engagement.

The Center for Democracy and Civic Life has taken the lead in our work to increase student electoral participation and voting. UMBC has joined the National Study of Learning, Voting, and Engagement, participated in the ALL in to Vote voter pledge drive, and led a campus-wide voting campaign in 2020 under the theme, "Cast Your Whole Vote." President Hrabowski kicked off the campaign in

2020 by signing the Higher Education Presidents' Commitment to Full Voter Participation. The Center organized issue-focused events and built a strong and diverse coalition on campus to disseminate messages that encouraged electoral participation.[66]

The success of this work is vital to the success of our political system and society.

6

Hope

While we in higher education may have "coddiwompled" through the first year or two of the pandemic, moving with purpose through a challenging period with an unknown ending, we have emerged into a new period in which we may refocus on our educational mission and the visions we hold for our institutions. Most of us have likely been forever changed by the pandemic experience and will not be returning to some old version of "normal." Instead, we will likely have conversations with colleagues about keeping what worked during the pandemic and adopting new visions for our campuses.

We will experience future crises and, if there is one thing we have learned, institutions must be well positioned and prepared ahead of time to meet them. We can focus on establishing financial reserves, cultivating a resilient staff, and developing a sense of community. These are all assets in times of crisis. Having the right mindset or attitude is an asset too. And so, we turn here to "hope," one that is grounded and communal, as an institutional asset to cultivate.

Grounded and Communal Hope

Hope is an expectation that what we want will happen. To be hopeful is to take a positive view of the future, or, in the midst of a crisis, to see the light at the end of the tunnel. The magic of hope is that it is empowering: those who are hopeful are therefore more likely to take the steps necessary to make what they want come true. "Without vision, there is no hope," George Washington Carver once said. It is also true that without hope, we may not realize our vision.

We, as university leaders, have what some have called "grounded hope."[1] We have built our hope on a knowledge of history and a re- alism about the challenges and opportunities we face in a society struggling with a public health crisis, economic upheaval, social un- rest, and political division. We acknowledge the hard times in our past, the progress we have made as a society, and the work we still need to do. We acknowledge the difficulties and anxieties we all face during a crisis. Nonetheless, we in higher education can shape our future, focusing on our goals with resilience, determination, and expectation.

Mary Dana Hinton, president of Hollins University, has asserted, "The president must always be the last optimist standing. Your cam- pus relies upon you absorbing all of their concerns and reflecting back joy and light."[2] Community members do turn to their leaders for guidance and, during tough times, what leaders do makes a dif- ference. If leaders panic, so do those around them. If leaders re- main calm and positive, others are reassured and more likely to be as well. Indeed, our leaders play an important role in shaping the campus response, not only setting a positive tone during a crisis by recognizing the seriousness of the situation but also communicat- ing a sense of hope.

Thus, we also embrace a hope that is not just grounded but com- munal. The campus community itself also plays an important role. When we believe in ourselves and in each other and when we deepen team connections and build collaboration, we bring a sense of com- munity that generates its own optimism and hope because of the empowerment we feel. We bring an energy to our work that helps overcome major setbacks and obstacles. We take on what is ur- gent but also embrace new opportunities to broaden and deepen impact.

As the pandemic became real and intensified, most of us felt some level of uncertainty, doubt, fear, and anxiety, and later also anger, grief, and exhaustion. Yet hope can exist even in the midst of crisis, challenges, and pain. It is hope that sustains us, providing an antidote to anxiety, cynicism, or detachment. Instead of fighting or fleeing, we stay engaged and do the work that brings us closer to our goals. A focus on the important issues, rather than sweating the small stuff, can also help us stay positive. So can humor. During the pandemic, Freeman Hrabowski signed off all of his virtual meetings by saying, "Keep Hope Alive!" It became a lighthearted tradition that everyone expected, however small or large the meeting. Everyone left these meetings with a collective, positive feeling and smile on their face.

During the pandemic, even as we were managing a frenzied shift to remote work and learning, we had to simultaneously deal with financial upheaval. At UMBC, we were truly shocked by the potential revenue losses we faced, as much as $80 million out of a budget of $500 million due to cuts in state appropriations, possible declining enrollment, and loss of student fee revenue. We tackled the intertwined ordeals of a public health crisis and a potentially cratering budget through an empowered community response. We reinforced our resilience by repeating our mantra, "We have been through tough times before, and we will get through this now." We then engaged in an honest assessment and discussion of our challenges and the work needed to overcome them, including tough choices and budget cuts.

Despite our shock and fear, we felt a surge of adrenaline and an excitement about tackling problems and finding solutions to make higher education work on our campus under challenging circumstances. We were flexible, we moved quickly, we innovated, we were resilient, and we had hope. We married grit to hope, optimism, high expectations, and a belief that we could accomplish our goals. We would not just survive, but thrive; we would not only emerge whole but also enact needed change. This was hope that was grounded, communal, and empowered.

Lessons Learned

We have hope for the future of higher education because we have learned lessons from our recent experiences that will make us wiser about our work in the future. Here we review our lessons learned.

Vision

Our first lesson: In times of calm or crisis, vision, planning, and flexibility matter.

Higher education has the potential to transform the lives of students, empowering them for life, careers, citizenship, and civic engagement. Higher education has the power to change or help society through the work of alumni and the research and creative activity of faculty. Higher education matters and, because it does, US residents of every political party send their children to college regardless of what the polls and media say about the partisan divide over the value of a college education.

Each college or university has the responsibility to ensure that higher education does matter. Each has the duty to support student success. This simple but potent vision provides leaders, their teams, and their campuses clarity and focus that enable successful navigation of challenges and opportunities. A strong vision also provides a lodestone to rally around in unsettled times.

Implementing a clear, communal vision requires planning, commitment, and action. While our vision defines our goals, we translate these into action through a strategic plan that outlines how we will achieve our objectives for student success, research and creative activity, and engagement with the community. Then we organize and take action to implement the actions in our plans. In these times, our vision and plans should address such critical issues as enrollment, diversity and inclusion, and innovation in teaching and learning. Our academic program should ensure that our students graduate with new knowledge, critical thinking skills, media and technology literacy, and the education they need to be good citizens in a democracy.

If done right, our vision and the plan to implement it are broadly shared by our community and guide us on our journey. A broadly participatory process leads to a plan that represents the collective aspirations of the community and captures the future we want to live in. There will always be naysayers, of course, but a plan that reflects a broad consensus becomes the foundation for community. Indeed, that sense of fellowship and unity, that sense that we are part of something that we have helped create, is powerful.

A strong and shared plan has further benefits. It allows leaders to communicate to others what our goals are and where we are going. It attracts people—like the new president of UMBC, Valerie Sheares Ashby—to our campus. When the USM Board of Regents announced her selection, someone asked what her vision was for UMBC. She responded, "I resonate with what UMBC already does."

Of course, during times of crisis, our vision may be blurred. We may be gazing anxiously into cloudy crystal balls or driving in a thick fog of uncertainty. All short-term plans are subject to change, but our long-term vision should not change even as we "coddiwomple" along.

One of the important lessons of our pandemic experience is that a "living" strategic plan is an asset for institutional sustainability and mission success in cloudy times. We must build flexibility into our plans, and we must be willing to change them as needed. We may even consider building into our plans a process for periodically monitoring our progress, assessing what we are doing, and adjusting our work as needed.

Higher education leaders should:

- Articulate a vision and develop a flexible strategic plan using an inclusive process.
- Establish a structured process for implementing the highest or most urgent priorities, monitoring progress, and adjusting the plan as needed based on changing circumstances and/or evaluation.

- Ensure that our academic programs provide our graduates with new knowledge, critical thinking skills, media and technology literacy, and the education they need to be good citizens in a democracy.

Openness

Our second lesson: Openness is a strength, particularly in times of uncertainty. Openness has two dimensions: (1) being open to participation and ideas and (2) communicating clearly, transparently, and frequently with our students, colleagues, and community.
Since early 2020, we have all participated in an unplanned experiment in institutional leadership. If ever we wanted to test our skills for leading through uncertainty, this has been the perfect opportunity. We experienced significant confusion and fear in the early part of the pandemic, while looking for a way forward. As there was no single way to navigate the pandemic, as university leaders we did not make the same decisions, though we all had to respond to the same difficult questions.

To mitigate the uncertainty and to make informed decisions, many of us followed the science and sought expert public health advice, as these were the best guides in an evolving crisis. The science could tell us much worth understanding but not everything we needed to know because science was often lagging behind the progression of the disease. So we talked to experts and peers to obtain critical information, informed opinion, best practice, and innovative ideas. We engaged on-campus experts and leveraged our networks within our systems and national organizations (APLU, NACUBO, Educause, and others). This openness to expert information and peer ideas was essential for understanding what we were dealing with.

With information available and expert advice in hand, leaders led according to their personal styles. Some leaders managed in a top-down manner. A top-down approach can be faster and is sometimes more efficient. It can, however, be more contentious and subject to pushback. This can require or deplete political capital. Other leaders took a more collaborative approach. This process can be slower and more time consuming. It can, however, be more collegial, produce more buy-in, and lead to sustainable solutions. This can increase goodwill and political capital.

Either way, we had to be prepared to change course due to pushback, new information and guidance, or an evolving situation. Most important, we had to learn to be comfortable with not having all the information and answers when we wanted them and to live with an iterative process in which we took action but were ready to change course. We also had to coach our campuses on being comfortable with uncertainty and flexibility. In a world of uncertainty, planning becomes more, not less, important. Informed by the notion that we may have to change plans as conditions change or we gain new information, we should chart alternate scenarios, be flexible and agile, and give people the "grace" to change plans.

Leaders who want their campuses to thrive and not merely survive must hold fast to an institutional vision that serves as moral compass, inspiration, and aspiration. They must be calm, hopeful, thoughtful, focused, and intentional. Most important, we believe that leaders who are open to different or new ideas, open to sharing information, open to broad participation, and open to collaboration will have, on average, the best outcomes. Openness involves risk, to be sure, but it also holds the promise of engagement, collective power, and the consideration of a broad range of solutions and innovations.

While the buck stops with the president, leaders who empower others do so by cultivating shared leadership and an institutional culture of openness, especially in times of uncertainty. When people are empowered, they have a sense of agency. That agency gives them both hope and the opportunity to do the work.

When we are open minded, we are willing to be honest about challenges and opportunities, ask good questions and listen actively, and empower the people we pull into the work. We engage in active listening to understand concerns, needs, perspectives, and ideas.

Secrecy erodes trust. Transparency facilitates participation, buy-in, and community. Expanding perspectives uncovers blind spots and avoids pitfalls, increases opportunities and solutions, and increases the potential for achieving ambitious goals.

It is easy to focus on and listen to the most powerful or the loudest. We all benefit when we listen more broadly, though, bringing more people into the conversation through surveys, focus groups, town halls, and meetings. We must not assume everyone ascribes to the same ideas and opinions as everyone else in the group with which they might identify. As one of our faculty reminded us, "We can't talk about the faculty as though we all believe the same thing."

When we are open, we create an empowered institutional culture characterized by the "five Cs":

- Clarity: Clarity of vision
- Community: Consensus about values, vision, and direction, born of conversation and shared leadership
- Commitment: A willingness to act on this vision, going above and beyond as needed to fulfill it
- Collaboration: A collaborative culture that allows us to work across silos, which is when much innovation happens, and to coordinate that work
- Communication: A sharing culture that facilitates the circulation of information, from the top down and from the bottom up

Communication is an essential component of openness, but it is a complicated act. We must do all that we can to get the word out about what we are doing and why. A critical operational lesson for leaders is that we cannot communicate often enough or on enough platforms when we really want or need to get a message through.

During the pandemic, we held online campus "town halls." During these conversations, we learned that our existing communication networks were insufficient during a crisis. We have always known that there are leaders on campus who do not have conversations about important issues and communicate what is going on with their units or departments. We also learned that there were many in our community who do not read campus messages, and they are often among those who are the most agitated or discouraged because they do not have information about what is happening. A high-stakes situation like a pandemic, though, requires wide dissemination of information.

Because of this, the University System of Maryland required each of its campuses to update their crisis communication plans. Our plan emphasized that communications must be credible and work to sustain community, or those who do read our communications will be cynical about them. During the pandemic, we embedded communications staff in our COVID-19 response operations. This helped our operations by allowing communications staff to highlight when and how to communicate. This helped communications because communications staff knew and could craft messages in real time about what was going on.

Over the past decade, leaders have found it necessary to communicate to their campuses with increasing frequency about sensitive cultural and political issues and events. People impacted by news—local, national, or global—want to hear from campus leadership about the issue, how it affects campus members, and how the campus is responding, if necessary.

We have found that there can be a trade-off between being timely in our communications and getting it right. The latter often means consultation that takes time, and while we are consulting, people may interpret the temporary silence as "not caring." Consultation, however, can be important to understanding how people feel, the nuances of issues, and striking the right balance in a campus communication. As tempting as it is to get a communication out quickly, on balance, we have found that getting it right ultimately matters more.

Higher education leaders should:

- Be open to different or new ideas, broad participation, and collaboration. When we are open, we create an empowered institutional culture characterized by the "five Cs": clarity, community, commitment, collaboration, and communication.

- Communicate as often as possible and on as many platforms as possible, during a crisis. Communication must be credible and work to sustain community. Leaders communicating with the campus community about sensitive issues will need to find a balance between timeliness and broad consultation before issuing a communication.
- Embed communications staff in crisis response operations. This helps response operations by allowing communications staff to highlight when and how to communicate, and it helps communications staff by allowing them to know in real time what is going on.

Resilience

Our third lesson: We build resilience on a foundation of community, financial health, human resources, digital infrastructure, a crisis management structure, and access to expert networks.
The community we have created through openness is critical to resilience. While people on our campus sometimes had different opinions on a range of issues, we all had the same fundamental goal of supporting students, faculty, and staff, which thus moved us in the same direction. When we were knocked down, we helped each other up. At some other institutions, we have seen people get knocked down and then start fighting. This creates a real problem.

We were temporarily knocked down during the pandemic by the news that we might lose $80 million in revenue. This was a tremendous shock. But we repeated our mantra: "We have seen tough times before, and we will get through this." And we did, together. We used reserves, we reduced spending, we used federal aid to replace foregone revenue, and in the end, we took base cuts of about $15 million. Because our vice presidents and deans understood both the situation and the budget process and agreed that we would do what was best for UMBC in the long run, we were able to agree on cuts with little pushback.

We moved deliberately and purposefully through a dense fog toward an unknown destination, getting up again each time we were knocked down. This was grit amid uncertainty. This was resilience, personal, communal, and institutional. At UMBC, people were already willing to go above and beyond in their work; during the pandemic, they stepped up and performed at a high level under challenging circumstances. Our strong shared governance was an asset. Our relationships and trust, built up over years, were a terrific source of energy and communication.

Facing a crisis, one is best positioned if one already has the resources and tools needed ahead of time. Of course, you cannot predict the timing of a crisis or what tools will be needed; however, certain resources can be helpful in almost every situation. These include effective leadership, financial resources, digital infrastructure, and human resources. These also include a collaborative culture, a sense that we are in this together, and the trust, grace, and goodwill these enable.

No matter how good you are, things will go awry at times. Someone will be unhappy and will complain. There will be mistakes. We have to make choices with partial information, knowing we cannot control the outcomes. Sometimes we can make a good choice and still get a bad outcome. We know that there is always more to do and that there are things we cannot control. Students have minds of their own and can upset our plans. (How many student parties led to spikes in COVID-19 cases?)

Cultivating the positive will help. How often do leaders dedicate a president's cabinet meeting to the question, "What are you grateful for at our institution?" We all sometimes have negative emotions or critical thoughts about our campuses and colleagues. They come easily to us. Our brains have a "negativity bias" designed to raise red flags and provide a measure of self-protection when things may not go smoothly or decisions are difficult, involving contending ideas and agendas, tensions and trade-offs, incomplete information, and nuanced deliberation. When we talk about what we are grateful for, we sense there is also much to hope for. To sustain a healthy community, we need to balance cynicism and criticism with gratitude, grace, and hope.

With the resources built up over time, our resilience will be stronger and our outcomes better. The experience will likely change us and, hopefully, we will be wiser and not regretful. Perhaps we will find opportunities amid the crises and emerge better than before.

Leaders in higher education should:

- Imbue their institutional cultures with the notion that we do what is best for the university, not what is best for the individual or their unit, department, division, or college. When we are knocked down, we help each other up.
- Position themselves for any crisis by proactively developing the resources and tools that may be helpful in almost every situation. These include effective leadership, a sense of community, financial resources, digital infrastructure, and human resources. Resilient institutions build these over time.
- Cultivate the positive, a collaborative culture and a strong sense of community. These can help a campus act productively with grit amid uncertainty. To sustain a healthy community, we need to balance cynicism and criticism with trust, goodwill, grace, and hope.

Courage

Our fourth lesson: We can muster institutional courage to put people first and summon the will to create a safe, equitable, inclusive, multicultural community.

We had to have courage to do what we considered "the right thing" again and again in the face of a public health crisis like COVID-19. As we made decisions about everything from health and safety to finances, we looked to our principles of supporting the academic program and the people who make up our community as a guide.

Not all decisions would be popular. For example, the campus was divided on some issues, such as whether commencements in 2020 and 2021 should be in person or virtual. Not all decisions would be easy. We knew that refunding some fees would be hard on our campus budget. In each case, though, we did what we thought was right for our campus, our students, and their families. Our decisions were campus specific—other university leaders came to similar or different decisions based on their situations.

We had to have the courage to push ourselves and our community to be inclusive. While we navigated our way through the pandemic, we continued our work to build a stronger Title IX program. We decided to take further actions to address structural racism as alumni and faculty raised issues in the wake of the murder of George Floyd. We sought to be more inclusive for LGBTQ+ members of our community. We invested more resources in supporting those students and employees struggling with mental illnesses, exacerbated by the anxiety and isolation of a pandemic.

Courage is critical: it is so easy to just float along without taking action. Taking action requires the will to do more, the will to tackle tough issues, and the will to have tough conversations with colleagues—including those who are friends. We often know what works to create an inclusive environment and support those who are from marginalized groups. We have the tools, we have the models, we know what to do, but we often fail to deliver on what we know or use what works. Institutional courage is about delivering on the tough issues.

The institution can have the courage to do the right thing only when leaders lead with integrity, guided by their personal and institutional values, as they make and communicate difficult decisions. Courage involves risk. It takes courage to do what is right rather than what is popular, including tackling difficult social issues that affect campus culture and student success. It takes courage to do the right thing—look in the mirror, be honest, have difficult conversations, and empower others.

Campus leaders must do more than articulate courageous goals; they must also be role models for courage on such issues as Title IX, race, LGBTQ+, and mental health. We learn to be courageous through experience, working through challenges, seeking advice from mentors and peers. Courage is not necessarily bold and fast—it can require patience, information gathering, deliberation, and risk assessment before action. We do not just manage short-term crises; we must do the right thing for the long term. Being a welcoming community is not an end, it requires ongoing work.

Changing culture is hard, but vision, openness, and resilience all help. When leaders make the choice to do more, they can articulate a culture of inclusion and well-being, build trust and working relationships around these issues, commit resources, and take meaningful action. They can make it clear that they are not just "checking the box" but are working for larger change, and providing a structure, resources, and accountability for a sustainable effort. Resources are critical, otherwise what may appear good (e.g., appointing a chief diversity officer) will be hollow, the new position a toothless tiger.

Student activism, a cherished and valued part of campus life, often plays a part in institutional reform and the courage required to tackle it. It is not surprising, for example, that student protest plays a role in the popular Netflix series *The Chair*. When confronted by protest or activism, leaders should invite conversations, convey genuine care, listen well, and be honest. Being angry or defensive erodes trust and progress, so leaders should avoid these. We take a deep breath and focus on facts, areas of agreement, areas that need further investigation, and charting a long-term path forward.

We have held town halls on tough issues, including sexual assault and racism. These were not easy conversations. We applaud the courage it took for people—students, staff, and faculty—to speak. In the town hall on sexual harassment and assault, survivors spoke about deeply painful experiences while speaking truth to power. This is bravery we admire and support. We tell people on our campus who raise challenging issues that we love that they care so deeply about our community. We create a space in which people can be honest; we create an opportunity for people to learn, participate, and take ownership.

Higher education leaders should:

- Muster the courage to face truths, make decisions without regard to their popularity, and then act. Leaders should make courageous decisions based on guiding principles that do not change, such as supporting the academic program and the people who make up our community.
- Have the courage to push campuses to be inclusive in our multicultural society. Taking action requires the will to do more, the will to tackle tough issues, and the will to have tough conversations with colleagues—including those who are friends. It also means being proactive rather than reactive, and continuing important work even when the pressure is off because it is still the right thing to do.
- Provide adequate resources to those we task with critical work, such as chief diversity officers, or they will be "toothless tigers" at best and their work will be undermined.

Passion

Lesson 5: A deep passion for our fundamental educational mission lies at the heart of the successful higher education institution. The passion and commitment of our staff and faculty got us through the first two years of COVID-19. Passion allows us to stick to our long-term vision for student success, despite disruptions, taking on initiatives that improve learning and outcomes.

We are unapologetically committed to our educational mission. We have stayed focused, despite disruption, on this mission—supporting and improving student success, research and creative achievement, and community engagement. Staying true to this mission required short-term action during the pandemic (e.g., the pivot to online learning and back) while also taking actions to achieve long-term goals and sustainability (e.g., enrollment and student support).

Leaders must decide which long-term goals we should pursue in the midst of a crisis and which we can postpone for the time being. At UMBC, we decided to focus on implementation of key priorities in our recently developed strategic enrollment plan. Enrollment was already an issue for higher education in general before the pandemic, then campus closures and online learning drove enrollment down overall. This was a good time for us to take action so that we could sustain enrollment despite national trends. We held relatively steady for the fall of 2021 and, through a series of actions, we were able to drive first-year enrollment to our highest level ever in the fall of 2022. This was a success for our institution and an opportunity to increase student access.

At the same time, leaders must learn lessons from crises, to change our academic program to meet the needs of students. We have learned through political, social, and health crises of the past six years that what our students learn about the wider world is important. In an age of technological change, social media, economic globalization, partisan rancor, and public health pandemics, we have a duty to educate our students for life, jobs, community, and citizenship. We should strongly consider whether we are educating knowledgeable and skilled citizens who understand our history, our political institutions, our society, and our varied media. Ron Daniels worries that "colleges and universities have blithely assumed our students had an understanding of democratic citizenship that they did not in fact have." He has recently postulated that universities should have a "Democracy Requirement," that provides students with civic knowledge, skills, values, and aspirations.[3]

Much of the recent discussion about teaching and learning has focused on course modalities, but there is more for us to consider. To be sure, the shift to online learning, the use of hybrid and hi-flex formats, and the availability of digital tools have all enriched our conversation and work about how faculty can and should teach. We have arrived at a point in which we understand that rather than one mode dominating others, faculty now have the tools, skills, and flexibility to deploy digital tools to maximize the learning for their particular students and circumstances.

Innovation in teaching also involves course design. Cognitive science has provided deeper insight into the way people learn, paving the way for new approaches to teaching and learning. Just as we know what works for inclusion, we also now know much about what works to improve student learning and outcomes. Some faculty have experimented with new approaches. On our campus, we have provided small grants to support faculty as they redesign and implement their courses. Still, not all faculty engage in course redesign, and when innovative faculty leave, they may be followed by faculty with traditional approaches that undermine all that has been gained.

We must channel our passion for student success into this long term effort to design courses, curricula, and experiences that provide them with the knowledge and skills they need and benefit our society. Those skills include writing and oral communication, leadership and teamwork, critical analysis, scientific and quantitative reasoning, facility with technology, media literacy, and intercultural competence. They should have the habits of mind that allow them to ask good questions, marshal evidence, and think critically. They should be open minded, able to live and work with people who are different, and participate in and defend democracy.

Leaders in higher education should:

- Decide which long-term goals to pursue in the midst of a crisis and which to postpone. We must also learn lessons from crises, including changing our academic programs to meet the emerging needs of students.
- Build on our experiences during the pandemic with digital tools, assessing what worked and what did not, and charting a new course for our institutions.
- Channel our passion for student success into a long-term effort to design courses and curricula that engage students

and provide them with the knowledge and skills they need. There is more to innovation in teaching than adopting new digital tools. Cognitive science has provided deeper insight into the way people learn, paving the way for new approaches to teaching and learning.

The Only Thing Permanent Is Change

The most resilient institutions are not static but dynamic, able to adapt in the face of challenges and act when presented with opportunities. These agile, innovative institutions derive strength from change. The only thing permanent is change, so the saying goes, and so the resilient institution is the one that is prepared for and embraces change, even in an environment of uncertainty. We have detailed the many ways that an institution can prepare itself for crises or change. We leave you with a final tool: conversation.

A resilient institution must continually change, and conversation is central to constructive change. Thus, cultivating the art of conversation is a practice we should adopt. It is through conversation, deep and sometimes difficult, that we arrive at common understandings, share information and ideas, discuss possible plans and solutions, and arrive at a way forward. We may not agree every step of the way, but we share information and perspectives that enrich the discussion and are transparent about how we arrived at decisions. Inclusion and transparency build trust and community, which are assets, now and for the future. When we have trust and community, we share both our vision and our collective aspirations for the future and then travel toward them together.

EPILOGUE

Transition

In spring 2022 Bridget Burns, CEO of the University Innovation Alliance, noted that leadership transitions at universities are inevitable and are happening with increasing frequency. She urged, "We need a strategy guide or playbook for institutions going through a leadership transition that will help campuses maintain momentum or, at the very least, not lose progress in the inevitable reorganization and reorientation that comes with a new president or chancellor."[1]

While it appears that the average tenure of university presidents has been declining, and the job of president has been getting more complex, we remain hopeful for both higher education in general and for our institution more specifically.

For higher education, we are hopeful because we are becoming more thoughtful about how to provide the next generation of leaders the opportunities and resources to lead, thrive, and take our institutions to the next level. Mentoring is key. The ACE Fellows program remains an important training ground for higher education leaders. Harvard's seminar for new presidents provides individuals who have been selected for this role with best practices to consider. The seminar covers the president's multiple roles as chief executive officer, senior personnel officer, and academic leader. It examines institutional culture, the senior executive team, and relations with the board of trustees. The American Association of State Colleges and Universities has established the New Presidents Academy, which provides new college and university presidents and chancellors an orientation to the position, along with insights on strategic planning, financial management, crisis management, fundraising, and equity-minded leadership.

Several years ago, an Aspen Institute commission examined the future of the college presidency and provided recommendations to campuses on how they can support new presidents. This commission urged a focus on professional development for presidents, particularly new ones during their first year. New presidents need support. They need to learn about the campus they have joined. They have to meet constituents from every stakeholder group. They must understand the data available about the university's students, faculty and staff, and financial resources.

When Freeman Hrabowski teaches in the Harvard seminar for new presidents, he reminds them that, while they have been deans and provosts in the past, their professional duties have changed. They have to let their old ones go and let those who currently hold those positions fulfill those duties. Leaders can mentor and push when needed, but ultimately the presidents must trust current provosts, vice presidents, and deans to do their jobs and then focus on what presidents need to do.

For UMBC, the departure of Hrabowski, president for three decades, is a major but hopeful transition. Even at the end of a positive presidency, an institution and the people it comprises experience anxiety as they pass through a period of uncertainty about what change will entail or where it will lead. Leaders must work to keep people calm, hopeful, and focused on the positive during this time. Even at the end of a successful presidency, an institution must embrace the change that will take it to the next level under the new president. Leaders must channel energy into the work of planning a new course and implementing new initiatives.

A new president brings a new leadership style and institutional agenda. The first year of a presidency should focus on learning and listening. A new president will benefit from a review of institutional data presented over time and compared to both national trends and the data of peer institutions. A new president will also benefit from meeting constituents, holding in-depth discussions that allow an understanding of whom they are and what concerns and ideas they have. A listening tour is a terrific opening for learning about the people on a campus and the institution's challenges and opportunities. This information can help shape thinking about a longer-term strategic plan.

Fortunately, the search for a new president for UMBC was a terrific success. We were able to attract candidates from public and private institutions we admire. The person selected, Dr. Valerie Sheares Ashby, Dean of Duke's Trinity College of Arts and Sciences, speaks volumes about both the progress of UMBC thus far and where it will go in the future. UMBC has focused on supporting its people, increasing student success, making inclusive excellence real, and addressing social issues. Sheares Ashby embraces this work and our vision of redefining excellence in higher education through inclusion. Her background as a polymer chemist who appreciates the humanities and her successful record as a leader at the University of North Carolina and at Duke once led Freeman Hrabowski to predict that she would one day be a university president. Now she is.[2]

Sheares Ashby's selection as UMBC president has brought to light a critical question for higher education. Which institutions are important and impactful? Sheares Ashby has noted that when she was at the University of North Carolina Chapel Hill and she took the job at Duke, not a single person asked her why she was going to Duke. They all assumed she was going because Duke was elite, private, and offered her more money. The only question people asked her was, "Who are you going to root for in basketball?" Meanwhile, when she took the job offer as president of UMBC, everyone asked, "Why UMBC?" "It tells me a lot about what people assume regarding which institutions are impactful," Shears Ashby remarked.

A decade ago, Isaacson Miller (IM) ran the search for a new dean of Trinity College of Arts and Sciences at Duke University. Duke hired Valerie Sheares Ashby, chair of the chemistry department at the University of North Carolina Chapel Hill. When IM approached her about applying for the position at UMBC, she said she was not interested. She already had a job she loved. She had no plans to leave it. The staff at IM argued that her values aligned with those of UMBC and encouraged her to apply to see what happened. Dr. Sheares Ashby agreed.

The first step in applying is submitting a statement of interest. Since Dr. Sheares Ashby was not initially interested; she had to do some research to determine if she might be interested and what she could say in her statement. "It took me two seconds," Sheares Ashby recalls. "I started with the UMBC vision statement and when I read 'Our UMBC community redefines excellence in higher education through an inclusive culture,' they had me. I said to myself, 'These are my people.'" Sheares Ashby was struck by the notion that an institution would be bold enough to aspire to "redefine" excellence. She was inspired that UMBC was an institution that was willing to change or evolve and to aspire to do it through inclusion. "What more noble cause is there?"

Although she recoiled at first when asked why she would choose UMBC, Sheares Ashby now wants people to ask her this question because she wants people to know why she chose this institution. "We cannot be the only people to know about the important work and successes at UMBC," she said. "We cannot appreciate just the Dukes or the Ivies. We must help people appreciate the impact of every institution—and give them the resources to most effectively carry out their missions."

The other question that people ask Sheares Ashby is, "How will you follow Freeman? How will you fill those big shoes?" She answers, "You don't try to be Freeman 2.0. What you do is embrace one of Freeman's favorite sayings, 'Success is never final.'" This is a terrific motto to live by, she argues. First, it states that "success"—or excellence, not mediocrity—is the goal. Second, it means we have the humility to know that we can always be better, and it means we are willing to look in the mirror, reexamine where we are, and consider the changes that will take our work to the next level. Sheares Ashby intends to lead UMBC as it strives for the next level.

Some presidents do not know how to leave. Fortunately, Hrabowski prepared his campus for his departure and was supportive of Sheares Ashby every step of the way. No one at UMBC has been through a presidential transition, unless they have been at another institution. There was some grief, to be sure, yet there was also excitement about what is possible, about what the future holds.

The presidential transition process was smooth and productive. On April 4, 2022, when the USM announced the selection of Sheares Ashby as UMBC's president, she surprised Hrabowski by coming to campus to thank him personally for all he has accomplished at UMBC. She was gracious and humble and impressed the campus community. In late April, during another visit, Hrabowski and Sheares Ashby attended a large campus event highlighting campus achievements. Hrabowski said goodbye to the campus, and Sheares Ashby said hello. When music started to play, the two presidents started dancing spontaneously, which thrilled the crowd. The spirit of celebration provided a great way to begin the transition.

In the months following, Sheares Ashby charted a transition process, which she has since been carrying out. Hrabowski's chief of staff at UMBC and Sheares Ashby's at Duke served as liaisons, facilitating communication, organizing meetings, and connecting the new president to people at UMBC on critical, immediate issues. Hrabowski and Sheares Ashby communicated frequently. Sheares Ashby also met with the provost, vice presidents, and deans to establish relationships and begin the process of getting to know UMBC as an organization. She met with her new communications team to plan a communications strategy and messaging themes for her first months.

By August 1, 2022, Sheares Ashby and her new team were able to hit the ground running. Day 1 on the job involved many phone calls, a tour of the administration building personally greeting staff, and a meet and greet for the university community. Then she and her team prepared for the beginning of the academic year with the Fall

Opening, a meeting for faculty and staff, and the Convocation, which brings together new students. These were formal opportunities to address the campus community and launch her first year on the job. In fall 2022 Sheares Ashby started a listening tour, learning more about the institution, meeting people, and appraising challenges and opportunities.

What was evident throughout this process were two themes. First, resilience enables a smooth transition. Second, a smooth transition builds further resilience and hope for the future.

Notes

Preface

1. Len Gutkin and Maximillian Alvarez, "Planning for the Fall Is Like 'Driving through a Dense Fog,'" *Chronicle of Higher Education* (April 29, 2020), https://www.chronicle.com/article/planning-for-the-fall-is-like-driving-through-a-dense-fog/. John S. Rosenberg, "Presiding during the Pandemic," *Harvard* (March–April 2022): 14, https://www.harvardmagazine.com/2022/03/jhj-presiding-during-pandemic.

2. Freeman A. Hrabowski III, Peter H. Henderson, and J. Kathleen Tracy, "Higher Education Should Lead the Efforts to Reverse Structural Racism," *The Atlantic* (October 24, 2020), https://www.theatlantic.com/ideas/archive/2020/10/higher-education-structural-racism/616754/.

Prologue. Empowerment

1. Eric Weiner, *The Geography of Bliss: One Grump's Search for the Happiest Places in the World* (New York: Twelve, 2008), 3.

2. David Kirp, *The College Dropout Scandal* (New York: Oxford University Press, 2019). http://www.davidkirp.com/book/the-college-dropout-scandal/.

1. Vision

1. Cheryl Norton, "Why a Higher Education Leader Should Have a Vision," *Inside Higher Ed* (October 22, 2019), https://www.insidehighered.com/advice/2019/10/22/why-higher-education-leader-should-have-vision-opinion.

2. Norton, "Higher Education Leader."

3. Norton, "Higher Education Leader."

4. UMBC, "Vision," accessed May 24, 2023, https://umbc.edu/about/mission-and-vision/.

5. Cary Funk and John Gramlich, "10 Facts about Americans and Coronavirus Vaccines," Pew Research Center (September 20, 2021), https://www.pewresearch.org/fact-tank/2021/09/20/10-facts-about-americans-and-coronavirus-vaccines/.

6. Anthony S. Fauci, "The Story behind COVID-19 Vaccines," *Science* 372, no. 6538 (April 9, 2021): 109, https://www.science.org/doi/10.1126/science.abi8397.

7. Sarah Hansen, "Her Science Is the World's," *UMBC Magazine* (June 10, 2021), https://umbc.edu/stories/her-science-is-the-worlds/.

8. Partnership for Public Service, "2021 Federal Employee of the Year," accessed May 24, 2023, https://servicetoamericamedals.org/honorees/Corbett-graham/.

9. Alice Park and Jamie Duchamp, "The Miracle Workers," *Time* (December 13, 2021), https://time.com/heroes-of-the-year-2021-vaccine-scientists/.

10. Sudip Parikh, "A Draft of History, a Template for the Future," *Science* (April 6, 2021), https://www.science.org/content/blog-post/draft-history-template-future.

11. Susan Thornton Hobby, "Retrievers on the Front Lines of the Pandemic," *UMBC Magazine* (May 2, 2020), https://magazine.umbc.edu/retrievers-on-the-front-lines-of-the-pandemic/. Jenny O'Grady, "UMBC Makers Shift Gears to

Pitch In," *UMBC Magazine* (April 14, 2020), https://magazine.umbc.edu/umbc -makers-shift-gears-to-pitch-in/.

12. Adrienne Jones, "Racial + Economic Justice Agenda" (February 11, 2021), https://www.mdspeakerjones.com/post/racial-economic-justice-agenda.

13. "Dzirasa Research," Dzirasa Lab, Duke University School of Medicine, accessed May 24, 2023, https://www.neuro.duke.edu/research/faculty-labs /dzirasa-lab.

14. Megan Hanks Mastrola, "UMBC Alumnus Kafui Dzirasa Is Named an HHMI Investigator, Elected to the National Academy of Medicine," *UMBC News* (October 26, 2021), https://umbc.edu/stories/umbc-alumnus-kafui-dzirasa-is -named-an-hhmi-investigator-elected-to-the-national-academy-of-medicine/.

15. "Kaitlyn Sadtler," National Institute of Biomedical Imaging and Bioengineering, accessed May 24, 2023, https://www.nibib.nih.gov/about-nibib/staff /kaitlyn-sadtler.

16. "The Growing Partisan Divide in Views of Higher Education," Pew Research Center (August 19, 2019), https://www.pewresearch.org/social-trends /2019/08/19/the-growing-partisan-divide-in-views-of-higher-education-2/.

17. "Growing Partisan Divide."

18. "Growing Partisan Divide."

19. "More Is Possible with Higher Education," National Association of College and University Business Officers (March 6, 2023), https://www.nacubo.org /Advocacy/State%20of%20Higher%20Education/More%20is%20Possible.

20. David Kirp, *The College Dropout Scandal* (New York: Oxford University Press, 2019). http://www.davidkirp.com/book/the-college-dropout-scandal/.

21. National Center for Education Statistics, Digest of Education Statistics, 2019, Table 326.10, https://nces.ed.gov/programs/digest/d19/tables/dt19_326.10.asp.

22. National Center for Education Statistics, "Undergraduate Retention and Graduation Rates" (May 2022), https://nces.ed.gov/programs/coe/indicator/ctr /undergrad-retention-graduation.

23. We have seen a significant decline in community college enrollment, which came in at just 4.7 million in fall 2021. National Center for Education Statistics, Trend Generator, "Student Enrollment: How Many Students Enroll in Postsecondary Education Annually?", accessed May 24, 2023, https://nces.ed.gov/ipeds /TrendGenerator/app/build-table/2/2?rid=1&cid=9.

24. National Center for Education Statistics, Table 326.10, https://nces.ed.gov /programs/digest/d19/tables/dt19_326.10.asp.

25. National Center for Education Statistics, Table 326.10.

26. Freeman A. Hrabowski III, Philip J. Rous, and Peter H. Henderson, *The Empowered University: Shared Leadership, Culture Change, and Academic Success* (Baltimore: Johns Hopkins University Press, 2019). https://www.press.jhu.edu /books/title/11838/empowered-university.

27. Hrabowski, *Empowered University*.

28. See, for example, Arthur Levine and Scott Van Pelt, *The Great Upheaval: Higher Education's Past, Present, and Uncertain Future* (Baltimore: Johns Hopkins University Press, 2021). https://www.press.jhu.edu/books/title/12757/great-upheaval.

29. National Center for Education Statistics, Digest of Education Statistics, 2017, Table 302.30, https://nces.ed.gov/programs/digest/d17/tables/dt17_302.30.asp.

30. U.S. Census Bureau, CPS Historical Time Series Tables, Table A-2, "Percent of People 25 and Over Who Have Completed High School or College, by Race, Hispanic Origin, and Sex: Selected Years, 1940–2022," https://www.census.gov/data/tables/time-series/demo/educational-attainment/cps-historical-time-series.html.

31. Commission on the Future of Undergraduate Education, "A Primer on the College Journey," American Academy of Arts and Sciences (September 22, 2016): 12, https://www.amacad.org/publication/primer-college-student-journey.

32. KPMG, "The Future of Higher Education in a Disruptive World," KPMG International website, 2020. https://assets.kpmg/content/dam/kpmg/xx/pdf/2020/10/future-of-higher-education.pdf.

33. Arthur Levine and Scott Van Pelt, *The Great Upheaval: Higher Education's Past, Present, and Uncertain Future* (Baltimore: Johns Hopkins University Press, 2021), 255.

34. KPMG, "The Future of Higher Education."

2. Openness

1. Terrence McTaggart, "The Personal Qualities of Leaders during the COVID-19 Era," *Trusteeship* (September-October 2021): 12–17, https://agb.org/trusteeship-article/the-personal-qualities-of-leaders-during-the-covid-19-era/.

2. "The State of Higher Education in 2020," Grant Thornton, 15. https://www.grantthornton.com/content/dam/grantthornton/website/assets/content-page-files/nfp/pdfs/2020/grant-thornton-state-of-higher-education-in-2020-new/grant-thornton-state-of-higher-education-in-2020-new.pdf.coredownload.inline.pdf.

3. Colleen Flaherty, "Undemocratic Civics at Purdue?" *Inside Higher Ed* (June 11, 2021), https://www.insidehighered.com/news/2021/06/11/some-purdue-professors-say-university-unilaterally-pursuing-civics-requirement.

4. Rick Seltzer, "The Slowly Diversifying Presidency," *Inside Higher Ed* (June 20, 2017), https://www.insidehighered.com/news/2017/06/20/college-presidents-diversifying-slowly-and-growing-older-study-finds.

5. Michael Nietzel, "More High-Profile College Presidents Are Leaving Office," *Forbes* (January 31, 2022), https://www.forbes.com/sites/michaeltnietzel/2022/01/31/more-high-profile-college-presidents-are-leaving-office/?sh=62b8fa062142.

6. "President's Video Series," Georgetown University, https://www.georgetown.edu/presidents-video-series/#_ga=2.20773627.2112841792.1644871172-1482942579.1644871172. Accessed June 25, 2023.

3. Resilience

1. Carol Dweck, *Mindset: The New Psychology of Success* (New York: Random House, 2006). Angela Duckworth, *Grit: The Power of Passion and Perseverance* (New York: Scribner, 2016).

2. Angela Duckworth, *Grit: The Power of Passion and Perseverance.*

3. Len Gutkin and Maximillian Alvarez, "Planning for the Fall Is Like 'Driving Through a Dense Fog'," *The Chronicle of Higher Education* (April 29, 2020), https://www.chronicle.com/article/planning-for-the-fall-is-like-driving-through-a-dense-fog/.

4. John S. Rosenberg, "Presiding during the Pandemic," *Harvard Magazine* (March-April 2022): 14, https://www.harvardmagazine.com/2022/03/jhj-presiding-during-pandemic.

5. "Here's Our List of Colleges' Reopening Models," *The Chronicle of Higher Education* (updated October 1, 2020), https://www.chronicle.com/article/heres-a-list-of-colleges-plans-for-reopening-in-the-fall/.

6. Emma Whitford, "August Wave of Campus Reopening Reversals," *Inside Higher Ed* (August 12, 2020), https://www.insidehighered.com/news/2020/08/12/colleges-walk-back-fall-reopening-plans-and-opt-online-only-instruction/.

7. Emma Marris, "Millions of Students Are Returning to US Universities in a Vast Unplanned Pandemic Experiment," *Nature* (August 17, 2020), https://www.nature.com/articles/d41586-020-02419-w.

8. Marris, "Millions of Students."

9. Charles Fishman, "The Risk Universities Can't Not Take," *The Atlantic* (October 1, 2020), https://www.theatlantic.com/health/archive/2020/10/16-weeks-and-5-days-university-arizona/616557/.

10. Marris, "Millions of Students."

11. Ian Bogost, "America Will Sacrifice Anything for the College Experience," *The Atlantic* (October 20, 2020), https://www.theatlantic.com/technology/archive/2020/10/college-was-never-about-education/616777/.

12. Chris Quintana and Mike Stucka, "'Astonishingly Risky': COVID-19 cases at colleges are fueling the nation's hottest outbreaks," *USA Today* (September 11, 2020), https://www.usatoday.com/story/news/education/2020/09/11/covid-cases-college-us-outbreak-rate-tracker/5759088002/.

13. John Schwartz, "How the University of Iowa Recovered from the 'Unfathomabble' Flood that Ruined It," *New York Times* (May 10, 2019), https://www.nytimes.com/2019/05/10/climate/iowa-floods-disasters-lessons-learned.html.

14. Richard J. Hatchett, Carter E. Mecher, and Marc Lipsitch, "Public Health Interventions and Epidemic Intensity during the 1918 Flu Pandemic," *Proceedings of the National Academy of Sciences*, 104, no. 18 (May 1, 2007): 7582–7587, https://www.pnas.org/doi/10.1073/pnas.0610941104.

15. Rosenberg, "Presiding during the Pandemic," 14.

16. KPMG. "The Future of Higher Education in a Disruptive World," KPMG International (2020): 16, https://assets.kpmg/content/dam/kpmg/xx/pdf/2020/10/future-of-higher-education.pdf.

17. Andy Altizer et al, "Preparing for the Next Pandemic: 11 Lessons Learned from COVID-19 by Universities," *Campus Safety Magazine* (November 21, 2021), https://www.campussafetymagazine.com/emergency/preparing-for-the-next-pandemic-11-lessons-learned-from-covid-19-by-universities/.

18. Kevin McClure and Alisa Hicklin Fryar, "The Great Faculty Disengagement," *The Chronicle of Higher Education* (January 19, 2022), https://www.chronicle.com/article/the-great-faculty-disengagement.

19. Dinah Winnick, "UMBC Ascends to the Nation's Highest Level as a Research University," *UMBC News* (February 2, 2022), https://umbc.edu/stories/umbc-ascends-to-the-nations-highest-level-as-a-research-university/.

20. Freeman A. Hrabowski, Philip J. Rous, and Peter H. Henderson, *The Empowered University: Shared Leadership, Culture Change, and Academic Success* (Baltimore: Johns Hopkins University Press, 2019): ix. https://www.press.jhu.edu/books/title/11838/empowered-university.

21. Kim Parker and Juliana Menasce Horowitz, "Majority of Workers Who Quit a Job in 2021 Cite Low Pay, No Opportunities for Advancement, Feeling

Disrespected," Pew Research Center (March 9, 2022), https://www.pewresearch
.org/fact-tank/2022/03/09/majority-of-workers-who-quit-a-job-in-2021-cite-low
-pay-no-opportunities-for-advancement-feeling-disrespected/.

22. Parker, "Majority of Workers."

23. "Future of Work Trends 2022: A New Era of Humanity," Korn Ferry (2022), https://www.kornferry.com/content/dam/kornferry-v2/featured-topics/pdf/FOW_TrendsReport_2022.pdf.

24. Marci Walton, "Right Now, Your Best Employees Are Eyeing the Exits," *The Chronicle of Higher Education* (February 16, 2022), https://www.chronicle.com/article/how-to-keep-your-staff-from-leaving.

25. Suzanne Smalley, "Colleges Cope with IT Staff Flight in Wake of Pandemic," *Inside Higher Ed* (February 2, 2022), https://www.insidehighered.com/news/2022/02/02/colleges-face-it-brain-drain-driven-covid-pay-disparities.

26. Hank Stuever, "Navigating the Return to Work," *Washington Post* (July 23, 2021), provided thoughts from readers about "What we dread about going back . . . and what we like about the office." https://www.washingtonpost.com/lifestyle/interactive/2021/return-to-the-office/.

27. Personal experience of Peter H. Henderson.

28. Sarah Brown, "What One University Learned About Pandemic Trauma and Its Workforce," *The Chronicle of Higher Education* (February 15, 2022), https://www.chronicle.com/article/what-one-university-learned-about-pandemic-trauma-and-its-work-force.

29. SHEEO, "State Higher Education Finance Report," 2021, Section on Education Appropriations, Figure 2.1, https://shef.sheeo.org/report/?report_page=distribution-of-revenue#education-appropriations-and-tuition-revenue. Michael Mitchell, Michael Leachman, and Kathleen Masterson, "A Lost Decade in Higher Education Funding," Center on Budget and Policy Priorities (August 23, 2017), https://www.cbpp.org/research/state-budget-and-tax/a-lost-decade-in-higher-education-funding.

30. The NACUBO standard is 0.40. KPMG, Prager, Sealy & Co., LLC, and Attain, *Strategic Financial Analysis in Higher Education: Identifying, Measuring, and Reporting Financial Risks* (7th ed., 2010): 113, https://emp.nacubo.org/wp-content/uploads/2017/10/NSS_Handbook.pdf.

31. Tracy Gordon, "State and Local Budgets and the Great Recession," *Brookings* (December 31, 2012), https://www.brookings.edu/articles/state-and-local-budgets-and-the-great-recession/.

4. Courage

1. "Courage," *Merriam-Webster Dictionary*. https://www.merriam-webster.com/dictionary/courage.

2. Tom Bartlett, "Why Are Colleges So Cowardly?" *The Chronicle of Higher Education* (July 23, 2021), https://www.chronicle.com/article/why-are-colleges-so-cowardly.

3. Alison Knezevich, "Judge Dismisses Claims against UMBC and Baltimore County in Lawsuit over Sexual Assaults," *Baltimore Sun* (October 2, 2020), https://www.baltimoresun.com/maryland/baltimore-county/bs-md-co-sexual-assault-lawsuit-order-20201002-ian67xefpfdp5jb3xhrl52dtym-story.html.

4. "Emma Sulkowicz," Wikipedia.org, https://en.wikipedia.org/wiki/Emma_Sulkowicz.

5. Haley Ott, "Hundreds Protest Campus Sexual Assault at Universities across the US," *CBS News* (February 10, 2021), https://www.cbsnews.com/news/college-sexual-assault-us-universities-protests/.

6. Maria Carrasco, "Students Gather in Washington to Protest Sexual Assault," *Inside Higher Ed* (October 7, 2021), https://www.insidehighered.com/news/2021/10/07/groups-deliver-edactnow-petition-education-department.

7. Freeman A. Hrabowski, Philip J. Rous, and Peter H. Henderson, *The Empowered University: Shared Leadership, Culture Change, and Academic Success* (Baltimore: Johns Hopkins University Press, 2019): 271. https://www.press.jhu.edu/books/title/11838/empowered-university.

8. Center for Institutional Courage, https://www.institutionalcourage.org/.

9. See https://www.institutionalcourage.org/the-call-to-courage.

10. Jennifer Freyd, "When Sexual Assault Victims Speak Out, Their Institutions Often Betray Them," The Conversation (January 11, 2018), https://theconversation.com/when-sexual-assault-victims-speak-out-their-institutions-often-betray-them-87050.

11. Jennifer Freyd and Pamela Birrell, *Blind to Betrayal: Why We Fool Ourselves We Aren't Being Fooled* (Hoboken, NJ: Wiley, 2013). Quoted in Tom Bartlett, "Why Are Colleges So Cowardly?" *The Chronicle of Higher Education* (July 23, 2021), https://www.chronicle.com/article/why-are-colleges-so-cowardly.

12. Center for Institutional Courage.

13. Office of Equity and Inclusion, "2020 Annual Update," UMBC, https://oei.umbc.edu/2020-annual-update/.

14. National Academies of Sciences, Engineering, and Medicine, *Sexual Harassment of Women: Climate, Culture, and Consequences in Academic Sciences Engineering, and Medicine*, (Washington, DC: National Academies Press, 2018). https://www.nap.edu/catalog/24994/sexual-harassment-of-women-climate-culture-and-consequences-in-academic.

15. National Academies of Sciences, Engineering, and Medicine. "Action Collaborative on Preventing Sexual Harassment in Higher Education," accessed June 6, 2023, https://www.nationalacademies.org/our-work/action-collaborative-on-preventing-sexual-harassment-in-higher-education.

16. National Academies of Sciences, Engineering, and Medicine, https://www.nationalacademies.org/our-work/action-collaborative-on-preventing-sexual-harassment-in-higher-education/about.

17. Maria Carrasco, "AAU Announces New Principles to Prevent Sexual Harassment," *Inside Higher Ed* (October 27, 2021), https://www.insidehighered.com/news/2021/10/27/aau-adopts-principles-prevent-sexual-harassment.

18. "AAU Principles on Preventing Sexual Harassment in Academia," AAU (October 26, 2021), https://www.aau.edu/aau-principles-preventing-sexual-harassment-academia.

19. Carrasco, "AAU Announces New Principles."

20. UMBC, Office of Equity and Inclusion, "Inclusion Council Recommendations," UMBC, accessed June 5, 2023, https://oei.umbc.edu/inclusion-council-recommendations/.

21. Freeman A. Hrabowski III, Peter H. Henderson, and J. Kathleen Tracy, "Higher Education Should Lead the Efforts to Reverse Structural Racism," *The*

Atlantic (October 24, 2020), https://www.theatlantic.com/ideas/archive/2020/10/higher-education-structural-racism/616754/.

22. NADOHE Anti-Racism Task Force, "A Framework for Advancing Anti-Racism Strategy on Campus," National Association of Diversity Officers in Higher Education (2021), https://nadohe.memberclicks.net/assets/2021/Framework/National%20Association%20of%20Diversity%20Officers%20in%20Higher%20Education%20-%20Framework%20for%20Advancing%20Ant-Racism%20on%20Campus%20-%20first%20edition.pdf.

23. NADOHE Anti-Racism Task Force, "A Framework."

24. UMBC, Office of Equity and Inclusion, "Inclusion Council Recommendations."

25. UMBC, Office of Equity and Inclusion, "Implementation Team," UMBC, accessed June 5, 2023, https://oei.umbc.edu/implementation-team/.

26. Howard Hughes Medical Institute. "HHMI's Commitment to Diversity, Equity, and Inclusion," HHMI, accessed June 5, 2023, https://diversity.hhmi.org/?_ga=2.98756254.1205047855.1658955152-2072524763.1654963351.

27. Howard Hughes Medical Institute. "New HHMI Program Pledges $1.5 Billion for Outstanding Early Career Faculty Committed to Diversity, Equity, and Inclusion," HHMI (May 26, 2022), https://www.hhmi.org/news/new-hhmi-program-pledges-1-5-billion-early-career-faculty-committed-diversity-equity-inclusion.

28. "Realizing Our Promise: The Second JHU Roadmap on Diversity, Equity, and Inclusion," Johns Hopkins University, accessed June 5, 2023, https://diversity.jhu.edu/second-jhu-roadmap-on-diversity-equity-and-inclusion/.

29. "Vivien Thomas Scholars Program," Johns Hopkins University, accessed June 5, 2023, https://provost.jhu.edu/about/vivien-thomas-scholars-initiative/.

30. Jocelyn Kaiser, "NIH Launches Grant Program Aimed at Closing the Funding Gap between Black and White Investigators," *Science* (June 17, 2022), https://www.science.org/content/article/nih-launches-grant-program-aimed-closing-funding-rate-gap-between-black-and-white.

31. Nick Anderson, "Black Professors Push a Major University to Diversify and Confront Racism," *Washington Post* (June 16, 2021), https://www.washingtonpost.com/education/2021/06/16/penn-state-black-faculty-racism/.

32. "What Has Higher Education Promised on Anti-racism in 2020 and Is It Enough?" EAB (November 16, 2020), https://eab.com/research/expert-insight/strategy/higher-education-promise-anti-racism/.

33. "What Has Higher Education Promised?"

34. Oyin Adedoyin, "How Can Colleges Advance Pledges of Racial Equity? A New Report Suggests Strategies," *The Chronicle of Higher Education* (November 17, 2021), https://www.chronicle.com/article/how-can-colleges-advance-pledges-of-racial-equity-a-new-report-suggests-strategies.

35. Alvin Powell, "President and Corporation Dedicate $100 Million to Implementation of Recommendations, *The Harvard Gazette* (April 26, 2022), https://news.harvard.edu/gazette/story/2022/04/slavery-probe-harvards-ties-inseparable-from-rise/.

36. NADOHE Anti-Racism Task Force, "A Framework."

37. President Donald J. Trump, "Executive Order on Combatting Race and Sex Stereotyping," The White House (September 22, 2020), https://trumpwhitehouse

.archives.gov/presidential-actions/executive-order-combating-race-sex
-stereotyping/.

38. Melissa Block, "Agencies, Contractors Suspend Diversity Training to Avoid Violating Trump Order," *NPR* (October 30, 2020), https://www.npr.org/2020/10/30 /929165869/agencies-contractors-suspend-diversity-training-to-avoid-violating -trump-order.

39. "Censorship of School Curricula in the United States," Wikipedia.org, accessed June 6, 2023, https://en.wikipedia.org/wiki/Censorship_of_school _curricula_in_the_United_States.

40. "2020–2021 Book Banning in the United States," Wikipedia.org, accessed June 6, 2023, https://en.wikipedia.org/wiki/2021%E2%80%932022_book_banning _in_the_United_States

41. Gregory Schneider, "What's in a Word? Youngkin Takes Aim at 'Equity'," *The Washington Post* (March 5, 2022), https://www.washingtonpost.com/dc-md-va /2022/03/05/whats-word-youngkin-takes-aim-equity/.

42. Schneider, "What's in a Word?"

43. Erin Cox, Ovetta Wiggins, and Lateshia Beachum, "Wes Moore's Campaign Pledges Created High Expectations. Can He Deliver?" *The Washington Post* (November 9, 2022), https://www.washingtonpost.com/dc-md-va/2022/11/09/wes -moore-campaign-promises/.

44. "A Bold Plan to Unlock Economic Opportunity for Maryland's Black Families," Moore-Miller for Maryland, accessed June 6, 2023, https://wesmoore .com/issues/unlocking-opportunity-for-black-families-maryland/.

45. "From Cradle to Career: Investing in Our students and Building a World-Class Public Education System," Moore-Miller for Maryland, accessed June 5, 2023, https://wesmoore.com/wp-content/uploads/2022/03/Moore-Miller -Education-Plan.pdf.

46. Kate Marijolovic, "For Black Students, 2 Obstacles to Graduation Loom Large: Discrimination and Responsibilities," *The Chronicle of Higher Education* (February 9, 2023), https://www.chronicle.com/article/for-black-students-2 -obstacles-to-graduation-loom-large-discrimination-and-responsibilities.

47. Ryan Quinn, "Fighting Racism in STEMM, *Inside Higher Ed* (February 15, 2023), https://www.insidehighered.com/news/2023/02/15/national-academies -release-antiracism-dei-recommendations.

48. Liam Knox, Shouting Down an Empty Hallway," *Insider Higher Ed* (February 3, 2023), https://www.insidehighered.com/news/2023/02/03/frustrated-dei -staff-are-leaving-their-jobs.

49. Heather Cox Richardson, "Letters from an American" (February 1, 2023), https://heathercoxrichardson.substack.com/p/february-1-2023.

50. Adrienne Lu, "Race on Campus: Diversity Efforts Under Fire," *The Chronicle of Higher Education* (January 31, 2023), https://www.chronicle.com/newsletter/race -on-campus/2023-01-31.

51. Knox, "Shouting Down."

52. Jack Stripling, "DeSantis Aims to Cut College Diversity Efforts; New College Ousts President," *Washington Post* (January 31, 2023), https://www.washingtonpost .com/education/2023/01/31/desantis-dei-tenure-florida-colleges/.

53. Francie Diep, "'Never Seen Anything Like It': New Bill Would Write DeSantis's Higher Ed Vision Into Law," *The Chronicle of Higher Education* (February 24, 2023), https://www.chronicle.com/article/never-seen-anything-like-it-new-bill-would-write-desantiss-higher-ed-vision-into-law.

54. Adrienne Lu, "South Carolina Requests Colleges' DEI Spending, Following Florida and Oklahoma," *The Chronicle of Higher Education* (February 8, 2023), https://www.chronicle.com/article/south-carolina-requests-colleges-dei-spending-following-florida-and-oklahoma. Kate McGee, "Texas Tech Reviews Its Hiring Practices as Efforts to Promote Diversity Come under Fire," *Texas Tribune* (February 8, 2023), https://www.texastribune.org/2023/02/08/texas-tech-hiring-diversity/.

55. Kendall Tietz, "University of North Carolina Moves to Ban 'Diversity, Equity, and Inclusion' Statements in Anti-woke Backlash," *Fox News* (February 24, 2023), https://www.foxnews.com/media/university-north-carolina-moves-ban-diversity-equity-inclusion-statements-anti-woke-backlash.

56. Adrienne Lu, Jacquelyn Elias, Audrey Williams June, Kate Marijolovic, Julian Roberts-Grmela, and Eva Surovell, "DEI Legislation Tracker," *The Chronicle of Higher Education* (March 9, 2023), https://www.chronicle.com/article/here-are-the-states-where-lawmakers-are-seeking-to-ban-colleges-dei-efforts.

57. Office of Human Resources, The Ohio State University, "Difficult Conversations: How to Discuss What Matters Most (A High-Level Summary of the Book by Stone, Patten, and Heen)." Department of Ophthalmology, Harvard Medical School, accessed June 5, 2023, https://eye.hms.harvard.edu/files/eye/files/difficult-conversations-summary.pdf.

58. "Getting Started with Difficult Conversations," American Association of University Women, accessed June 5, 2023, https://www.aauw.org/resources/member/governance-tools/dei-toolkit/difficult-conversations/. "Guidelines for Discussing Difficult or High-Stakes Topics," Center for Research on Learning and Teaching, University of Michigan, accessed June 6, 2023, https://crlt.umich.edu/publinks/generalguidelines.

59. "Cast Your Whole Vote," Center for Democracy and Civic Life, Division of Student Affairs, University of Maryland, Baltimore County, accessed June 5, 2023, https://civiclife.umbc.edu/learning-engagement/election-resources/castyourwholevote/.

60. "Theodore Parker," Wikipedia.org, https://en.wikipedia.org/wiki/Theodore_Parker.

61. Kristen Renn, "LGBTQ Students on Campus: Issues and Opportunities for Higher Education Leaders," *Higher Education Today* (April 10, 2017), https://www.higheredtoday.org/2017/04/10/lgbtq-students-higher-education/.

62. LGBTQ+ Student Union, myUMBC, accessed June 5, 2023, https://my3.my.umbc.edu/groups/lgbtqstudentunion.

63. "UMBC's Queer and Trans People of Color Community," myUMBC, accessed June 5, 2023, https://my3.my.umbc.edu/groups/qpoc.

64. "The Pride Center," i3b, Division of Student Affairs, University of Maryland Baltimore County, accessed June 6, 2023, https://i3b.umbc.edu/spaces/the-pride-center/.

65. Manil Suri, "Why Is Science so Straight?" *The New York Times* (September 4, 2015), https://www.nytimes.com/2015/09/05/opinion/manil-suri-why-is-science -so-straight.html.

66. Renn, "LGBTQ Students on Campus."

67. Email, Keith Bowman to Peter Henderson, April 27, 2022.

68. "Employment Nondiscrimination," Equality Maps, Movement Advancement Project, accessed June 5, 2023, https://www.lgbtmap.org/equality-maps /employment_non_discrimination_laws.

69. "SafeZone: LGBTQIA+ Allyship Development Workshop," i3b, Division of Student Affairs, University of Maryland Baltimore County, accessed June 5, 2023, https://i3b.umbc.edu/programs-events/event/105944/.

70. "Nondiscrimination Laws," Equality Maps, Movement Advancement Project, accessed June 5, 2023, https://www.lgbtmap.org/equality-maps/non _discrimination_laws.

71. Thomas Insel, *Healing: Our Path from Mental Illness to Mental Health*, (New York: Penguin Random House, 2022). https://www.penguinrandomhouse.com /books/670329/healing-by-thomas-insel-md/.

72. "Mental Illness," National Institute of Mental Health (March 2023), https://www.nimh.nih.gov/health/statistics/mental-illness.

73. "2020 Mental Health by the Numbers: Recognizing the Impact," National Alliance on Mental Illness, accessed June 30, 2023, https://www.nami.org/NAMI /media/NAMI-Media/Infographics/NAMI_2020MH_ByTheNumbers_Adults-r .pdf.

74. Roosa Tikkanen, Katharine Fields, Reginald D. Williams II, and Melinda K. Abrams, "Mental Health Conditions and Substance Use: Comparing U.S. Needs and Treatment Capacity with Those in Other High-Income Countries," *The Commonwealth Fund* (May 21, 2020), https://www.commonwealthfund.org /publications/issue-briefs/2020/may/mental-health-conditions-substance-use -comparing-us-other-countries.

75. John Elflein, "US Adults Reporting Symptoms of an Anxiety or Depressive Disorder, Jan.-June 2019 to Jan. 2021," *Statista* (March 16, 2021), https://www .statista.com/statistics/1221102/anxiety-depression-symptoms-before-since -covid-pandemic-us/.

76. Valerie Straus, "Surprising College Research from Multiple-Intelligences Theory Creator," *Washington Post* (March 24, 2022), https://www.washingtonpost .com/education/2022/03/24/surprising-new-college-research-new-study/.

77. "2020 Mental Health by the Numbers: Youth and Young Adults," National Alliance on Mental Illness, accessed June 4, 2023, https://www.nami.org/NAMI /media/NAMI-Media/Infographics/NAMI_2020MH_ByTheNumbers_Youth-r.pdf.

78. Melissa Ezarik, "Reading Between the Lines to Support Struggling Students," *Inside Higher Ed* (February 17, 2022), https://www.insidehighered.com /news/2022/02/17/identities-and-traumas-students-struggling-most -infographic.

79. Olivia Sanchez, "Rethinking Campus Mental Health to Better Serve LGBTQ+ Student and Others," *The Hechinger Report* (March 22, 2022), https:// hechingerreport.org/rethinking-campus-mental-health-to-better-serve-lgbtq -students-and-others/.

80. Ezarik, "Reading between the Lines."

81. UMBC's Faculty Development Center links to this site: "Trauma Informed Pedagogy Series," Office of the Provost, Azusa Pacific University, accessed June 6, 2023, https://www.apu.edu/provost/posts/27814/.

82. Daniel Eisenberg, Sarah Ketchen Lipson, and Justine Heinze, "The Healthy Minds Study," Healthy Minds Network. For 2015–2016 data see https:// healthymindsnetwork.org/wp-content/uploads/2019/04/HMS_national _DataReport_15-16.pdf. For 2018-19 data see: https://healthymindsnetwork.org /wp-content/uploads/2019/09/HMS_national-2018-19.pdf. For 2021 data (during the Pandemic) see: https://healthymindsnetwork.org/wp-content/uploads/2021 /09/HMS_national_winter_2021.pdf.

83. Active Minds, American College Health Association, American Council on Education, Healthy Minds Network, JED Foundation, Mary Christie Foundation, and The Steve Fund, "Mental Health, Higher Education, and COVID-19: Strategies for Leaders to Support Campus Well-Being," American Council on Education (2020), https://www.acenet.edu/Documents/Mental-Health-Higher-Education -Covid-19.pdf.

84. National Academies of Sciences, Engineering, and Medicine, Mental Health, *Substance Use, and Wellbeing in Higher Education: Supporting the Whole Student* (Washington, DC: National Academies Press, 2021). https://www.nap.edu/catalog /26015/mental-health-substance-use-and-wellbeing-in-higher-education -supporting.

85. National Academies, *Substance Use, and Wellbeing*, 3.

86. National Academies, *Substance Use, and Wellbeing*, 5.

87. National Academies, *Substance Use, and Wellbeing*, 5.

88. Active Minds, "Mental Health."

89. National Academies, *Substance Use, and Wellbeing*.

90. National Academies, *Substance Use, and Wellbeing*.

91. National Academies, *Substance Use, and Wellbeing*.

92. National Academies, *Substance Use, and Wellbeing*.

93. National Academies, *Substance Use, and Wellbeing*. Active Minds, "Mental Health."

94. "Warren, Wyden, Brown, Casey, Smith Introduce New Bill to Build Child Care Infrastructure and Availability," Senator Elizabeth Warren, U.S. Senate (May 27, 2021), https://www.warren.senate.gov/newsroom/press-releases/warren -wyden-brown-casey-smith-introduce-new-bill-to-build-child-care-infrastructure -and-availability.

95. National Academies of Sciences, Engineering, and Medicine, *The Impact of COVID-19 on the Careers of Women in Academic Sciences, Engineering, and Medicine* (Washington, DC: National Academies Press, 2021). https://nap.nationalacademies .org/catalog/26061/the-impact-of-covid-19-on-the-careers-of-women-in-academic -sciences-engineering-and-medicine.

96. Liz McMillen, "The Pandemic Hit Female Academics Hardest: What Are Colleges Going to Do about It? *The Chronicle of Higher Education* (July 27, 2021), https://www.chronicle.com/article/the-pandemic-hit-female-academics-hardest.

97. Coleen Flaherty, "Something's Gotta Give: Women's Journal Submission Rates Fell as Their Caring Responsibilities Grew due to COVID-19," *Inside Higher Ed*

(August 20, 2020), https://www.insidehighered.com/news/2020/08/20/womens
-journal-submission-rates-continue-fall.

98. Flaherty, "Something's Gotta Give."

99. Sarah Brown, "What One University Learned about Pandemic Trauma and Its Workforce," *The Chronicle of Higher Education* (February 15, 2022), https://www.chronicle.com/article/what-one-university-learned-about-pandemic-trauma-and-its-work-force.

100. Brown, "What One University Learned."

101. "National Health Education Week Launches Today," myUMBC (September 27, 2021), https://my3.my.umbc.edu/groups/training/posts/112690.

5. Passion

1. Maria Carrasco, "Most Students Believe Faculty Adjusted Well to the Pandemic," *Inside Higher Ed* (February 23, 2022), https://www.insidehighered.com/news/2022/02/23/teaching-and-learning-year-disruption.

2. Carrasco, "Most Students Believe."

3. Carrasco, "Most Students Believe."

4. Xingyu Li, Miaozhe Han, Geoffrey L. Cohen, and Hazel Rose Markus, "Passion Matters but Not Equally Everywhere: Predicting Achievement from Interest, Enjoyment, and Efficacy in 59 Societies," *Proceedings of the National Academy of Sciences*, 118, no. 11, (March 12, 2021): e2016964118, https://www.pnas.org/doi/10.1073/pnas.2016964118.

5. Kenneth I. Maton, Freeman A. Hrabowski, Metin Ozdemir, and Harriette Wimms, "Enhancing Representation, Retention, and Achievement of Minority Students in Higher Education: A Social Transformation Theory of Change," in Marybeth Shinn and Hirokazu Yoshikawa, eds., *Toward Positive Youth Development: Transforming Schools and Community Programs* (New York: Oxford University Press, 2008): 120–121.

6. Daniel F. Chambliss and Christopher Takacs, *How College Works* (Cambridge, MA: Harvard University Press, 2014). https://www.hup.harvard.edu/catalog.php?isbn=9780674049024.

7. Peter Felten, John N. Gardner, Charles C. Schroeder, Leo M. Lambert, and Betsy O. Barefoot, *The Undergraduate Experience: Focusing Institutions and What Matters Most* (San Francisco: Jossey-Bass, 2016). https://www.wiley.com/en-us/The+Undergraduate+Experience%3A+Focusing+Institutions+on+What+Matters+Most-p-9781119051190.

8. Felten et al., *Undergraduate Experience*, vii.

9. Nathan D. Grawe, *Demographics and the Demand for Higher Education* (Baltimore: Johns Hopkins University Press, 2018). https://www.press.jhu.edu/books/title/11859/demographics-and-demand-higher-education.

10. Grawe, Demographics and the Demand. Nathan D. Grawe, *The Agile College* (Baltimore: Johns Hopkins University Press, 2021). https://www.press.jhu.edu/books/title/12234/agile-collegehttps://www.press.jhu.edu/books/title/12234/agile-college; Nathan D. Grawe, "How to Survive the Enrollment Bust," *The Chronicle of Higher Education* (January 13, 2021), https://www.chronicle.com/article/how-to-navigate-the-demographic-cliff.

11. Todd Sedmak, "Undergraduate Enrollment Declines Show No Signs of Recovery from 2020," *National Student Clearinghouse* (October 26, 2021). https://www.studentclearinghouse.org/blog/undergraduate-enrollment-declines-show-no-signs-of-recovery-from-2020/.

12. "Planning Instructional Variety for Online Teaching," University of Maryland, Baltimore County. https://pivot.umbc.edu/pivot-live/.

13. Data from John Fritz, in written response to questions posed to Jack Seuss, Damian Doyle, John Fritz, and Robert Carpenter, May 24. 2021. Jack Seuss, email to Peter Henderson, May 24, 2021.

14. Lucille McCarthy, email to Freeman Hrabowski, May 20, 2020.

15. UMBC Faculty Senate, Faculty Workload Survey, October 2021. Presentation slides provided to Peter Henderson by Orianne Smith, March 13, 2023.

16. These lessons were informed by the oral and written responses to questions we posed to Jack Seuss, Damian Doyle, John Fritz, and Robert Carpenter, May 24. 2021. Jack Seuss, email to Peter Henderson, May 24, 2021.

17. "Student Guide to Online Learning," Academic Engagement and Transition Programs, University of Maryland, Baltimore County, accessed June 4, 2023, https://aetp.umbc.edu/student-guide-to-online-learning/.

18. Commission on the Future of Undergraduate Education, *The Future of Undergraduate Education, The Future of America* (American Academy of Arts and Sciences, November 2017). https://www.amacad.org/publication/future-undergraduate-education.

19. Beth McMurtrie, "Why the Science of Teaching Is Often Ignored," *The Chronicle of Higher Education* (January 3, 2022), https://www.chronicle.com/article/why-the-science-of-teaching-is-often-ignored.

20. Felten, *Undergraduate Experience*, 9.

21. Commission on the Future, *Future of Undergraduate Education*.

22. Colleen Flaherty, "Required Pedagogy," *Inside Higher Ed* (December 13, 2019). https://www.insidehighered.com/news/2019/12/13/online-conversation-shines-spotlight-graduate-programs-teach-students-how-teach.

23. Flaherty, "Required Pedagogy."

24. Jessey Wright and Melissa Jacquart, "Teach Graduate Students How to Teach," American Philosophical Association blog (August 29, 2017), https://blog.apaonline.org/2017/08/29/teach-graduate-students-how-to-teach/.

25. Flaherty, "Required Pedagogy."

26. Center for the Integration of Research, Teaching, and Learning, https://www.cirtl.net/, and CIRTL at the University of Maryland, Baltimore County, https://cirtl.umbc.edu/

27. Beth McMurtrie, "A 'Stunning' Level of Student Disconnection," *The Chronicle of Higher Education* (April 5, 2022), https://www.chronicle.com/article/a-stunning-level-of-student-disconnection.

28. Stephanie Riegg Cellini, "How Does Virtual Learning Affect Students in Higher Education," Brown Center on Educational Policy, The Brookings Institution, August 13, 2021, https://www.brookings.edu/blog/brown-center-chalkboard/2021/08/13/how-does-virtual-learning-impact-students-in-higher-education/.

29. Cellini, "How Does Virtual Learning."

30. David Asai, Bruce Alberts, and Janet Coffey, "Redo College Intro Science," *Science* (March 24, 2022), https://www.science.org/doi/10.1126/science.abq1184.

31. Ronald J. Daniels, Grant Shreve, and Phillip Spector, *What Universities Owe Democracy* (Baltimore: Johns Hopkins University, 2021). https://www.press.jhu.edu/books/title/12802/what-universities-owe-democracy.

32. "Preventing Gender-Based Harm at UMBC: Designing and Teaching a Multidisciplinary Course," Spring 2021 awardees, Hrabowski Innovation Fund Grant Recipients, Faculty Development Center, University of Maryland, Baltimore County, https://calt.umbc.edu/academic-innovation-competition/past-recipients/.

33. Tara Carpenter, "Do Students Carry 'Lessons Learned' from One Course to the Next?" Presentation, March 10, 2022, Learning Analytics Community of Practice, University of Maryland, Baltimore County. Copy provided by email to Peter Henderson by Robert Carpenter, March 31, 2022.

34. McMurtrie, "Why the Science of Teaching."

35. Steven Mintz, "Strategies for Improving Student Success," *Inside Higher Ed* (May 28, 2019), https://www.insidehighered.com/blogs/higher-ed-gamma/strategies-improving-student-success.

36. Mintz, "Strategies for Improving."

37. "Powered by Publics," Association of Public and Land-grant Universities, accessed June 5, 2023, https://www.aplu.org/our-work/1-driving-equitable-student-success/achieving-university-transformation-and-systemic-changes/center-for-public-university-transformation/powered-by-publics/.

38. "The Student Experience," Strategic Planning Steering Committee Final Report, University of Maryland, Baltimore County, https://strategicplan.umbc.edu/the-student-experience/.

39. "Strategy Group: Student Experience," Strategic Planning Steering Committee Final Report, University of Maryland, Baltimore County, https://strategicplan.umbc.edu/files/2015/08/SE-background-narrative.pdf.

40. "Strategy Group."

41. "Strategic Plan Implementation Inventory of Accomplishments, August 2019," Strategic Planning Committee, University of Maryland, Baltimore County, https://planning.umbc.edu/files/2019/08/Inventory-of-SP-Implementation-2019.pdf.

42. "University Innovation Alliance," accessed June 4, 2023, https://theuia.org/.

43. Catalina Sofia Dansberger Duque, "$21 Million Sherman Family Foundation Gift Supports UMBC's Bold Commitment to PreK-12 Research, Teaching, and Learning," *UMBC News* (February 24, 2022), https://umbc.edu/stories/21m-sherman-family-foundation-gift-supports-umbcs-bold-commitment-to-prek-12-research-teaching-and-learning/.

44. Sherman STEM Teacher Scholars Program, University of Maryland, Baltimore County, https://sherman.umbc.edu/.

45. Jill Barshay and Sasha Aslanian, "Colleges Are Using Big Data to Track Students in an Effort to Boost Graduation Rates, But It Comes at a Cost," *The Hechinger Report* (August 6, 2019), https://hechingerreport.org/predictive-analytics-boosting-college-graduation-rates-also-invade-privacy-and-reinforce-racial-inequities/.

46. "Using Analytics to Improve Student Success," Ellucian, accessed June 5, 2023, https://www.ellucian.com/blog/student-success-analytics.

47. Tara Carpenter, "Do Students Carry 'Lessons Learned' From One Course to the Next?" Presentation, March 10, 2022, Learning Analytics Community of Practice, University of Maryland, Baltimore County. Copy provided by email to Peter Henderson by Robert Carpenter, March 31. 2022.

48. Robert Carpenter, email to Peter Henderson, March 31, 2022.

49. Commission on the Future, *Future of Undergraduate Education*.

50. UMBC General Education Distribution Requirements, UMBC, https://catalog.umbc.edu/content.php?catoid=31&navoid=2045#general and UMBC General Education Competencies. UMBC, General Education Functional Competencies, https://calt.umbc.edu/wp-content/uploads/sites/50/2015/02/General_Education_Competencies_0805.pdf.

51. UMBC General Education Competencies.

52. Commission on the Future, *Future of Undergraduate Education*.

53. "The State of Higher Education in 2020," Grant Thornton, 15. https://www.grantthornton.com/content/dam/grantthornton/website/assets/content-page-files/nfp/pdfs/2020/grant-thornton-state-of-higher-education-in-2020-new/grant-thornton-state-of-higher-education-in-2020-new.pdf.coredownload.inline.pdf.

54. Carl Bergstrom and Jevin West, quoted in Kay Kupferschmidt. "On the Trail of Bullshit," *Science* (March 26, 2022): 1334. https://www.science.org/doi/epdf/10.1126/science.abq1537.

55. Commission on the Practice of Democratic Citizenship, *Our Common Purpose: Reinventing American Democracy for the 21st Century* (American Academy of Arts and Sciences, 2020), https://www.amacad.org/ourcommonpurpose/report.

56. Ronald J. Daniels, Grant Shreve, and Phillip Spector, *What Universities Owe Democracy*, (Baltimore: Johns Hopkins University, 2021), 87. https://www.press.jhu.edu/books/title/12802/what-universities-owe-democracy.

57. Daniels, *What Universities Owe*, 87, 93.

58. Daniels, *What Universities Owe*, 90, 99, 122.

59. Daniels, *What Universities Owe*, 129.

60. Sandra Feder, "Stanford Pilots a New Citizenship Course for First-Year Students," *Stanford Report* (March 17, 2021), https://news.stanford.edu/report/2021/03/17/citizenship-course-piloted/.

61. University of Virginia, "Strengthening American Democracy," UVA Today, paid content in *The Chronicle of Higher Education*. https://sponsored.chronicle.com/StrengtheningAmericanDemocracy/index.html.

62. Freeman A. Hrabowski III, Peter H. Henderson, and J. Kathleen Tracy, "Higher Education Should Lead the Efforts to Reverse Structural Racism," *The Atlantic* (October 24, 2020), https://www.theatlantic.com/ideas/archive/2020/10/higher-education-structural-racism/616754/.

63. Freeman A. Hrabowski III, Philip J. Rous, and Peter H. Henderson, *The Empowered University: Shared Leadership, Culture Change, and Academic Success* (Baltimore: Johns Hopkins University Press, 2019). https://www.press.jhu.edu/books/title/11838/empowered-university.

64. James F. Smith, "Harvard Kennedy School Offers New Race and Policy Course for Incoming Students," Harvard Kennedy School (November 10, 2020), https://www.hks.harvard.edu/faculty-research/policy-topics/fairness-justice/harvard-kennedy-school-offers-new-race-and-policy.

65. "The Inclusion Imperative," University of Maryland, Baltimore County. https://inclusionimperative.umbc.edu/about/.

66. "Voter Friendly Campus Designation" and "National Study of Learning, Voting, and Engagement," Center for Democracy and Civic Life, University of Maryland, Baltimore County, accessed June 6, 2023, https://civiclife.umbc.edu/learning-engagement/election-resources/plans-and-reports/.

6. Hope

1. Lee Daniel Kravetz, "Facing Adversity through Building Resilience: A Guide to Grounded Hope," based on David Feldman and Lee Daniel Kravetz, *Supersurvivors: The Surprising Link Between Suffering and Success*. Option B. https://optionb.org/advice/steps-to-grounded-hope.

2. Mary Dana Hinton, "The Antidote to Pandemic Disillusionment: Shepherding Your Community with Intention and Care," Academic Impressions (November 2, 2021), https://www.academicimpressions.com/blog/the-antidote-to-pandemic-disillusionment/.

3. Ronald J. Daniels, Grant Shreve, and Phillip Spector, *What Universities Owe Democracy*, (Baltimore: Johns Hopkins University, 2021), 87.

Epilogue. Transition

1. Bridget Burns, UIA Monthly Newsletter, May 4, 2022.

2. Hrabowski and Sheares Ashby did not have any contact during the search process.

Index

DEI. *See* diversity; equity; inclusion
democracy, 207–9, 227. *See also* Center for
Democracy and Civic Life
DeSantis, Ron, 136, 137
Difficult Conversations: How to Discuss What Matters Most (Stone, Patton, and Heen), 138
disabilities, people with, 10, 32
diversity: constraints on initiatives to improve, 133–39; courage to achieve, 13, 107, 120, 124–25, 127–33, 134–35, 138–40; culture change of commitment to, 4; higher education addressing, 8–12; openness to, 39; politicization of, 10, 133–39; vision for, 16, 30, 31–32
DocuSign, 93, 94
Dodson-Reed, Candace, 119
Doyle, Damian, 93
Drake, Brent, 201–2
Driving Change Program (HHMI), 129
Drucker, Peter, 38
Duckworth, Angela, 56
Duke University, 21–22, 232–33
Dweck, Carol, 56
Dzirasa, Kafui, 21–22
Dzirasa, Letitia, 20

Ebbinghaus, Hermann, 193
Educause, 76, 86
elections, engagement in, 209, 210–11
empathy, 12
employees: Great Resignation by, 74, 85, 87, 162; in-person vs. remote work for, 88–92; labor market changes for, 85–87; as mental health counselors, 162; university (*see* faculty and staff)
Empowered University, The (Hrabowski, Rous and Henderson), 1, 36, 78, 85, 115–16, 130, 158, 195, 197
empowerment: communication and, 6, 44, 54–55; courage to support, 106; course redesign to include, 193; culture reflecting, 5, 38–39, 77–79, 219; hope as source of, 213; by leadership, 1–14, 36–37, 42–45, 106; openness and, 13, 36–37, 38–39, 42–45, 218–19, 220 21; passion with, 170–71; for racial justice improvements, 8–9, 11, 127–28; resilience through, 77–79

engagement: change supported through, 7, 44; community, 68; courage for, 106–7, 116; electoral, 209, 210–11; by leadership, 7, 12; student affairs initiatives to encourage, 82–83
enrollment: COVID-19 pandemic effects on, 99, 109–10, 171–72, 173–74, 177; demographic changes and, 172–73; expansion of opportunities for, 173; institutional level goals for, 174–76; passion driving, 171–77, 227; services to support, 199; statistics on, 32, 97; strategic plan for, 46–47, 75, 94–95, 104, 172, 174–76, 196, 227; student characteristics and, 176–77
equity: constraints on initiatives to improve, 133–39; courage to achieve, 13, 119–20, 125–33, 134–35, 138–40; definition of, 126; higher education addressing, 8, 10–12; politicization of, 10, 134–39; vision to address issues of, 24–25, 30
"excellence," as code for exclusion, 17

faculty and staff: communication by/with (*see* communication); community of colleagues among, 85–87; culture change among, 3–5 (*see also* culture); DEI initiatives for, 2, 12, 130–31; empowerment of (*see* empowerment); financial issues affecting, 102, 104–5, 110–11; in-person and remote work by, 88–92 (*see also under* COVID-19 pandemic); LGBTQ+ advocacy among, 142–43, 144–47, 149; mental health and, 162, 163–66; online instruction shift for, 80–81, 94, 178–80, 194 (*see also* online and hybrid instruction); passion and commitment of, 169–70, 226 (*see also* passion); pedagogical instruction for, 189–91; resilience and reliance on, 72, 77, 80–81, 85–92 (*see also* resilience); shared leadership with, 1, 3, 5–6, 44–45, 52, 74, 77; student success role of, 188–94 (*see also* student success); tensions with, 39–40; Title IX protestors requesting termination of, 115–16; vision development by, 16–17 (*see also* vision)